Taken to Extremes

Frank Darnell and Anton Hoëm

Taken to Extremes

Education in the Far North

SCANDINAVIAN UNIVERSITY PRESS
Oslo – Stockholm – Copenhagen – Boston

Scandinavian University Press (Universitetsforlaget AS)
P.O. Box 2959 Tøyen, N-0608 Oslo, Norway
Fax +47 22 57 53 53

Stockholm office
SCUP, Scandinavian University Press
P.O. Box 3255, S-103 65 Stockholm, Sweden
Fax +46 8 20 99 82

Copenhagen office
Scandinavian University Press AS
P.O. Box 54, DK-1002 København K, Denmark
Fax +45 33 32 05 70

Boston office
Scandinavian University Press North America
875 Massachusetts Ave., Ste. 84, Cambridge MA 02139, USA
Fax +1 617 354 6875

ISBN 82-00-22588-7

Published with a grant from the Institute for Educational Research,
University of Oslo

Design: Astrid Elisabeth Jørgensen
Cover illustration: Mittet Foto
Typeset in 10.5 on 13 point Photina by HS-Repro A/S
Printed on 90 g Partner Offset by HS-Trykk A/S, Norway 1996

Teachers say that culture cannot be taught in schools,
that it should be taught in the home.
But they teach culture in the schools,
in fact that is all they teach.

Bristol Bay Native Association
Bristol Bay, Alaska

Contents

Part Three

Conclusions

List of Maps and Illustrations

Maps

Photographs

Textbook Examples

Figures

Foreword

While reviewing the draft manuscript for this book I was struck with how much of it reflects my own years as a young Alaska Native student and, in later life, a member of the education profession. As a young man-child growing up in a Tlingit community located in Southeast Alaska on the west coast of Prince of Wales Island in the village of Klawock, I had the distinct privilege of spending my early summers with my grandparents. I had the responsibility of helping them gather and prepare the indigenous foods of the area for the winter months. It was a time when I was introduced to activities that began to teach me many of the skills that I would use after the age of nine when I graduated to working with my paternal uncles during the summer months (they were my early mentors). Traditionally, the young men were trained by their maternal uncles (but paternal uncles on occasion) and other elders of a clan community. My formal schooling took place during the winter months, first in a Bureau of Indian Affairs school, then an Alaska Territorial school in my village. I later went to a mission boarding school started by Dr. Sheldon Jackson, in Sitka, Alaska; a private denominational school in Seattle, Washington, and three colleges and universities on my way to earning a doctorate.

I am recognized as Tlingit (although I have Oglala-Lakota blood in my veins). I do not have to *act* in a certain way. My beliefs are based on what my grandparents, my uncles, my parents, and other members of the Tlingit community taught me. The extended family is recognized as important; the formal leadership structure is still intact and recognized. I was taught that I should not waste the food that we harvested, that I must leave enough for the next time and the next person. I was taught how to live on the high seas, live and hunt in the forest, and taught how to think and anticipate by my uncles. I was also given a chance to develop skills important for today: to exist in today's social, cultural and economic environment. I was taught that I must be prepared for a changing world, that there was a knowledge base I must have access to through my schooling. My grandparents taught me the songs and dances of the family. I did not retain the Tlingit language because of the schools' and government's policies on learning English only.

In direct contrast to all of this I have a Doctor of Education degree from Harvard University. I spent most of my winters going to school: kindergarten, elementary, secondary, and college. I have worked as a bus driver, physical education teacher, coach, elementary and secondary school teacher. I have served as a US Deputy Commissioner of Education, the Director of Education for the Bureau of Indian Affairs, the Commissioner of Education for the State of Alaska, and as a professor in several universities. My education has occurred in a context created by my grandparents and uncles that has given me a unique cultural perspective. My teachers in the schools I have attended have given me insight into the context of middle-class America and what it means to be part of the larger society in which I find myself. There are people that say that this is living in two worlds. To me it is living in one world and adjusting to what I find in the same way that my grandfather, my father and my uncles adjusted to their worlds. Environments change and we adjust to those changes. To me these are challenges that are exciting, exciting because they are new and different; exciting because I am given an opportunity to form my actions and thoughts to these new environments. Am I no longer a Tlingit because I live in a modern world?

I think not. I am Tlingit in spite of all of this! I have just adjusted to a new period of history in the life of an *Indian* in the same way my great grandfather, my grandfather, and my father adjusted as *Indians* to their different environments. There has been adjustment by all. Some of it by design, but much of it dictated by the circumstances we find ourselves in. Our personalities and training have much to do with how we react to the world that is out there. There have to be thousands, if not tens of thousands, that have adjusted to a constantly changing world and yet remain *Indian*.

Taken to Extremes: Education in the Far North is a glimpse of the educational and political situations that my grandparents' generation, my parents' generation, my generation, and the generation my children represent have been exposed to in our schools and schooling. The primary focus of this text is the Circumpolar North, but the circumstances surrounding the events in this publication are the same among many of the Native peoples of the world over that were colonized. The situations are very similar in nature. The culture and genesis of the people of the North are tied to a subsistence culture. Native people in other parts of the Americas were also hunters and food gatherers while others were more agricultural in nature. In all cases the Native people are indigenous to the land.

Among my current activities I chair the Steering Committee for a Series of International Cross-Cultural Education Seminars in the Circumpolar North. Many of the members of this committee, a mix of Native and non-Native people, have been directly involved in the school systems that are described in this book; they have been brought up in its schools, taught in them, and studied their systems and consequences. The committee is unique in its standing among education associations. It has no official standing, its members are not appointed by any official group and it has little sustainable funding other than a grant from the Ford Foundation that enabled it to initiate its work and acquire status. The international series of seminars initiated by the committee have been specifically designed to address the education needs of indigenous peoples in the Far North. They have been jointly planned in partnership with local planning committees to insure that the issues and policies addressed were important to the communities in which the seminars were held and a local sense of ownership was developed.

This concept and the committee have survived for twenty years because of the commitment of its individual members. Professors Darnell and Hoëm were among the founding members of this group. As they mention in their first chapter, many of their impressions of the Far North, its people, and problems of providing an adequate education among them, derive from their involvement in the seminar series and their work with the committee. Indeed, it is their close association with the committee and the concepts that have emerged from the committee's work that have contributed in part to the emergence of this book. Both authors have experienced remarkably long careers in the Far North. Frank Darnell is Emeritus Professor of Education at the University of Alaska Fairbanks, where he taught and carried out research for many years. Anton Hoëm is Professor of Education and Director of the Institute for Educational Research at the University of Oslo. He grew up in the Finnmark district of Norway where he has maintained a life-long personal and professional interest in Saami affairs.

In one sense *Taken to Extremes: Education in the Far North* is a benchmark in the Circumpolar North: it draws together for the first time the problems of schooling in that remote part of the world. It cuts across international boundaries and looks at the peoples found there as an entity with much in common despite the variety of national states of which they are a part. As such it serves well the need to move forward the debate on how best to improve education among the indigenous peoples found there, especially for the next generation of pupils only now entering school.

Dr. William G. Demmert, Jr.*

---

* Dr. William G. Demmert, Jr., is Chairman of the Steering Committee for the Series of International Seminars on Cross-Cultural Education in the Circumpolar North, and Visiting Professor of Education, Woodring College of Education, Western Washington University.

Acknowledgments

The publication of a book that is the result of many years of experience and travel means that we have come under the influence of a great number of people who have given us support and encouragement for our work. Acknowledging all of them is an impossible task, but we want to draw attention to – and thank – those that stand out.

The time and the financial means required for writing this book were made possible when the US Norway Fulbright Foundation for Educational Exchange awarded a Fulbright scholarship to Frank Darnell for a residency at the Institute for Educational Research at the University of Oslo for a full academic year. Therefore, we owe a particular debt of gratitude to Barbara Lysholt Petersen, Director of the US Norway Fulbright Foundation, for her support. Funds for the award were made available to the Fulbright Foundation by the Norwegian Ministry of Church, Education and Research. Without the interest of Dr. Gudmund Hernes, Minister for Church, Education and Research, in education in multicultural societies this book would not have been possible. Furthermore, the University of Oslo generously provided funds to the Fulbright Foundation to enable the Fulbright scholarship to be extended six months beyond its original duration.

Financial assistance for our early work in the 1970s came primarily from the Ford Foundation. Ralph Bohrson, then Program Officer of the Foundation, not only was instrumental in helping us obtain funds, but was a source of new perspectives on how problems in education might eventually be resolved. More recent financial support has been provided by the Norwegian National Research Council. Their contributions to the process are appreciated.

People who have encouraged us over the years have come from every region of the Polar world. In particular, we are appreciative of the contributions by members of the International Committee for Cross-Cultural Education in the Circumpolar North. They include the late Roger Lang, first chairman of the Committee and President of the Alaska Federation of Natives. Former members include Ralph Eluska of Alaska, Tagak Curley and Mary Cousins, of the Northwest Territories, Ami Poppet from Arctic Quebec, Dr. Terence Armstrong of Cambridge University, Marcus Bjarnarson, formerly of the Greenland Department of Education, and, from Norway, Aslak Nils Sara, former director of the Nordic Saami Institute and former vice president of the World Council of Indigenous Peoples (WCIP), and Ellena Hellander, also a former director of the Nordic Saami Institute. Current members include Dr. William Demmert, Chairman of the Committee, Visiting Professor of Education, Woodring College of Education, Western Washington University; Dr. Edna Ahgeak MacLean, President of Ilisagvik College of Barrow Alaska; Joseph L. Handley, Deputy Minister of Renewable Resources, Northwest Territories; Ingmar Egede, former director of the Greenland Teacher Training College at Nuuk; Karl Kristian Olsen (Paartoq), Director of Culture, Education and Church for the government of Greenland; and Jan Henry Keskitalo, Director of the Saami Cultural College at Guovdageaidnu, Norway.

Over the years personnel of the Scott Polar Research Institute at the University of Cambridge have been a constant source of assistance in furtherance of our work. Among the many courtesies of the institute, grant funds for operation of the International Steering Committee for Cross-Cultural Education in the Circumpolar North were administered through the institute's office for several years. In particular we want to acknowledge with gratitude the contributions of Dr. Terence Armstrong, for many years Deputy Director of the institute. Dr. Armstrong has been a constant source of inspiration to us. Furthermore, our warmest thanks are extended to the always courteous personnel of the institute's library where an incredible wealth of printed material that pertains to the Far North can be found.

We are indebted to Jon Tolgensbakk of the Geography Department of the University of Oslo for his excellent work in preparing the maps that are found in the text. Also, we wish to thank Ron Inouye of the University of Alaska Fairbanks, Dave Wilman, Director of the Nunatt Campus of the Arctic College, Iqaluit and Karl Kristian Olsen, for their assistance in identifying pictures and teaching materials used to illustrate the text.

We are appreciative of the "beyond the call of duty" efforts of the following who have reviewed the draft manuscript and offered their constructive comments and suggestions: David Wilman, Ray and Carol Barnhardt, Jan Henry Keskitalo, Ingmar Egede, and Edna Ahgeak MacLean. Their contributions have kept us focused on our task in a substantial manner and improved the text in many ways.

In like manner, we are especially indebted to the great number of village and settlement residents and teachers with whom we have come in contact over the years who ultimately have contributed the greatest amount to our understanding of the subject of schooling and given us insight into the complex way of life in the Far North. Without their intelligence and willingness to share, this book could not have been written.

Part One
Conceptual Framework

Chapter 1

Purpose and Premise

> I have lived in this village all my life and never went to school. I speak only my Native language. Why is it that the kids who finish school do not know any more than I do?[1]

This question, posed in 1991 by an elder in the Yup'ik Eskimo village of Tununuk, located on the shores of the Bering Sea in Southwest Alaska, could have been asked just as well in any number of villages and settlements across the Far North. At the time he was addressing, through an interpreter, a small group of Alaska State Legislators who had traveled to the village to take testimony on the status of village education. The question speaks to a common perception and frustration found throughout the Polar Rim. In a roundabout way this book attempts to answer it.

Taken to Extremes: Education in the Far North might well have been further subtitled *Cross-Cultural Perspectives on School and Society*, for it is a book about relationships between the indigenous peoples of the Arctic and Subarctic and systems of formal education that have been introduced over the years in the remote villages of North America, Greenland, and the Nordic countries of Norway, Sweden, and Finland. The indigenous peoples of the Far North are but a small, isolated segment of the world's population. Nevertheless, aspects of lessons learned through a review of the development of education and an analysis of current issues there may have relevance for minority populations in other intercultural societies as well as Circumpolar peoples themselves. The book

1. Tununuk village elder, cited in Alaska 1991, p. 104.

is an attempt to demonstrate this premise, offer suggestions for improved schooling among minority populations in the Far North and elsewhere and develop theoretical notions of education appropriate to multicultural societies.

Unknown to us at the time, the book had its genesis at a brief meeting 25 years ago when we first discovered that we had mutual interests in the education of indigenous minority peoples living in the Far North. In our early discussions we discovered that we held many similar views concerning the problems of providing education in the Polar regions of the countries with which we were familiar. At that time provisions for schooling were developed and controlled almost exclusively by governmental education agencies hundreds of miles to the south. Concepts that dealt with education across cultures were seldom considered by educational bureaucrats or those who made policy. Terms such as intercultural, cross-cultural, and multicultural education were rarely part of the vocabulary of those who were responsible for schooling. Nor was there notable controversy respecting the appropriateness of the ethnocentric, monocultural systems and programs of education then being deployed in each of the Circumpolar countries. Nevertheless, in our studies of education systems and the societies in which they were found we had independently concluded that something was not right with much of what passed for formal schooling in the Far North.

We did not, however, believe that any one segment of the educational establishment – teachers, administrators, the policy making bodies, or a combination of these groups – was necessarily at fault. Indeed, stories abound that tell of the extraordinary character and achievements of those people responsible for establishing schools and teaching in small isolated communities during the early years. Instead of blaming the inadequacies of the enterprise on a specific cause, we attributed the predicament to a set of complex societal, intercultural and geographical circumstances. Little known or infrequently understood cultural characteristics of the peoples of the Far North, the physical and psychological demands of their environment, and ill-considered notions of the purposes and methods of teaching across cultures all contributed to the situation. These factors all spoke of a need for more information on the subject than was then available. This book, then, draws together what we have learned over the years trying to understand the problems of education among the indigenous peoples of the Far North and of working closely with them as they emerged from passive acceptance of an alien system of education to political activism in search of a better way. In so doing we have organized the book around four objectives or purposes and attempt to answer a number of questions that can be derived from them.

First of all, if nothing else, the indigenous peoples of the Circumpolar world have in common high latitudes, isolation, and what much of the rest of the world perceives as a harsh physical environment. These features alone, and the cultural adaptations they require for survival, make the development of formal education among them fraught with problems. The first purpose of the book, therefore, is to document the historical development of schooling in the Far North for its own sake and to subsequently identify some of the reasons for problems in contemporary schools.

Secondly, it is our purpose to compare and analyze current educational issues concerned with programs and policies of education in each of the geographic regions and groups of people covered in the book.

Our third purpose is to bring about a better understanding of theories of education in multicultural societies. Thus, we account for our notions in their development both in the opening section of the book and the conclusion. In the first instance, we define how we use various culture-related terms and introduce our perspectives on school and society as they pertain to the book as a means to set the theme for the narrative that follows. In the last chapter we depart from our format by becoming less regionally specific when setting forth our general notions and theories on education in multicultural societies in the hope that they will lead to better schools and a population more able to cope with the changes taking place around them.

To fulfill these objectives we attempt to answer three fundamental questions:

1. What are the historical events and conditions that have had an influence on the nature of systems of education over time?
2. What are the most contentious education issues that persist today and what are some of the arguments advanced to resolve them?
3. What lesson can be said to have been learned from answers to the first two questions?

By declaring these purposes and examining these questions, it is not our intention to reach definitive conclusions as to the direction education in all multicultural societies should take. We do, however, hope that lessons we have learned as observers of, and participants in, a complex educational process in a unique and little known part of the world have the potential to contribute to the debate on productive ways to provide improved schooling for minority populations anywhere.

To accomplish this we rely heavily on our individual work over a lifetime of study of education systems in the North and our analysis of the consequences of those systems on Northern societies. Although our findings and conclusions are not necessarily the result of empirical research or structured analytical models, we are confident that they are based on careful observations over many years in the field and reliable testimony by indigenous residents of the Far North. In this sense the book is a personal narrative based on our experiences and study among an inadequately known segment of the world's population.

Working with persons from another culture on projects of mutual interest is believed to be one of the best ways to learn about that culture.[2] Certainly in our case this has been true. Much of our understanding of education in the Far North is derived from a composite of personal observations and research in each of the geographic areas covered in the book. But it also is drawn from the insight of many Northern Natives who have come under the influence of formal Western education systems in the normal course of their lives. In our case we were fortunate to have

2. Walsh 1973, p. 193.

been accepted among a large segment of that population and because we came to work with a long-standing international study group made up mostly of indigenous leaders. That group, the Steering Committee for a Series of International Seminars on Cross-Cultural Education in the Far North, has been the inspiration for much of our work, and the seminars they have sponsored the source of much of our data. As founding members of the committee and as active members continuously since, we have had the opportunity to be exposed to countless ideas and experiences pertaining to education in the multicultural Far North. Consequently, the seminar sessions and the papers they have generated form the basis for some of the material that we have drawn on to prepare this book, although we want to emphasize that by use of these materials we do not presume to speak for the Native population. This they do effectively and most eloquently on their own terms.

With many parallels in their surroundings, life styles, and historical circumstances, all indigenous peoples of the Far North have experienced similar problems and changes due to the introduction of Western culture and schooling. Since education often motivates and facilitates change, it is reasonable to expect that the effects of Western education on the various Northern indigenous societies have been similar in many ways. Therefore, although we come from opposite sides of the Pole it is important to note, but it should not be surprising, that our individual understanding of the situation, is, for the most part, remarkably similar.

The purposes of the authors in publishing this book, their understanding of terms related to cross-cultural situations and concepts, and a brief description of the peoples and areas they consider are covered in Chapter 1. Chapter 2 introduces certain perspectives on schooling and society upon which the authors have based their discussions as they developed the body of this book. Moreover, Chapter 2 serves as the foundation for the discussion in the final chapter where their theories of education in multicultural societies are the main subject.

In Chapter 3, education is examined in relationship to the places and physical setting in which the people of the Far North live and their demographic characteristics are summarized. The historical development of formal education in each of the countries under consideration is presented in Chapter 4. Chapter 5, in which topics in education that currently are at issue are examined, concludes Part Two.

In Part Three we briefly return to the history of education and the issues we have discussed in Chapter 5 as a means to better tie the four domains of our subject together. This will allow us to make comparisons between countries and summarize what we have learned over the years as a foundation for Chapter 7. There, we expand the perspectives and notions we introduced in Chapter 2 into tentative theories of education in multicultural societies as a conclusion to the book.

Places included and ethnic groups considered

Because education among the people of the Far North is the focus of the book, it is necessary to explain what we mean by this term and identify the groups of people with whom we are concerned.

All of what we refer to as the Far North lies in the Arctic and Subarctic geographic/climatic zones of the world. Much of the area borders the Arctic Ocean. Identified by national group, this area includes the USA, but in that country only the American state of Alaska; Northern Canada, including the Yukon Territory, the Northwest Territories, Arctic Quebec, and Labrador; Scandinavia, including Northern Norway, Sweden and Finland; and, finally, Northern Russia (see Map 1).

Circumpolar peoples inhabiting these regions are comprised of many groups with a wide variety of ethnic origins. Collectively, they are Alaska Eskimos, Aleuts, and Indians; Canadian Inuit, Dene, and Metis; Greenlandic Inuit; and in Norway, Sweden, and Finland the Saami. Although not covered in this book, by far the largest Arctic and Subarctic land masses and the most numerous Northern indigenous groups are in the Republic of Russia. Approximately 750,000 indigenous minority people live above the 60th degree of latitude in that country. They range from the Saami on the Kola Peninsula in the West, to the Komi, the many

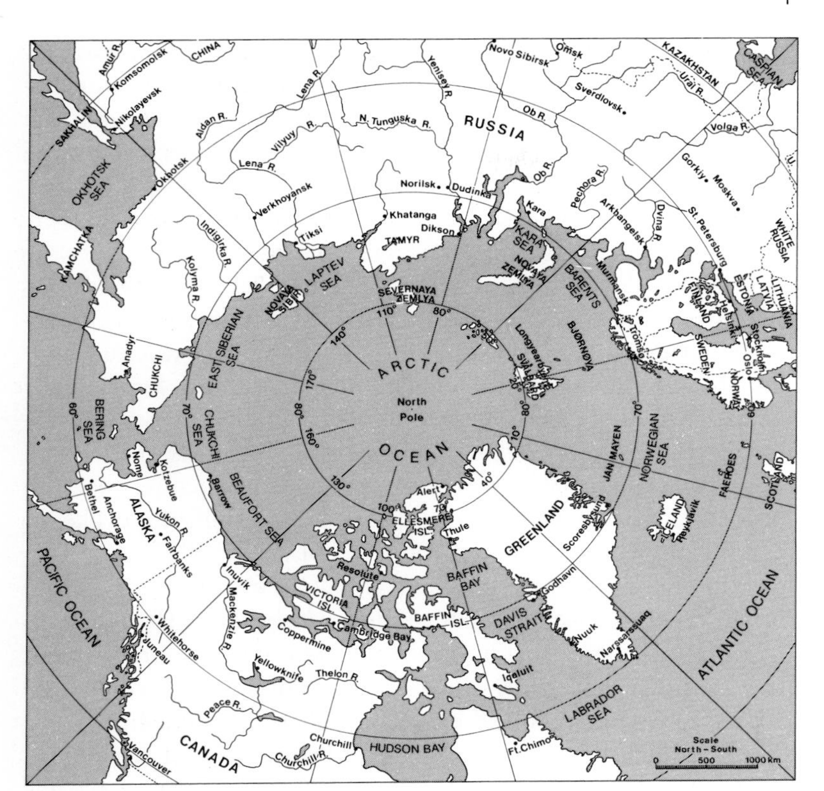

Map 1. Polar projection of the Circumpolar North.

small groups who speak the Samoyedic language across central Russia, to the Yakuty in the Lena Basin, and finally to the Chukchi and Eskimos on the shores of the Bering and Chukchi Seas in Siberia, to name only a few.

As beneficial as it would be both from an academic point of view and in terms of the appropriateness of learning from the practical experience of still others, it has not been possible for us to include the indigenous peoples of the Russian Far North. Little is known about education among these people, and there is much more to be learned from their history and current practices. And both the extensive land mass and numbers of indigenous peoples living there far exceed those of other Northern countries. The decision not to include Russia is due entirely to the fact that neither our experience nor our knowledge is sufficient to adequately describe the situation there. Nevertheless, even without the Russian Far North, the area with which we are concerned is more than one-half of the entire Circumpolar world.

Terms defined

Education is such a commonly used word it hardly seems necessary to define it here. However, it is used in various ways depending on personal preference and circumstances; thus, for the sake of clarity in this book we have selected a definition from the literature that best suits our need. In his book *Traditions of American Education,* Lawrence A. Cremin has defined education as "the deliberate, systematic, and sustained effort to transmit, evoke, or acquire knowledge, attitudes, values, skills, or sensibilities."[3] This definition is especially consistent with our experience and appropriate to the way we relate education to the way we define culture.

Although there are innumerable definitions of culture found in the literature, especially since anthropologists and sociologists who specialize in this field have decided on many meanings, we need to establish how we use the term.[4] Simply stated, we see culture as the stored composite of knowledge a nation or a people has at its disposal. In keeping with this use, culture forms the basis for understanding and mastery, for a single individual, a society or a nation. As such, it is the mechanism of group survival and, according to Bullivant, "consists of the public knowledge and conceptions embodied in the behavior and artifacts, or cultural forms, that enable the group to adapt to [the] environment."[5]

It follows, therefore, that if social groups are to survive, and this is one of the basic dilemmas of all indigenous peoples in the Far North, their cultures must be transmitted from generation to

---

3. Cremin 1977, p. viii.
4. For a thorough discussion of the definition of culture, see Kluckhohn 1966, pp. 19–73.
5. Bullivant, Brian M., "Culture: Its Nature and Meaning for Educators." In Banks and Banks (eds.) 1989, p. 43.

generation. Education and systems of education, regardless of form and locus of control, are inextricably a part of this process.

Since there are many definitions of culture it is also important for us to state how we do not use it. Culture is sometimes used by others, in a loose way, as a substitute for 'society.' Since we look upon culture as the stored knowledge of a society or sub-society that enables the society to survive as a group, it is an apparatus of, not a synonym for, society. As explained by Pullman, "People belong to, live in, or are members of social groups; they are not members of culture."[6]

Two related terms, cultural pluralism and cultural homogeneity, are often used in association with education in multicultural societies that we also need to differentiate. Both express ideological positions that have polarized some elements of contemporary society in recent years. In some circles cultural pluralism has become a term used to denote cultural imperialism. In this context, the separation of cultural groups with different and separate beliefs is inflexibly advocated as a means to assert cultural identity and minority rights at the expense of the larger society as a whole. (Unfortunately, some critics of contemporary education mistakenly see this concept as being synonymous with multicultural education – more correctly defined below.) Cultural homogeneity, the ideology of a uniform or "melting-pot" society, on the other hand, is the antithesis of cultural pluralism. Proponents of this ideology advocate that minority cultural identity be relinquished in favor of a thoroughly uniform society. When taken to extremes either cultural homogeneity or cultural pluralism prevent a dynamic multicultural society from developing in an orderly fashion.[7]

As a conceptual term more appropriate to our discussion, we favor the use of 'ethnic pluralism' to describe a middle course between cultural pluralism and cultural homogeneity. Ethnic pluralism, unlike cultural pluralism, has been used as an empirical concept to describe relationships between groups in society.[8] In

6. Ibid., p. 28.
7. For an extensive attack on multicultural education, see Schlesinger, Jr. 1992.
8. Banks, James A., "Issues and Trends in American Education – Pluralism and Educational Concepts: A Clarification." In Borg (ed.) 1981, pp. 26–29.

this sense, according to James Banks, "ethnic pluralism describes a society composed of various ethnic groups fully participating in ethnic sub-societies but having allegiances to the nation state and accepting its idealized values."[9] Acceptance of this concept as a goal of education is seen as a necessary step to develop better schools in the Far North. It follows, therefore, that the extent to which indigenous minorities participate in the larger society of which they are a part, but are able to retain some patrimonial cultural characteristics, will have a direct bearing on the extent to which schools will prove to be a success.

Ethnicity and minority, two other terms we use throughout this book, also require clarification as to what they mean to us. Race, as a term, while related, is not used in our discussions because of fluctuations in the way the word is interpreted, and because it is sometimes confused or substituted for ethnicity. As characterized by Van den Berghe, race refers to a group that is socially defined only on the basis of physical criteria. Ethnic groups, while also socially defined, are distinguished on the basis of cultural criteria.[10] Ethnicity refers to a number of people who perceive themselves to be in some way united because of their sharing a common cultural background but not because of the way others may perceive them, and especially not because of physical appearance.[11] Furthermore, ethnic groups are products of distinct histories, irrespective of physical characteristics. Perlman has made the point, that "[we] need not seek the single, constantly primary factor creating ethnic distinctiveness, nor even a single generalization that will cover the relationships among several factors, far better, with a comparative perspective and an eye on theory, to explore the individual ethnic histories."[12]

As for the terms minority/majority, it is paradoxical that in many instances, minority peoples are in the numerical majority in the Far North. This is to say they may account for the greatest number of individuals in a society, but are in a minority position

9. Ibid.
10. Lee 1993, p. 75.
11. Cashmore and Troyna 1990, p. 2.
12. Perlman 1988, p. 219.

because of the political, economic, and educational dominance of others. Minority, then, refers to a state of relative power and is not necessarily dependent on numbers.

Throughout the book we use two terms, Native and indigenous, to identify the minority population. These terms are at present the most extensively used in the literature and the ones most often used by the people themselves as a generic descriptive term that portrays the original minority residents of the Far North. As we use it, then, Native may be defined as "an original inhabitant of a place as opposed to an invader, explorer or colonist" or as "the first or earliest known inhabitant." Indigenous may similarly be defined as it is a synonym for Native. We do not see a stigma attached to either Native or indigenous, although we recognize that historically "native" has been used in a prejudicial manner to describe minority groups and individuals in some parts of the world. Aboriginal is preferred in place of Native or indigenous in some circles and is replacing them in some locations, but it too is a synonym for Native. More recently "First Nations" peoples is the preferred term for indigenous individuals, communities, or societies in some locations and is currently finding favor among some indigenous peoples, especially in parts of Canada.

Both assimilation and acculturation are terms often associated with schooling in multicultural societies. We see assimilation as meaning the cultural absorption of a minority group or individual into the main cultural body of which they are a part. Absorption in this sense implies becoming like someone or something else. Acculturation, a separate but related term, on the other hand, is the process of conditioning an individual or group to the patterns or customs of another culture.

Multicultural education, currently a topic of contention in many parts of the world, is concerned with the acquisition, development and transfer of knowledge from many cultures in societies where either two or more ethnic groups are living together. In addition to this sense of the term, multicultural education also is concerned with mono-ethnic minority groups that are, nevertheless, in contact with and under pressure from external formal institutions, such as school systems, commercial advertising, and mass media, including film, TV, and print. These influences make it necessary for education systems to be sensitive to, include specifics of, and respect minor cultures wherever found. However, these considerations not withstanding, regardless of the need for and worth of minority cultures in school programs, they should not predominate at the expense of the need for minority students to acquire the knowledge of scientific and cultural thought from other cultures.

Because of this we reject monocultural education in any society. Simply put, it is often biased toward the dominant group. In monocultural education, as Nieto has pointed out, "those who decide what is most important generally reflect the dominant view and make choices that are of necessity influenced by their own background."[13] Furthermore, there is the requirement that goals and objectives of the culture in question are accepted without question.

On the other hand, a recipient of multicultural education, the universal person, to take Walsh's position,

> finds himself facing a much wider range of possible goals.... He discovers that another culture [or] other cultures, open up vast new perspectives to him and add wholly new dimensions to his thinking. Most often he does not at all want to relinquish the values and goals of the culture into which he was born, but at the same time he finds himself drawn toward, and directed by new goals which transcend any one particularized culture.[14]

Cross-cultural education (sometimes used as a synonym for intercultural education), a term closely related to multicultural education, came into prominence in the Far North earlier than multicultural education. It differs little in principle from multicultural education. As defined by Walsh, it is

> that process by which the people of one culture arrive at new and deeper knowledge of, and a better understanding and appreciation of, the nature and functioning of different contemporary cultures.... [It] aims to change the negative attitudes of the people of one culture toward those of another, and to reinforce positive attitudes.[15]

---

13. Nieto 1992, p. 212.
14. Walsh 1973, pp. 46–47.
15. Ibid., pp. 62, 63.

Defined this way, the term suggests that there need not necessarily be a multicultural population in the community to benefit from cross-cultural education. People in monocultural communities, such as were first found at the time of contact, are as likely to benefit from this form of education as are those in multicultural societies. However, the prefix "cross" indicates that knowledge flows both ways between two cultures and that school personnel and policy makers from outside the culture of the subject community have an obligation to learn about and respect the culture of the society in which they work as much as they expect their students to learn about the culture they bring with them.

Both multicultural education and cross-cultural education require teaching/learning strategies and processes that enable people to participate in and value their respective sub-societies, while providing the means to acquire the knowledge necessary to be successful members of the multicultural society at large. Equally important, they reduce discrimination against stigmatized ethnic groups. They do not, as contended by antagonists of multicultural or cross-cultural concepts, divide societies; on the contrary, they teach the richness and value of diversity. By providing all components of the society with equal educational opportunities, the ultimate purpose of either cross-cultural education or multicultural education, then, is to provide the means by which an aggregate society may become ethnically pluralistic and egalitarian in character.[16] To achieve these goals it is the responsibility of the school to develop in its students the competencies necessary to master the complexities of multiple cultures in a balanced fashion, free of stigmatized or pretentious perceptions of any single culture.

The emergence of widespread commingling of peoples of diverse ethnic patrimony in many regions of the world has given rise to a proliferation of multicultural societies. This movement in turn has created numerous problems of social adjustment for both the minority and majority components of those societies. It

16. For a more thorough discussion of multicultural education along these lines, see Banks and Banks (eds.) 1989.

has become apparent that educational problems concerned with this development can be identified in many places among the world's various societies, the Far North being no exception. But, unlike many large populations, the Far North, because of its unique position among regions of the world, and its small numbers of people, affords a singular, manageable example of the role of formal education in societies undergoing cultural transformation. Lessons learned in the Far North may have applicability worldwide. The most profound aspects of multiculturalism point to inclusiveness and egalitarianism rather than exclusion and racism.[17] Thus, whereas the focus of this book for the most part is about education among indigenous minorities, some of our observations and conclusions may apply to the education of immigrant minority students as well.

Worldwide, mass movements of people from less to greater developed countries are substantially reshaping the population composition of countries heretofore predominantly monocultural. The full impact of this development on society in general and education in particular has yet to be realized by many of those responsible for the essence of schooling. Writing on the move to change the constitution of Canada in a way that would have redistributed decision-making authority that more closely reflected that country's multicultural population (a good example of a means to cope with this problem, but an effort, incidentally, that failed at the ballot box), Martin Woollacatt expressed the view that "giving adequate representation to people in diverse and geographically widespread societies, reconciling minorities, and dividing up powers between various levels and centres of government in a workable way has a fair claim to be the single most important political problem of our time."[18]

Woollacatt's view applies to both indigenous and immigrant minorities, and although there are similarities between the two groups, there are differences between them that need to be kept in mind, especially in regard to policy formulation. Except for those

---

17. Fredrickson 1993, p. 17.
18. Woollacatt 1992.

seeking political asylum whose lives otherwise are at risk, immigrants are, to use Ogbu's term "voluntary minorities." That is, they have chosen to live in a society with a culture different from the one into which they were born. As Ogbu has explained, "Immigrant minorities have generally moved to their present societies because they believe that the move would lead to more economic well being, better overall opportunities or greater political freedom."[19] Conversely, indigenous minorities had little or nothing to say about why or how they acquired their minority status.

These differences notwithstanding, in the ideal school system goals of education in multicultural societies will be much the same for both indigenous and immigrant populations. However, the policies and means by which these goals are reached may differ from group to group. In our final chapter we elaborate further on this notion as we look at emerging theories of education in multicultural societies.

19. Ogbu, John U., "Immigrant and Involuntary Minorities in Comparative Perspective." In Gibson and Ogbu (eds.) 1991, pp. 8–9.

Chapter 2

Perspectives on School and Society

School systems for the indigenous peoples usually are limited to the years of compulsory schooling and, in North America, non-compulsory secondary schools. However, in recent years educational programs for indigenous peoples that comprise all stages from the primary level to the university have been developed. In this book our discussion is primarily concerned with compulsory elementary and elective secondary education except in the section on teacher training where higher education is included.

Schools have existed among the indigenous minorities for as long as three hundred years in some regions and as few as forty in others. Controversies about educational materials and methods over these years have been resolved more often in favor of a conservative and inflexible approach to schooling than by innovations and adoption of new ideas.[1] Consequently, schools are more static than dynamic places of learning. At first they provided only the means to learn to read, followed in turn by writing and arithmetic. It has only been in recent years that schools have included provisions for equality of opportunity among members of multicultural societies by assuming responsibility for the maintenance of the indigenous culture while simultaneously providing the means to succeed in the contemporary multicultural society.[2]

There are circumstances and considerations which intrinsi-

1. Walle-Hansen and Hoëm 1992, pp. 94–107.
2. Hoëm 1990a, pp. 185–94.

cally determine the efficacy and outcomes of these schools, just as in education systems and programs in all societies. In effect, they are the factors that enable us to frame the subject of this book and to set the tone of the chapters that follow. The way we have perceived them in the Northern setting has guided us in our analysis of the education systems described in the following chapters.

Problems of developing a general theory of education in multicultural societies

In the ideal situation, a society and its system of education are congruent. That is, the levels and composition of education programs will be compatible with the society's technological, economic, social and cultural development, a point we return to throughout the book. Therefore, in societies that rely on a subsistence economy for much of their daily living, a Western-style school, if lacking in conformity with the community, would be as inappropriate and as dysfunctional as a rural, one-room school emphasizing a subsistence life style in a large, modern, technological society. In short, to be functional and predictable, a school must be in accord with and integrated into all aspects of that society of which it is a part; otherwise the enterprise is at risk. Furthermore, technology, economic systems, and cultural and social characteristics are variable over time, thus their power to interact with and influence the character of the school is similarly variable.

Congruence between society and the school is also at risk when the education system is the center of tension because of antagonism between extreme ideologies. This is most apparent when purposes and goals of education are being debated, especially when the debate includes differences of opinion as to the value of such things as locus of control, curriculum content or the meaning of equality of opportunity. Similarly, tensions surface when pressures are applied in favor of certain political ideologies that are contrary to educational principles of the community. The perennial debate on language of instruction for minority children is a good example of this type of tension, with elements of both political ideologies and pedagogical doctrines in contention for dominance.

Furthermore, there always will be protagonistic and antagonistic positions between the various forces at odds in any community, regardless of its size and stage of social development. The extent of power of any one of a number of community forces and their ability to interact with other forces will determine the educational goals of the community as well as the level and style at which the community will be able to function in general. Moreover, the effectiveness of each force will vary as each strengthens and weakens over time.

The challenge to create a successful education system that fulfills community needs while simultaneously relieving or avoiding destructive ideological tensions, then, is to identify and understand these forces and their relationship. In the chapters that follow we identify some of the forces and elements of the community and their relationships for their own sake, but also as a means to develop a general theory of education suitable for multicultural societies that may explain them.

Of course, there are problems in formulating any theory that attempts to explain situations with complex variables. Such is the case with education; thus we have focused on three particular aspects of the Circumpolar milieu to frame our conclusions: 1) the local community as a basic unit of society and the focal point for all activities and considerations; 2) the school system as an entity within the society and the extent to which it relates to local needs; and 3) change as a phenomenon in Native societies. Most components of the people's lives and the changes they experience are interconnected by these influences. Thus, it is the local community, the school, and, ultimately, the nature of change that inform our assumptions and give our theme direction.

The local/ethnic community and the school

Usually small in population, villages and settlements across the Far North generally have fewer than 300 to 500 persons, with only a few larger units that range in size from 2,000 to 16,000, the two largest being Nuuk, Greenland (14,000), and Yellowknife, Northwest Territories (16,000). The extent of exposure to outside cultural influence in local settlements or villages has varied over time across the Far North. In the case of a some locales, such as the Far North in Canada and remote locations in Alaska, it has only been in recent times that they were not isolated. In others, such as communities in Northern Scandinavia, coastal Alaska and Southwestern Greenland, Native contact with Western culture has been extensive for many years, hundreds in some cases. Regardless of the length of time since contact has had a bearing on local customs and the ethnic composition of the communities, there are certain pre-contact ethnic and cultural characteristics that persist today in Native societies.

Daily life reflects an interwoven web of phenomena representative of different levels of society, both at the macro- and microlevels. In Native communities, especially those with tenacious ethnic characteristics, traditional values require that activities at both levels be in accord with those values. However, as stated by the Alaska Native scholar Angayuqaq Oscar Kawagley,

> the incursion of western society on indigenous peoples has brought about many cultural and psychological disruptions in the flow of life in traditional societies. Indigenous people have become subservient to the western system and are confronted with new social structures which they do not always find compatible with their needs.[3]

For example, if a family is striving for cultural and economic freedom along traditional lines, it may be inconsistent with this purpose to send their children to a Western-style, culturally homogeneous school. The paradox in this situation is illustrated by the family ideologically advocating Native culture while adopting a Westernized non-Native life style. However, an awareness of this contradiction of principle and the ability to see a lack of integration between the different levels of their indigenous community has the potential to give uniqueness and character to ethnic cul-

3. Kawagley 1993, p. 1.

tures and school programs. Conversely, it is the inability to recognize this form of uniqueness and insistence on a strict Western-style education that produces tension between the school and society.

Also significant in the maintenance and modernization of indigenous cultures are the means to preserve and advance traditional institutions within the community. Kinship systems and their interconnected social networks are among the most important of these traditional institutions. They are complex, multifunctional, and their parts intrinsically interrelated. As such, the kinship system is the basic unit in the structure of the community; it allocates the work that has to be done, it takes care of religious and other ceremonies, provides for social welfare, and preserves the economic system.

This list of functions, typical of most traditional institutions, can be extended to cover almost all social and economic elements in the community. The main function of the kinship system, then, is to bring about interaction of all aspects of the society thereby giving it its multifunctional character. For example, the institution for the upbringing of children illustrates the interconnectedness and multifunctionality of this phenomena. In a traditional indigenous society child rearing takes part throughout all of the different activities that make up daily life in the community. This is in sharp contrast to the structure of modern Western institutions, where each function of the society usually is carried out independent of the other, child rearing included.

Also at the community macrolevel, the theme of ethnic minority sovereignty and autonomy is of importance. Often this topic is related to issues of land and water rights and the capacity to keep and develop indigenous culture. It can be shown that historically indigenous peoples have developed their culture through a long struggle with nature. Thus, it is argued, to be able to maintain their uniqueness as a people there is a need to retain historic fundamental rights, including the responsibility for controlling traditionally occupied lands.

By raising the subject of sovereignty and autonomy, a central issue among indigenous peoples, the even more fundamental question of whether it is possible to ever retain and further develop traditional societies and cultures is broached. Furthermore, an awareness of differences between traditional and contemporary Western society evokes an equally fundamental question: What still actually remains of the traditional culture and what does it really mean to revitalize and modernize it? While answers to these questions can only be speculative at best, an awareness of them is fundamental to resolving problems in education. By invoking them we at least add to the background of our theme even though answers can only be suggested by inference.

In the minority society there are often conflicting interests and different views as to what issues actually are important and intercommunity controversy can arise over the most practical and achievable ways to resolve differences. One explanation for this problem is the accelerating speed at which changes in society are taking place and a corresponding lack of ability to determine what are and what are not important changes. Indigenous minorities in the Far North undergoing changes as profound as those found everywhere about them are bound to experience unrest. Thus, schools are caught up in the struggle of the people to regain a new form of stability – a struggle compounded by a paradox that exacerbates the problem. Education, as an element of Western society, is a source of strain on the traditional indigenous society caused by the schools' failure to recognize their worth or values while simultaneously having the potential to provide a means to cope with change.[4]

In this regard, technological innovations are of special interest, both because they are so immediately available and adaptable and because often they are seen as culturally neutral. In actuality, technological innovations create tension between those favoring adaptation and those adhering to traditional ways of doing things. Moreover, this condition is more convoluted in indigenous societies in the Far North than it might be elsewhere because of the indirect social and cultural consequences of such innovations.

4. Darnell 1980.

Traditional societies, development, and change

The phenomenon of change and the concept of traditional culture and their effects on the development of education applies to much of our perspective in the chapters to follow.

A common way of looking at traditional Native customs is to define 'traditional' as the culture that was prevalent at the time of contact with Western societies. When used this way the user is dependent on reports from the first Western voyages of "discovery" and historical data describing Native societies through the work of early anthropologists and missionaries. While this is a worthwhile field of research it provides only a partial picture of the traditional societies today. Native cultures are intrinsically dynamic and do not need to be "protected" from external forces of change, a policy sometimes advanced in the past by governmental authorities as justification for limiting their responsibilities toward minority populations.[5] Indigenous peoples in the North are as interested in innovations that enhance their quality of life as people anywhere. It is demeaning to think otherwise. But like change anywhere, not all change results in positive development. The correct stratagem for those responsible for education systems is to recognize the difference between those changes that have a positive potential and those that do not.

Northern societies, rather than being culturally static, have had the need and ability to keep pace with the vicissitudes of nature over the centuries. One of their most unwavering cultural characteristics is the ability to cope with ever-changing conditions of daily life, especially changes in nature that affect subsistence resources and general living conditions in their harsh natural environment.

But along with changes in nature, man-made factors, especially factors from the South that have influenced re-evaluation of traditional life style have been introduced in Native societies,

---

5. Thuen, Trond, "The Ethnic Dimension in Future Arctic Cultural Research, Some Anthropological Viewpoints." In Broadbent (ed.) 1992, p. 16.

thereby putting a strain on their ability to maintain social stability. Therefore, while traditional ways that existed at the time of contact are a consideration in the relationship of Native societies to contemporary education systems, so too are the traditions that are relatively recent societal or cultural innovations due to outside influences. So it is that we find both historic tradition and more recent traditions born of innovation and constantly changing conditions that make up contemporary tradition.

Accordingly, it can be said that contemporary cultures derive from different traditions; they are a mixture of ancient cultures and adaptations due to changes over time, both in nature and because of the introduction of man-made elements from other cultures. This is also the case with societies; they are ever changing through adoption of characteristics from other societies, in various forms and stages of development. This is especially so in indigenous societies in the North. For example, in local communities both traditional kinship systems and systems of family relationships typical of the outside world can be found simultaneously. So too are both ancestral tools and modern technological equipment, subsistence economies and Western market systems, Native languages and second languages, and traditional and foreign religions all found side by side in Far Northern societies.

Therefore, those responsible for education policies and programs need to understand how changes take place, what generates them, the degree and pace at which they are taking place and the extent to which they alter the situation, for better or worse. For example, Kawagley illustrates the complexity of change processes by showing that they can have both positive and negative consequences at the same time:

> most villagers have no qualms about taking advantage of Federal and State grants for generating electricity, roads, airports, housing, and assistance to the needy. This has brought new opportunities to the village and local administrators have learned to account, budget, report on activities, and to live by the rules and regulations attached to these institutions. From the point of view of some elders, however, this is seen as a disease of the newer generation, especially with respect to assistance to the needy.

> In their view, it has effectively relieved villagers to their self-esteem, self-reliance, self-sufficiency and self-determination.[6]

Some innovations, however, apparently are free of the cultural and psychological disruptions associated with cultural change. These, while enriching Native life styles, apparently do not endanger or compromise that life style. A good example of this kind of adaptation to Western culture has also been pointed out by Kawagley:

> An interview with a middle-aged dog musher illustrates how some people have successfully integrated old and new ways on their own. He has 35 dogs in his kennel. He feeds his dogs fish until the fall, then switches to commercial dog food interspersed with fish. He has a brand that has worked best for him. He had to develop a knowledge of nutrition, stamina, disease of the dog, and looking for signs of non-producers.... He must be able to diagnose disease.... He must be able to remedy these. He has had to work with a veterinarian and read materials on the above.... He has been adapting to new knowledge and ways with dogs and sleds.[7]

Even though Native societies in the North have a tradition of coping with change as a natural phenomena and making it a characteristic of their typical way of thinking, not all change has been integrated in society smoothly. This predicament is due primarily to the differential rate or pace of change among the various sectors or categories of change factors. Of these, the most powerful are modern technology, market economic systems, Western social organization and Western cultural value systems. But, by comparing the rate of change in society due to these factors, it can be shown that categories of change are not necessarily introduced at the same rate nor are they accepted in the Native society at the same rate. Modern technology is introduced the most often and brings about change at the fastest rate, followed in turn by market economics. Social organization and Western cultural value systems typically become integrated at the slowest rate.[8]

It is this differential rate of influence and adaptation, resulting

6. Kawagley 1993, pp. 116–17.
7. Ibid., p. 118.
8. Hoëm 1990b.

in a subtle form of cultural incongruity and incompatibility between the different categories of change, we believe, that have created the most profound tensions in society. Such tensions in turn create further changes, namely changes in social order, leading to social dissonance and unrest. This tension is almost always related to ethnicity. For example, when all terrain vehicles were introduced in Saami communities it was thought of as just another technical innovation. But immediately social and cultural consequences due to the innovation emerged. Their presence gave rise to a new and emotionally charged question: did the innovation interfere with the purpose of reindeer symbols of ethnic identity? In like manner, this concern gave rise to the question of whether ethnicity is more closely connected to the modern mastery of technological matters or to the historic tradition of mastery of animals?

As mentioned above, technological and economic innovations are more frequently introduced and integrated with less effort than are social and cultural phenomena. The main reason for this difference is because technological and economic innovations are erroneously perceived as being culturally or socially neutral. Often they have immediate utility and are easily replaced or improve existing functions of traditional technology or economies with little regard for the immediate consequences on social or cultural values. Often it is through the school that such innovations are first introduced, making the school a fundamental agent of change. Furthermore, when schools limit their subjects to a body of knowledge from Western culture at the expense of Native culture, it intensifies the differential rate of change. This is often perceived as an expression of disregard for the Native store of knowledge and implies that such knowledge is of little or no value. There have been many well-intended but misguided developments in school programs because this phenomenon is little understood. Also, it is this situation, in part, that has given rise to many contemporary problems in Native societies in general. How these have evolved and how they are now constituted are the subjects of the next three chapters.

Part Two
Places, Programs, and Issues

Chapter 3

The Physical and Demographic Setting

The Far North in general

To better understand the problems of providing education among the indigenous peoples of the Far North, it is helpful to examine the environment in which these people live and the circumstances that have influenced their lives. Natural surroundings, political histories, and social relationships all have contributed to the present cultures of Northern indigenous societies. These factors, and the ever increasing in-migration of people from societies to the south, along with widespread introduction of their value systems and technology, have been especially instrumental in bringing about cultural changes among the indigenous minorities. Thus, the following background material sets the stage for discussions on schooling and society to come later.

Indigenous peoples of the Far North, as a general category, are comprised of many groups with a wide variety of ethnic origins. As mentioned in Chapter 1, collectively, they are Alaska Eskimos, Aleuts, and Indians; Canadian Inuit, Dene, and Metis; Greenlandic Inuit; and in Norway, Sweden, and Finland, the Saami. Thus, it can be seen that the Circumpolar World, even excluding the Republic of Russia, is a vast, sparsely populated region comprised of all of Greenland and the most northerly parts of the United States (Alaska), Canada (The Yukon, Northwest Territories, Arctic Quebec, and Labrador), Norway, Sweden, and Finland. The combined political units of Northern Canada account for the largest of these "polar" areas with approximately 4,648,545 sq. km

(1,794,805 sq. miles). These include the Northwest Territories (1,304,903 sq. miles), the Yukon Territory (207,076 sq. miles), Arctic Quebec (170,000 sq. miles), and Labrador (112,826 sq. miles). Greenland is next in size with 2,175,600 sq. km (840,000 sq. miles), followed by Alaska with 1,518,776 sq. km (586,400 sq. miles), and Scandinavia (excluding Denmark) with 1,369,560 sq. km (528,803 sq. miles).

Regardless of the huge expanse of land over which Circumpolar people live, similarities among them are more prevalent than dissimilarities. Fundamentally it is a shared affinity for the land and the demands of its extremes that have given them a high degree of similitude over a realm that encircles more than one-half of the globe.

In this book, political divisions which characterize the lives of indigenous people of the Far North have been arbitrarily used as one of the means to distinguish the groups under discussion. Although this organizational scheme is more in keeping with conventional ways of looking at regions of the world, it is an unnatural division. Physiographic features, on the other hand, and the distribution of ethnic groups discussed are not necessarily confined to specific political units. For example, because of shared climatic and topographic features and dependence on similar natural resources, there are many common cultural characteristics among the Inuit of Alaska, Canada, and Greenland, irrespective of the flags under which they live. The Inuit range from northwestern Alaska to Labrador and the east coast of Greenland, a distance of 4,800 km (3,000 miles) across some of the most physically hostile (although strikingly beautiful) country in the world. Until quite recently, some of these people, cut off from contact with the rest of the world, lived by means of the most basic subsistence life style possible. In like manner, the Saami have been one people with the same cultural characteristics for centuries, yet their land cuts across the frontiers of Norway, Sweden, Finland, and Russia. And Indians of Alaska and Canada share a common cultural heritage, shaped in large part by the environment in which they live, without reference to the international boundary that separates them.

By any comparative standard, Arctic and Subarctic lands are among the most physically severe in the world. In the higher latitudes temperatures during the long winters drop below –50°C and the sun fails to rise above the horizon for as long as three months during the winter in some communities or settlements. Nevertheless, these areas have been inhabited by indigenous peoples for thousands of years. It is only natural, therefore, to expect that such an environment has exerted a strong influence on the nature of the various groups of indigenous people found there. Compelled in part by the severity of this environment, complex cultures with sophisticated languages, value systems, and knowledge bases as well as an ingenious although limited material culture have developed over time. Moreover, physical constraints under which Northern indigenous peoples live and the limited resources available to them have given rise to unique life styles and survival mechanisms with common features throughout the Far North. These same constraints have kept the population small in number simply because the limits for human survival, based on available food and shelter, were reached long ago.

Since the geographic areas with which we are concerned are in the Arctic and Subarctic, it should be noted that, depending on the observer, these terms are used with different meanings. To many, the Arctic simply is limited to lands above the Arctic Circle, while the Subarctic lies below it. A more acceptable way to others is to designate the Arctic as a geographic zone that comprises all areas above the tree line, i.e., that line beyond which trees are unable to grow regardless of altitude or latitude. Others designate it as the area above the 10°C July isotherm or use the permafrost (perennially frozen ground) line in like manner. All three, the tree line, the 10°C July isotherm, and the permafrost line, each being a climatic phenomenon, are closely related and are a more natural delimitation of the Arctic zone than the inflexible Arctic Circle. In some places these boundaries fall far south of the Arctic Circle.

Polar geographers continue to refine the terms that describe the North and debate the merits of a variety of criteria that are used in polar terminology. Fine gradation of terminology aside, there is another aspect of polar terms that is relevant to our subject. According to Stager and McSkimming,

> [Arctic regions] have a unique and distinguishable physical environment that is a consequence of an overriding characteristic, the relative absence of heat energy. It is the high latitude location that is paramount as a climatic control and enables the Arctic to be recognized as different from similar environments, like Alpine regions, that are cold because of high elevation. With a climate of low heat energy there are corresponding biological and physical responses that have become incorporated in the definition of the boundaries of the Arctic.[1]

This condition explains why there is such a limited variety of naturally occurring flora and fauna in the Arctic available to sustain human life. Accordingly, this condition has had a profound effect on the culture of Arctic peoples and speaks to the necessity for a high level of resourcefulness and ingenuity necessary to survive in such an environment. It also explains one of the reasons for cultural similarity among the peoples who inhabit the Arctic sector of the Far North.

Below these climatic lines that encompass the Arctic, the land gives way to the Subarctic. However, there are great differences within the Subarctic zone in vegetation, climate, geology, and physiography. Subsequently, the Subarctic as a zone is more difficult to delineate than is the Arctic. In some cases the Subarctic penetrates the higher latitudes substantially north of the Arctic Circle. Yet it is generally characterized by a large variety of flora and fauna, much of it more or less within the boreal forest, another term not easy to define. As described by Gardner,

> the great expanse of the Subarctic precludes detailed presentation of all its spatial and temporal variability.... [However], environmental elements [are] of particular significance to Whites ... for it is they that have stimulated a new dynamism. The impact of Euro-Americans and industrial technology on the environment and people of the Subarctic has been, and will continue to be profound.[2]

---

1. Stager, John K., and Robert J. McSkimming, "Physical Environment." In Damas (vol. ed.) 1984, p. 27.
2. Gardner, James S. "General Environment." In Helm (ed.) 1981, p. 5.

While Northern people have much in common historically due to a demanding natural environment, so too have all of them come under pervasive and, at times, disruptive influences of cultures from the south. It is the impact of Euro-Americans and industrial technology on the indigenous people found in both the Arctic and Subarctic that is of particular interest when considering the nature of formal education in these regions.

Although we are primarily concerned more with the ethnographic characteristics of peoples of this zone than those of the environment, it is necessary to recognize that it is the environment in the Subarctic as well as the Arctic that has contributed substantially to the ethnographic and demographic characteristics of the people. So too have natural resources been an incentive for the in-migration of non-indigenous people into the region. Consequently, the environment has given rise to cultural adaptation of the indigenous and non-indigenous alike. By way of elaboration, Gardner has made the point that

> the Subarctic environment is complex and dynamic. The physiography, climate, hydrology, flora, fauna, and soils, all interacting, provide the stage and context for human life and activity. By the standards of the temperate regions and modern postindustrial society, it is a harsh and rigorous environment. Yet viable cultures and economies have developed and thrived within it ... [and] one can not ignore the fact that elements of the environment have been, and will continue to be, attractive to outsiders. By this process, the physical environment of the Subarctic and the social, economic, and technological context of life there is being transformed.[3]

This northward movement of society and technology has been the stimulus for profound changes in the lives of indigenous minorities, in both the Arctic and the Subarctic. More often than not it has been characterized by Western-style resource development at the expense of the traditional life style of indigenous minorities, especially in those areas where the people have only recently come under the sustained influence of industrial development. Much of the responsibility for enabling all Northern peoples, Native and non-Native alike, to cope with this situation now falls

---

3. Ibid., p. 14.

to those who develop policies and practices for systems of education among the multicultural populations that now inhabit these regions. Moreover, it speaks emphatically to the need for all concerned to have a better understanding of the types of programs of education that are appropriate to the vicissitudes of multicultural societies in such a unique environment.

Physical characteristics within each political unit

Alaska

At the time Alaska was purchased from Russia in 1867, the Russians had nearly exhausted the then-known resources of the land, notably fur-bearing marine animals. The *New York Post*, which was opposed to the purchase, editorialized that the United States had purchased a "sucked orange." Of course, Alaska is no longer looked upon in such deprecating terms. That Alaska was perceived as an unknown frozen waste by many for nearly two hundred years after first being described to the Western world by European navigators, however, is not surprising. Given its distance from the world's population centers of that time and other regions of the world competing for development capital during the 18th and 19th centuries, it is understandable that little attention was given to Alaska.

Although occupied by the Native population for thousands of years, it was not until the voyage of the Dane Vitas Bering in 1741, on behalf of Imperial Russia, that the location of the Northwest Coast of North America was known to the rest of the world. Soon after the voyage of Bering, British explorers, notably Cook and Vancouver, followed, as did explorers from Spain, France, and Germany. Reports of their voyages, while monumental for their time, did not leave the impression that Alaska held promise as a place for large or permanent settlements. Nor did these first voyagers adequately describe the nature and scope of the land beyond the coast line or the extent and diversity of the Native population, although valuable ethnographic data was collected.

It was not until the American presence in the late 1880s, including the explorations of American scientists and participants in several notable gold rushes of that period, that Alaska's principal physical characteristics became better known. Even then there remained many misconceptions about the physical nature of Alaska and its indigenous inhabitants. Only in recent times have most of these been set aside. Although much of Alaska has long winters, low temperatures, high winds, and short, cool summers, certain climatological factors provide for a temperate climate and comfortable living conditions in several areas. Nevertheless, there are vast, sparsely uninhabited areas that are apt to remain so because of their severe climate, inadequate economic potential, and inaccessibility. It is in these regions that many of the Native villages are found, scattered over hundreds of thousands of square kilometers. This condition is one of the factors that complicates the problems of providing programs that meet educational needs of village residents

Alaska is by far the largest state of the United States. (It is more than twice the size of Texas, the largest of the contiguous states.) Geographically, it extends from 54°40' north latitude in the south (on a parallel with Copenhagen) to 71°23' north latitude at Point Barrow (on a parallel with the northern tip of Norway) and from 132°41' west longitude near Stewart, British Columbia to 172°26' east longitude at the end of the Aleutian chain, the same longitude as New Zealand. The east to west southern boundary of the state, extends 5,120 km (3,200 miles) from point to point.

Although conspicuous by its large size, Alaska is an entity primarily because its residents are bound by a common set of laws within specific political boundaries. Otherwise, there are many regional Alaskas, making it what is sometimes described as a "federation of subsystems." It can be divided into several physiographic, and climatic provinces. These in turn have been responsible, in part, for the differences in the development of the various cultures found among the indigenous population.

In a generally accepted classification of land forms, the state has been divided into four principal areas: 1) the Pacific Mountain System, with several ranges (Coast, Fairweather, St. Elias, Chugach,

Alaska, and Aleutian), which form the Pacific boundary of the state from the tip of Southeast Alaska to the end of the Aleutian Chain; 2) the Brooks Range, which extends across the northern section of the state entirely above the Arctic Circle; 3) the Interior Basin, which is a vast intermontane plateau between the Pacific Mountain System and Brooks Range, having a continental climate with extremely cold winters; and 4) the Arctic Slope, which lies north of the Brooks Range to the coast of the Arctic Ocean.

Within these geographic provinces a full range of climatological conditions are encountered, from temperate to severe. Slightly over one fourth of the state lies north of the Arctic Circle and 56 percent between the Arctic Circle and the 60th parallel. North of the 60th parallel most areas exhibit some Arctic or Subarctic characteristic of which the true Arctic consists of approximately 388,500 sq. km (150,000 sq. miles).

The climatic belts of the state tend to follow the general land forms because of the influence of the two mountain systems. The Pacific Mountain System shields the Interior of the state from the warm, moist air of the Pacific and provides a sharply breaking line between the continental climate of the Interior and the cool, temperate climate of the Pacific coast. Similarly, the Brooks Range in the north provides a transition zone between the Arctic climate of the North Slope and the climate of the Interior.

Climatically, then, the state can be divide into four major zones, affected by, but not identical to, the four physiographic zones: 1) a temperate maritime zone along the Pacific Coast bounded by the Pacific Mountain System and the Pacific Ocean with temperate climatic conditions; 2) the Interior Basin zone between two major mountain systems, with extreme cold in the winter and warm, dry days in the summer; 3) a coastal zone along the Bering Sea without clear-cut boundaries but merging gradually into the Interior zone on the east and the Arctic zone on the north, typified by cold, wet winds and low, mean temperatures; and 4) the Arctic or North Slope from the Brooks Range northward to the Arctic Ocean with below-freezing temperatures possible the year round.

Thus, as a large peninsula, or more nearly a subcontinent, surrounded by water on three sides, the climate of Alaska is powerfully influenced by ocean temperatures, and the intensity of storms moving inland from the sea. Contact between the cold waters of the Arctic Ocean and the warm waters of the Pacific is through the Bering Sea. But the entry of the warm Pacific waters into the Bering Sea is blocked by the Aleutian Island Chain, a segment of the Pacific Mountain System protruding above the Pacific Ocean floor as a submarine wall. As a result, the Bering Sea is cold, and the winter ice pack extends further south in this area than in any other part of the Northern Hemisphere. The net effect is to give the Bering Sea Coast a harsh, Arctic climate. This is reflected in the barren, windswept terrain which extends northward from Bristol Bay in the south until it finally merges with the Arctic Coast. Such extremes have profoundly influenced the life style of its inhabitants and their educational needs.

Many remote Native villages are located in the Bristol Bay–Bering Sea–Chukchi Sea coastal region and the Interior Plateau (where temperatures reach as low as –55°C and as high as +25°C), giving rise to the need for a large number of very small schools in small villages in an extremely harsh climatic environment. Inadequate or inaccurate information about living conditions in these and most of the rest of rural Alaska has accounted for numerous errors, both in the administration of territorial/state services and provisions for schooling.

Canada

The Canadian Far North accounts for approximately 40 percent of the total land mass of Canada. On a north–south line it extends from the tree line at approximately the 48th parallel in the south (the most southerly dip in the tree line is located in Quebec) to Cape Aldrich on the northern tip of Ellesmere Island at 83°6' north latitude, the northernmost point of land in Canada. The southern border of the Far North extends across Canada for 4,800 km (3,000 miles) and is common along four of Canada's provinces at the 60th parallel. Its eastern boundary is along Advise Strait and Baffin Bay, bodies of water adjacent to Greenland on their eastern side, while the western boundary of the Yukon Territory (and therefore Canada's most westerly border) shares the 141st meridian with Alaska.

Because of its extreme size and great distance from easily navigated seaways and rivers it has only been during the latter half of the 20th century that there has been widespread interest in the potential value of the Canadian Far North. Although romanticized in literature through the exploits of early polar explorers and French-Canadian voyagers, other than by the Native population, the true nature of such a vast land is known to only a few still today.

Canada's Far North consists of four primary political divisions: the Yukon Territory, the Northwest Territories, Arctic Quebec, and the Labrador section of Newfoundland (see Map 2). Except for the Belcher Islands of the Northwest Territories, Labrador, and portions of Arctic Quebec, the rest lies above the 60th parallel. However, lines of latitude are innovations of mankind and although convenient devices for purposes of political demarcation they do not necessarily coincide with population classifications or the traditional land use and occupancy patterns of indigenous peoples. Therefore, in addition to Native peoples that reside in the Canadian Far North many indigenous peoples in the northern parts of each of the Canadian provinces have experienced problems in education and social relations similar to those found north of the 60th parallel. To the extent conditions and situations in the provinces are similar to those in the Far North, our observations and conclusions most probably hold true for those places further south as well. Incidentally, many geographers consider the northern sections of all Canadian provinces to be part of the true Canadian Far North. This is especially so where the tree line falls below the 60th parallel, such as it does in Ontario and Quebec where it is found at the lowest latitude of anywhere in the world. When these areas are included in the definition of the Canadian Far North, it comprises approximately 7,000,000 sq. km (2,750,000 sq. miles), about three-fourths of the entire country. Nearly four-tenths of this area is above the tree line and for the most part is underlain with perennially frozen ground.

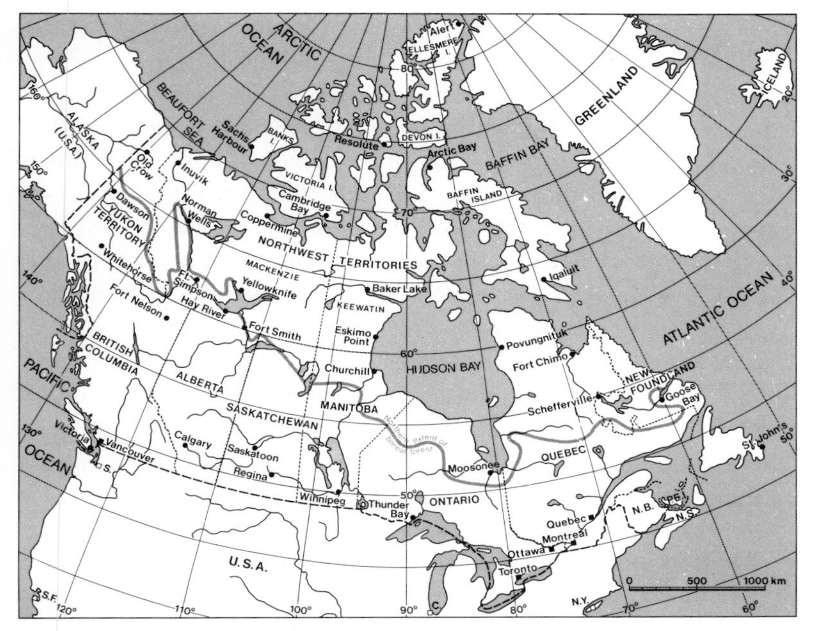

Map 2. Canada, with tree line shown.

Though much greater in size than Alaska, climatic characteristics of the Canadian Far North are not as complex, albeit in much of the country they are more severe. This is so because so much of the Canadian land mass is cut off from the moderating effects of the oceans by extremely high mountains. On the western edge of the country in the Yukon Territory, there are several peaks above 4,000 meters (13,120 feet), the highest being Mt. Logan at 6,052 meters (19,850 feet). Relatively rugged mountains, but not as high as those in the west, are found on the eastern fringe of the country along the coast of the Atlantic Ocean, Advise Strait, and Baffin Bay. Furthermore, the Canadian Arctic Archipelago, that large group of islands north of the North American continent, contains the highest mountains in the Eastern Arctic, the highest, at 2,600 meters (8,500 feet), being on Ellesmere Island.

The vast interior between these coastal mountains is extremely rough and barren with many lakes but few mountains to interrupt the movement of cold air masses. Indeed, the most commanding feature of the Canadian landscape is the Canadian shield, a vast extent of ancient Precambrian rock stretching across the country that comprises almost two-thirds of the entire Canadian Far North. The result of these factors are long winters in much of the country and extremely low temperatures over much of the land, –62°C (–86°F) at Snag in the Yukon Territory being the record recorded low at an inhabited place. Winter lows of –45°C all across the continental mass are not uncommon. Winter freeze-up varies somewhat due to local conditions, but ice can be expected on lakes and rivers in most locations by early to mid-October and spring break-up between the first part of June to early July. Furthermore, winds are severe much of the year, especially along exposed coastal stretches, exacerbating the harshness of the environment. Offsetting this effect, the continental climate found throughout much of the Canadian Far North accounts for summer conditions that can be very warm, as high as 35°C (95°F) on brief occasions in a few locations. Nevertheless, summer is brief even in the warmest areas and along the Arctic coast temperatures can fall below freezing during any summer month. But putting temperature extremes aside, it is the low annual mean temperature and persistent wind that account for the severe living conditions across Northern Canada. These conditions demand the most ingenious cultural adaptations to sustain life and for centuries severely limited the number of people the land was able to support.

Greenland

Greenland, the largest island in the world, is physically the most dramatic land mass of all the polar regions. It covers an area of 2,175,600 sq. km (840,000 sq. miles) that extends a distance of 2,670 km (1,669 miles) from Cape Morris Jesup at 83°39'N, the most northerly land mass in the world, to Cape Farewell in the south at 59°46' north latitude, about the same latitude as Oslo and Anchorage (see Map 3). Greenland's most striking feature is its great ice sheet which covers four-fifths of the island. The ice sheet, or ice-cap, reaches a maximum altitude of 3,330 meters (10,800 feet) while the highest mountain in Greenland is 3,733 meters (12,265 feet). At its greatest, the ice is as much as 3,500

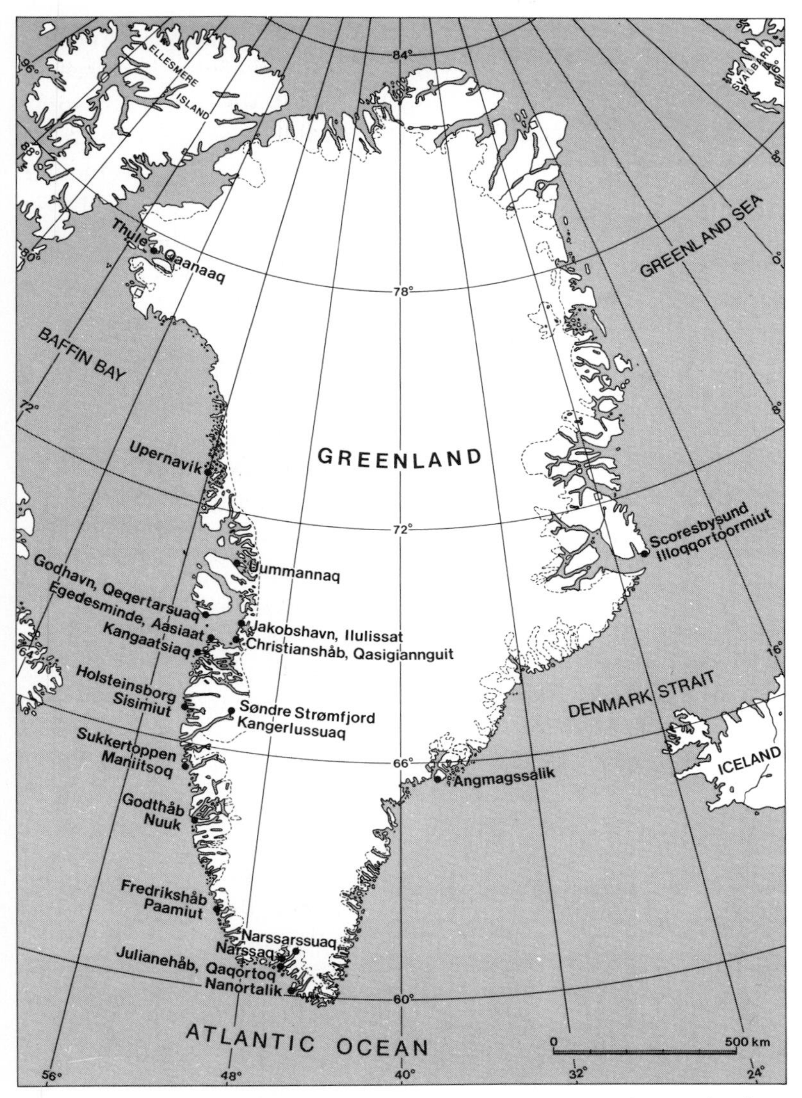

Map 3. Greenland, with place names shown in Danish and Greenlandic.

meters (11,480 feet) thick, the average being 1,500 meters (4,920 feet). It is estimated that if the ice sheet were to melt it would raise the level of the sea worldwide by 6.5 meters (21 feet).

Those portions of Greenland not covered by ice are fairly well divided between the north, east, and west coasts, an area of approximately 350,000 sq. km (135,000 sq. miles). In some places these stretches of coast are imposing examples of the most majestic mountain topography in the world. Long, spectacular fjords, unequalled for beauty, characterize both the east and west coast. It is along the shores of this dramatic setting that the indigenous peoples of Greenland are found in small and large settlements, some of which have been inhabited for hundreds of years.

Only the Antarctic continent has more severe weather than Greenland. On the ice sheet temperatures have been recorded as low as –70°C (–138°F) and it is seldom above freezing in the summer. The mean annual temperature on the ice sheet is –20°C to –30°C (–4°F to –22°F). However, due to the moderating effects of ocean currents the climate in the southwest of Greenland is, relative to its latitude, fairly mild. In this region fertile grasslands today support sheep farming, first introduced by Norsemen a thousand years ago. This mild area notwithstanding, severe storms are also the rule even there; all locations in Greenland come under the influence of harsh weather conditions.

Scandinavia

The Scandinavian countries comprise that portion of the Circumpolar World covered in this book that is in the Eastern Hemisphere. The Nordic countries of Denmark, Iceland, Finland, Sweden, and Norway are all known as the Scandinavian countries although only Norway and Sweden are on the Scandinavian Peninsula. However, we cover neither Iceland nor Denmark; Iceland because it has no indigenous minorities and Denmark because it is south of the Subarctic (except as the history of Denmark applies to the early rule of the Scandinavian Peninsula and to Greenland as a Danish colony).

Map 4. The Nordic countries: Norway, Sweden, and Finland.

Among the Polar countries the physical characteristics of Scandinavia are probably the best known to the general public. With an extensive tourist industry and a reputation for some of the most attractive scenery in the world, all of the Scandinavian countries have been well publicized. Even those portions that comprise Saamiland/Lappland are fairly well known, although they do not get the volume of travelers that are found in the south of Norway, Sweden, and Finland. Located as far north as Alaska and much of the Canadian north it might be expected that the Scandinavian climate would be similar to other northern lands. But this is not entirely the case, latitude being only one criterion that influences climate. Because the climate over parts of Scandinavia is moderated by the warming effects of Atlantic Ocean currents, many areas are temperate, especially along the Norwegian coast.

Sweden is the largest of the Scandinavian countries with 449,675 sq. km (173,620 sq. miles). Finland is next in size with 337,008 sq. km (130,119 sq. miles), and Norway has the least area with 323,916 sq. km (125,064 sq. miles). Collectively the three countries cover an area of 1,369,600 sq. km (528,803 sq. miles), similar in size to Alaska. The northernmost extent of Scandinavia is at North Cape in Norway (71°11'N) and in the south at the tip of Sweden at approximately 55°10'N, close to the latitude of the southern boundary of Alaska.

Although there is much worldwide interest in Scandinavia, much of it focused on Scandinavian culture, it is only the northern portion or "Northern Cap" as it is sometimes called, that is pertinent to the subject of this book. The Saami population is, for the most part, confined to the area north of the Arctic Circle, consisting of Finnmark, Troms, and Nordland counties in Norway, Norrbotten in Sweden, and Lappi in Finland. It is in this part of Scandinavia that the physical characteristics of the land come the closest to the rest of the Circumpolar World. Compared with the rest of Europe the Northern Cap is remote, severe in character, sparsely populated, and cold. Nevertheless, when the climate is compared with Greenland and North America it is relatively mild. Neither the Norwegian Sea nor the Barents Sea on the Atlantic Ocean and Arctic Ocean side of the peninsula freeze over, although the Gulf of Bothnia at the head of the Baltic Sea does. There, because of its distance from the Atlantic, a more continental climate is found so portions of Finland and Sweden have colder winters than western and northern Norway. And, of course, over the whole Northern Cap the sun is below the horizon in winter for several weeks and heavy snowfall is the rule along the coast. In the interior of Finnmark, in Norrbotten and Lappi counties, temperatures can be depended on to drop as low as –50°C (–58°F).

The terrain along the coast is rugged with glaciated mountains as high as 2,000 meters (6,560 feet). Long, spectacular fjords, considered to be some of the most spectacular scenery in the world, distinguish much of the coast. Inland a plateau supplants the mountains with vast stretches of rolling tundra so characteristic of reindeer grazing range. It is here that the Saami are most numerous and form the majority population.

Demographic composition

Although the demographic composition of the Circumpolar North was briefly covered in Chapter 1, it is complex enough and pertinent enough to our subject that it is informative to describe it in more detail. In all the countries we cover, indigenous minorities are the majority population in certain sections of the countries in which they are found, but are small minorities in the total population of their respective national states. Indeed, it is this relationship and intermingling of ethnic groups that has given rise to many of the problems associated with schooling throughout the North.

Alaska

Of the several ethnic groups that comprise the population of Alaska, the largest segment is made up of white, English-speaking Euro-Americans. This group, consisting of 438,900 people, accounts for approximately 77 percent of the total Alaska population of 570,000. The indigenous population as a whole consists of 15.1 percent of this total with approximately 86,000 individuals (but 21 percent of the school-age population). The remainder consists of blacks (3 percent), Asian/Pacific Islanders (2 percent), and "others" (just under 2 percent).[4]

Although it is not possible to reconstruct the demographic composition of Alaska at the time of contact with Western society in 1741, it is estimated that the total population then was

4. US Department of Commerce 1992.

74,700. Of this number, approximately 40,000 were Eskimo, 16,000 Aleut, 6,900 Athabascan, and 11,800 Tlingit-Haida-Tsmishian.[5]

Contact with non-Natives, at first only by Russians seeking furs, brought tragedy to the Native population. Exploited as hunters, victimized in massacres and subjected to epidemics of smallpox, the Native population was reduced to an estimated 39–40,000 by 1839. Over the following years other diseases, such as influenza and tuberculosis, added to the toll. These diseases were aggravated by the destruction or reduction of essential elements of the natural resource base on which people depended and by the many unfortunate changes resulting from the head-on clash of two disparate cultures. Russian fur seal hunters in the Bering Sea, whaling fleets from many countries, and, later on, unregulated commercial fishing methods that depleted salmon runs all contributed to a decline in population.[6]

Such adversity is reflected in the population figures which declined to an all time low of 25,331 by 1910, at which time a slow return to higher figures took place. Increases in population notwithstanding, it was in 1939 that the Native population ceased to constitute the majority population of Alaska as a whole. The ratio of Native to non-Native has continued to decline, although the total Native population continues to increase; today, with approximately 86,000 individuals, it is the largest ever.

Most Alaska Natives live in 180 small, isolated villages randomly scattered across approximately 1,295,000 sq. km (500,000 sq. miles). Over 52,000 of Alaska's Natives, approximately 61 percent of the state's total indigenous population, live in this area, sometimes called "village Alaska." It is comprised of nearly 87 percent of the land mass of Alaska (geographically divided between Arctic/tundra, the interior plateau, and maritime areas). Outside of village Alaska the largest number of non-Natives live in five urban centers of the state, the greater Anchorage area being the largest by far, where nearly 50 percent of the total population

5. Rogers 1962, p. 75.
6. Fitzgerald 1967, pp. 13–14.

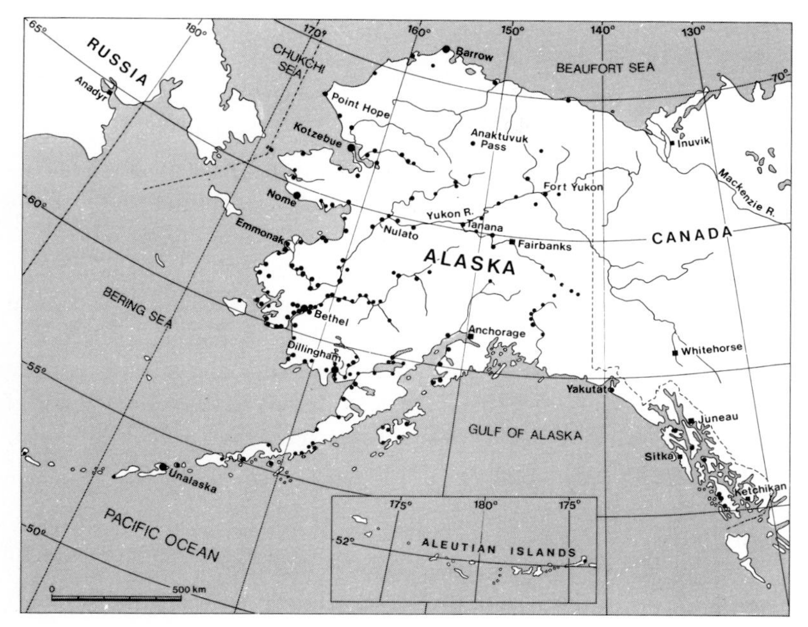

Map 5. Alaska, showing distribution of village sites.

of the state live. The urban centers of Fairbanks, Juneau, Ketchikan, and Sitka account for the bulk of the remaining total. The significant aspect of this demographic feature is that Alaska Natives comprise a majority in rural places and non-Natives make up an urban majority. However, this Native superiority in numbers in rural areas does not necessarily assure them a major share of Native decision-making authority or influence in political, economic, or education concerns in rural areas.

Although we use the term Alaska Native to identify the indigenous population, it is a term used to collectively identify all distinctly different Native groups found in Alaska. It is the term preferred by the Native people to identify themselves as a pan-Alaskan population with common needs and aboriginal rights. Included in this broad category are 1) the Eskimos, composed of two distinct groups, the Yup'ik, generally found in Southwest Alaska adjacent to the Bering Sea, and the Inupiaq, for the most part on the Chukchi Sea and Arctic Ocean Coasts (however, a few

Inupiaq villages are located some distance from the sea); 2) the Aleuts, who are distantly related to the Eskimos, inhabiting the Aleutian Islands; 3) the Athabascan Indians, who live south and east of the tree line (the divider between Indian and Eskimo domains) and accordingly are found mainly in the Interior Yukon River Basin, the Copper River Basin, and Cook Inlet area (part of a much larger group of Athabascans living in Canada and the southwestern United States); and 4) the Tlingit, Haida, and Tsimshian Indians, the coastal people of Southeast Alaska.[7] Climatically, Southeast Alaska can not be classified as Subarctic, being part of the great Pacific Coast rain forest. However, because the Native population there belongs culturally to the broad classification of Alaska Native, they are as much a subject of this book as those who live to the north of them.

Canada

Two features of the population composition of the Canadian Far North bear on the problems of developing an appropriate education system for the indigenous peoples living there. First of all, the tree line divides the country into two ethnological domains; Inuit to the north of it, Indians to the south. The tree line, as an outermost feature of nature has given rise to distinct cultural, societal, and economic differences between the Indian and Inuit populations. However, it is not only the harshness of the Inuit habitat delineated by the tree line that has shaped the Inuit way of life; it is the very remoteness of their world which limited cultural contact for such a long period of Western history as well. Thus, with the abrupt introduction of formal education, culture contact was accelerated at a previously unknown rate, especially in the Canadian Eastern Arctic.

There is another demographic characteristic of Canada's indigenous population that has had a profound effect on the development of education. As previously pointed out in the Alaska case (as well as will be seen in Greenland and Scandinavia), in nearly

7. Oswalt 1967, pp. 2–10.

all rural sites, the indigenous population is the majority population in sheer numbers, but the minority population in cultural and economic leverage. Schools with their uniform, state-prescribed standardized education systems often failed to take this phenomenon into account.

An extremely small number of inhabitants in relation to the size of the land mass characterizes Canada's demography in the Far North. The population density is very low. Of the four primary political units in Canada that we consider, the Northwest Territories has the greatest number of residents, 57,649, but that is only 0.2 percent of the Canadian total of 29,100,000 in 1994. Of these, approximately 20,300 are Inuit, the name preferred by that group of indigenous people previously referred to as Eskimo; 9,300 Dene (Athapaskan); 3,200 Metis; and 1,200 multiple indigenous. Thus, the Inuit account for 35 percent of the total population of the Northwest Territories and occupy about 30 settlements, all but one coastal, the greatest number in the Eastern Arctic where they comprise about 85 percent if the population. The Dene represent about 16 percent of the population, the Metis 5.5 percent, and 2.2 percent are multiple indigenous, most of whom live in the West.

Arctic Quebec has the next largest number of Natives with 4,500 Inuit who live in 12 coastal settlements. And there are approximately 1,000 Inuit and 1,000 Algonkian who live in the Labrador section of the province of Newfoundland. The Yukon Territory had 27,791 residents in 1991, only 0.01 percent of the Canadian total. Of that number there are approximately 5,400 Indians and no Inuit.

While Inuit and Indians are the two legally recognized ethnic groups in Canada, a third category of indigenous peoples exists. Unlike other Polar countries, Canada separates Indians of "mixed blood" into a distinctive classification of people based on the fact that they are the progeny of mixed parentage. The term used for this classification, Metis, is derived from the French word for a "cross-bred" or "half-caste" person, that is, a "half-breed." In particular, it referred at first to the offspring of a French-Canadian and Canadian-Indian couple. Some observers believe that it now applies to a person of either Indian or Inuit and "white" parentage and may have lost some of its earlier prejudicial tone. Richard Slobodin, in his studies among the Metis of the Mackenzie District in 1966, observed that

> a consensus among the people of the North, including those called Metis, would, it is believed, agree that Metis are non-treaty Indians and unlisted Eskimos; that is, persons of Indian and Eskimo ancestry who are not in the legal position of Indians and Eskimos.[8]

Although in the eyes of government Metis do not exist officially in the lexicon of governmental provisions for Native Canadians, in recent years more attention has been paid to their social, educational, and economic needs, depending in part on where they live. As their particular status is related to schooling, many have experienced the same problems of cultural dissonance in the school setting as Indians and Inuit. Likewise, where discrimination is shown to exist, be it in social, commercial or school settings, the Metis experience differs little from that of other Native North Americans. Where we refer to schooling among the Native people of the Far North, our observations and conclusions apply, for the most part, to the Metis population as well.

Greenland

The first inhabitants of Greenland are believed to have arrived there from the West more than 4,000 years ago. Archaeological evidence suggests that they emigrated from nearby Ellesmere Island in Arctic Canada, a mere 20 km from the northwest corner of Greenland. In all likelihood these immigrants were in the same wave of early people who started in Norton Sound in Alaska and slowly moved across the Arctic rim until they eventually reached Greenland. These early arrivals are not thought to have survived and there is little they left behind as evidence of their way of life. However, through a series of newer arrivals more suited to the climate and terrain, the population increased and the culture

8. Slobodin 1966, pp. 4–5.

became more complex. The last of these people in the eastward migration, identified as the Arctic Whale Hunting Culture, or better known in Alaska and Canada as the Thule Culture, can definitely be traced to their origins in Alaska. They arrived in Greenland about 1,000 to 1,100 years ago. Clearly they were Inuit whose culture can be linked to the Bering Sea, where it had evolved, most likely a thousand years before they arrived in Greenland. Because they were marine mammal hunters and not solely dependent on land animals as had been their predecessors, much larger communities than those previously established were both necessary and viable. It was at this same time that Norse settlers arrived in southern Greenland and the pattern for eventual co-mingling of vastly different ethnic lineages and cultures was set in place.[9]

When the first European missionary, Hans Egede, arrived in Greenland in 1721 it is thought that there were as many as 8,000 Inuit living there. The first official census was not taken until 1805 at which time 6,046 Greenlanders were counted, but the residents of the far north and east coast were not included in the count as their existence was not then know to the Danes. Since there were only a few hundred Inuit found to be living on the north and east coasts, and if the census of 1805 is to be trusted, the estimate of 8,000 given for the time of Egede may be too high.

Between the early 19th and the mid-20th century, the population gradually increased to about 20,000. However, it was during this period that there was considerable contact between the Inuit and Europeans, at first among the whalers followed by Danes who came to settle. There was considerable intermarriage between the Inuit and Danes and mixed families were not uncommon. Following World War II, with the opening of Greenland to the Western world, the population grew even faster. By the mid-1970s the population was approximately 50,000. Much of this was due to Danish immigration since the birth-rate among Greenlanders fell during this time because of widespread contra-

9. Larsen, Helge, "The Origin and Cultural Development of the Population." In Hetling et al. (eds.) 1975, pp. 115–20.

ceptive use. Among the current population of 55,553 (census of 1991), approximately 80 percent can claim Inuit ancestry.

Scandinavia

Determining accurate population figures for the Saami, the only indigenous minority people in Scandinavia, has always been problematic. At first this was due to the remoteness and vastness of the land over which they were distributed as well as to their nomadic life style. In more recent years it is more a matter of deciding how each individual should be counted, the criteria differing among the various census takers and countries. Moreover, Saami populations are intermixed with other Scandinavians, except in a few small communities. Saami physical appearance is not as distinct from the majority of Europeans as appearance of Native North Americans and Greenlanders is from Euro-Americans, and there has been a fair amount of intermarriage between the Saami and other Scandinavians. Scandinavians have never had a system similar to the Americans by which indigenous people were officially given Native status by virtue of the amount of Native blood. Formal distinctions between Saami and non-Saami have been rare; rather, it has been a matter of the use of language, costume, and declarative statement that have set them apart, identifying factors that neither have been nor are uniform. Complicating this situation has been stereotyping and prejudice against the Saami by the non-Saami population with the result that the Saami have been forced "to acquire majority cultural traits for economic and social advantage but to display minority traits, mostly the Saami language, for purposes of intimate relations and group identity."[10]

Problems of demography aside, it is estimated that the current Saami population numbers 40,000, as large as it has ever been. Of this number, 21,000 are in Norway (approximately 0.50 percent of the population of Norway); 12,000 in Sweden (0.13 percent of the population); 5,000 in Finland (0.07 percent of the pop-

10. Roland 1993, p. 79.

ulation); and 2,000 in Russia, mainly on the Kola Peninsula. Although the Saami population is small compared to many minority groups, it accounts for a large percentage of the total population to the whole in some regions of the sparsely populated North. The population can be divided into three distinct subgroups: coastal or sea Saami; reindeer herders who live in the mountains; and the forest Saami in Finland and Russia. In each of these regions the Saami have a viable (although endangered), complex culture. The Saami population has also been broken down into sub-categories based on economics, geography, or dialect. For example, the Hoëm Committee of 1982 subdivided Norwegian Saami into four groups: the Northern, the Southern, the Lule Saami, and mixed or bilingual–bicultural Saami.

The term Saami has originated from Saapmi, which means the land where the Saami live. In recent years it has become the name the people prefer to use about themselves. Used this way, it is both singular and plural, and may be used collectively to designate an individual, a society, the culture, and the language.[11] Lapp, a designation still used to identify the people of Northern Scandinavia, is still accepted in some circles, but in others it has a negative connotation. Lappland, on the other hand, is still used as the accepted term for the Saami region of Sweden.

Archeological evidence shows that the northern part of Scandinavia has been populated for over 10,000 years. It is not known for certain if the Saami are the descendants of the original inhabitants, but they are considered to be so and thus are now recognized as the indigenous population of the Scandinavian Far North. The earliest written description of the Saami is attributed to the Roman historian Tacitus (circa 100 A.D.), in which he describes them as primitive people with no horses, dressed in animal skins and using bone weapon tips for hunting because of their

11. Writing of the Saami, Robert Paine has pointed out that "the people's own name for themselves is, in nominative singular, *sabmi;* in accusative and genitive singular, *sami;* and in nominative plural, *samit.*" He uses, as we do, Saami for both the singular and plural, as well as for an individual person and the society, culture, and language. As Paine further explains, "the 'aa' is phonetically appropriate [in speaking English], avoiding the sounds of 'Sam' and 'same.'" Paine 1994, p. 215.

ignorance of iron.[12] The anthropologist Christian Meriot has divided the history of the discovery of the Saami people by southern Europeans into three periods: prehistory, which extends into the 9th century; the second period, a time of "discovery," colonization, and subjugation lasting into the 18th century; and the third period, characterized by scholars, travelers, and missionaries moving about throughout Saamiland and describing it in accurate terms. These investigators, in the words of Meriot,

> were certainly more driven by demands of administration and evangelism, but their investigations, while not always directly fired by a zeal for pure knowledge, show a concern for accuracy and a critical appreciation from which can be drawn the indispensable foundations of ethnological observation.[13]

Present-day Norwegians and Swedes also are thought to be descendants of other early settlers in the North, but came later than the antecedents of the Saami. Finns, on the other hand, did not move into Saamiland until well into the 16th century.

---

12. Meriot 1984, p. 373.
13. Ibid., p. 373.

Chapter 4

Historical Development of Schooling

The historical development of schooling reported in this chapter is not intended to be a definitive history of education in the Far North. Instead it is a survey of events that have contributed to the most notable characteristics and problems of schooling as we now find them. As might be expected, covering as broad a geographic area as we do here, historical events are found to vary from place to place, but, remarkably, there is greater similarity among them than there is difference. In each of the countries we cover, similar cultural conflicts and institutional forces have shaped education policies. Furthermore, throughout the history of formal education school systems have, for the most part, been designed as instruments for the assimilation of the Native population into the dominant national culture. Seldom, until recent times, did they provide a means to maintain or enhance the distinctive cultures of Native groups.

Alaska

The history of formal schooling in Alaska can be divided into four parts: the Russian period; the early American period; the period during which Alaska was a territory of the United States; and, finally, the years since Alaska became a state of the United States.[1]

1. Much of the early history reported in this section is adapted from Darnell 1970.

The Russian period

The first instance of Western schooling in Alaska occurred at Three Saints Bay on Kodiak Island in 1784, site of the first permanent Russian settlement. The Russian presence in Alaska was then, and throughout the Russian occupation, primarily for the purpose of exploiting natural resources, mostly the harvesting of marine fur animals. As private entrepreneurs acting with profit motives, and with little interest in establishing permanent settlements or carrying on scientific work, there emerged "one of the most shameful chapters in the annals of white man's conquest."[2] It has been estimated that in the first hundred years of Russian occupation the number of Aleuts, the Native group most affected by enslavement and other adverse effects of the Russian occupation, declined from a pre-contact population of 16,000 to 2,200.[3]

There were random efforts, however, on the part of some Russians, particularly through the Russian Orthodox Church, to change the tyrannical methods of the fur traders. Catherine II made these efforts official in 1766 when she ordered, "make it clear to the promyshlennicks [fur hunters] that they are to treat their new brothers, the inhabitants of these islands, kindly and without the slightest persecution and deceit."[4]

The founder of the first school, Gregory Shelikov, as head of the fur-trading company seeking a monopoly on all fur-harvesting activities, reported that the Aleut Natives were starting to imitate Russian customs as a result of his efforts at schooling, which was seen as a positive consequence of their presence because, in his opinion, "only literate people can be good and accurate interpreters, so needed in this country." In order to further this trend he stressed the need to train the Natives so as to make them good navigators and seamen and to teach them crafts, especially carpentry.[5]

Nevertheless, efforts to start the first school, as altruistic as the

---

2. Harjunpää 1967.
3. Rogers 1962.
4. Tikhmenev 1978.
5. Ibid., pp. 87–88.

motives of the founder may or may not have been, were primarily inspired by the need to demonstrate to the empress and the head of the Church that the organizers were worthy of being granted a monopoly in the fur trade and to better equip the Natives to work for the company.

With Western European and American traders arriving in Alaska on a regular basis and with Russian vessels over-extending their range, the need for permanent Russian bases became more acute. In 1799 the formation of the Russian-American Company was accomplished by imperial charter from the Russian government and an element of Russian permanence in North America was established. The company was to become the dominant force in Alaska for the next 68 years and, due to the terms of its charter from the Russian monarch, the *de facto* government.

The charter required the company to establish schools in connection with its trading activities. Subsequently, a primary goal of education from the point of view of the Russian-American Company was to benefit itself by providing schooling that would support company middle management and clerical skills. For the privilege of attending school some students were required to remain in the service of the Company for a period of 15 years.[6] Church schools, which taught the rudiments of reading, writing, and Christian doctrine at several missions, a few of which were located in remote Native villages, were established in addition to company schools.

Natives were allowed to attend company schools, but no special effort was made to use the schools as a "civilizing" force. For the most part, company officials were only interested in the forced labor of Natives and at times were compelled to find ways to discourage increased conversions by the Church, especially because the company had to support the mission schools.[7]

Throughout the Russian period, one figure stands out as the exception to Russian ruthlessness. Ivan Veniaminov, a Russian priest who lived and worked among the Native people for many

6. Okun 1951, p. 215.
7. Ibid., pp. 211–21.

years during the first half of the 19th century, considered the overall intellectual as well as spiritual welfare of the Native people the responsibility of the Church. He developed an Aleut alphabet and compiled a grammar of the Aleut language as well as similar work among the Tlingit. In this way he predated the movement for bilingual education in Alaska by more that one hundred years. Eventually, Veniaminov became metropolitan of the Russian Orthodox Church at Moscow, which may explain in part why Russia continued to support mission schools in Alaska until 1916, long after the United States purchased Alaska.

The educational activities of both the Church and the company are difficult to separate because the company financed the Church at the same time as it opposed its presence. Except for the work of Veniaminov, neither made any real attempt to bring education to large numbers of indigenous peoples for education's sake, especially since it would not have been in their interests to provide Natives with the means of progressive self-improvement or an interest in a more egalitarian society.

In summarizing the activities of the company, Okun concluded that the ultimate reason educational efforts were deficient was because

> the policy of the Company was identical with that of the government, and that it was actually the government which handed over the original inhabitants of the colonies to the Company in absolute bondage. And only when the question of liquidating the Company had been decided, did the government assume the attitude of a disinterested defender of the Natives and utilize facts, that it had known for decades, to accuse the company of the illegal exploitation of those Natives.[8]

With the Russian-American Company's activities and influence waning in the final years of its operation, all educational activities of the company ceased. A few years previous to the transfer of Alaska to the United States, the Russian-American Company discontinued its schools as a result of increasing expenses and lack of purpose for their existence. However, that was not a great loss

8. Okun 1951, p. 210.

since the Russian-American Company, and even the Russian Orthodox Church, lacked purely munificent motives, being mostly concerned with replicating their cultural order to enhance Russian commercial enterprises.

The early American period: 1867–1918

Development of education during the early period of the American presence in Alaska was influenced by three factors: the cultural underpinning of the dominant society which defined the objectives and structure of schooling in general; Presbyterian Church officials, who were the controlling figures in the implementation of early schools; and the slow execution of any government policies across such a vast and inaccessible tract of land.

Under a treaty signed by the United States and Russia, concluded March 30, 1867, by which Alaska was sold to the United States, all inhabitants who did not reserve their natural allegiances to Russia, with the exception of so-called uncivilized Native tribes, were "admitted to the enjoyment of citizens of the United States." Unprepared for the acquisition of such an extensive territory and with such a small and inconsequential population in the view of most Americans, the US Congress gave little attention to Alaska.

Between 1867 and 1877 Alaska was placed under the control of the US Army, a ten-year period during which there were no government programs of any type. The US Collector of Customs in Alaska was the only official with authority to oversee government affairs for the next two years, 1877–79. During the next five years, until 1884, the commanding officer of a small unit of the US Navy represented the government. Failure of the US Congress to provide for any form of local government meant there were no provisions for education during the first 17 years following the purchase of Alaska by the United States. Schooling was left to the American missionary movement of the 19th century, and the few schools of the Russian Orthodox Church that remained active after the sale of Alaska to the United States.

During this period American attitudes toward racial and ethnic minorities were a powerful determinant in shaping public policy. There was widespread belief that the human race could be divided into higher and lower groups and that Caucasians "were the most lofty." Distinctions between ethnocentrism and racism were not clearly drawn and the concept of ethnic pluralism had not been set forth. The power elite came primarily from politically conservative, Protestant backgrounds, explaining in part why the federal government subscribed to the policy of full Native assimilation into white, American society. For example, a US Commissioner of Indian Affairs during this period declared,

> They [Native Americans] must abandon tribal relations; they must give up their superstitions; they must forsake their savage habits and learn the arts of civilization; they must learn to labor, and must learn to rear their families as white people do, and know more of their obligations to the Government and society.[9]

Many of the leading protagonists of this policy were Protestant clergymen and missionary teachers. Attitudes prevalent among Indian reformers viewed American Native culture and life styles as inferior. These negative views of Native customs and their advocacy of cultural replacement put them at the forefront of the assimilationist movement. The head of the missionary movement in Alaska, Reverend Sheldon Jackson, who later became the US government's first General Agent for Education in Alaska, continually stressed that "teachers must try to educate [the Natives] out of and away from the training of their home life," that they must be true to their mission, and "give prominence to moral as well as intellectual instruction."[10] Jackson's strongly rooted view of the role of schools were, in the tradition of sectarian Protestantism, at the time the prevailing moral force in much of American society. As put by Cremin,

> In their attempt to create a new republican individual of virtuous character, abiding patriotism, and prudent wisdom, the churches developed an American paideia that was for all intents and purposes a Protestant pai-

9. US Congress 1886, p. 5.
10. US Congress 1886.

> deia. Indeed, they did everything in their power to render the two indistinguishable and therefore interchangeable.[11]

Regardless of how motives of American missionaries may now be perceived, they alone were the first American teachers in Alaska, the first school having been established in 1877 by a Presbyterian missionary. By 1884 several other Presbyterian mission schools had been established along the southeast coast, staffed by 17 teachers working with 500 pupils. Missionaries from other denominations, including Roman Catholics and Anglicans, were also at work during this time with the introduction of Western education in a few interior villages. Early on an informal agreement had been struck between the major religious denominations to divide Alaska regionally among themselves to avoid sectarian competition and duplication of effort.

With pressure from a scattering of new American settlers, mostly miners and fishermen, and the Presbyterian Church, the US Congress, after 17 years of neglect, took action and established Alaska as a Judicial District of the United States with a restricted civil government that included a court system and the first provision for local government and schools. Specifically, the act that established these governmental services, as meager as they were, provided "that the Secretary of Interior make needed and proper provision for the education of children of school age ... without reference to race, until such time as permanent provisions shall be made for the same."[12]

With schools provided for by Congress, the US Commissioner of Education, as expected, appointed Reverend Jackson to the position of General Agent of Education in Alaska. Schools were to be 4,000 to 6,000 miles from his headquarters in Washington and from 100 to 1,000 miles from one another. A large majority of the students did not speak English. School facilities had to be constructed and teachers recruited from outside Alaska. Only $25,000 was appropriated to enable this work to get under way.

---

11. Cremin 1977, p. 49.
12. United States 1884.

As inadequate as the act proved to be, it did appropriate the first American funds for education. However, the provision "without reference to race" in the legislation set the stage for confrontation between miners and missionaries and competition for those funds that was to last for years. It eventually led to a dual federal territorial/state system of education.

Because of insufficient funds to establish and maintain a school system in a vast, unsettled area, a policy that proved to have a long-lasting effect was adopted. The Reverend Jackson persuaded federal government officials that the American constitutional principle of separation of Church and state should be ignored and his office be allowed to subsidize mission schools with government funds. The goals of education promoted by Jackson further advanced the development of schools along religious lines and closely aligned government programs with the aims of the missionary movement.

The policy of stressing distinct Protestant moral attitudes and Western social values and educating Natives "out of their home life" became as much part of the programs of education as the teaching of basic subject matter. Advertisements placed in newspapers for teachers in the government schools illustrate this point: "The work being both educational and missionary, applicants will send not only certificates as to the their aptness as teachers but also testimonials from their pastor or others as to their Christian activity."[13]

The policy of subsidizing Church-related schools did have the desired effect of rapidly building an education system, although it was not always made clear in official reports which schools were mission schools and which were government schools. By 1890 the total number of Alaska schools had increased to 54, but of this number only 16 appeared to be wholly controlled by the government.[14] They were scattered over thousands of miles, mostly along the coast, which made it impossible for the General Agent

13. Unpublished document on file in the archives of the Bureau of Indian Affairs, Seattle, Washington.

14. Jenness 1962, p. 11.

to visit them all, as stipulated in the rules for governing the schools.

It was inevitable that once the school system consisted of so many elements from missionary societies that there would be objections. A broader cross section of the American population was arriving in Alaska. There was extensive governmental exploration during the last two decades of the 19th century and increased development in fisheries and mining. Gold rushes in the interior as well as along the coasts had resulted in a large influx of population from throughout the United States, a population not necessarily inclined toward the missionaries' point of view. Thus, with a broader based population and with Congress better informed about conditions in Alaska, the practice of subsidizing missions schools became increasingly criticized. As a consequence the practice was discontinued by order of the Secretary of Interior.

Although the Act of Congress in 1884 had specified an educational system "without reference to race," it became apparent at an early date that the emphasis in government schools was on Native education. As Reverend Jackson, as a government agent as well as a missionary, became more concerned with "civilizing" the Native population, the white population came to look upon the system as biased against their interests. From the outset of the appointment of a Presbyterian missionary to the position of General Agent for Education, fears had been expressed by whites that education for their children would be slighted.

Pressure from new residents, especially miners, and a better informed Congress resulted, in 1900, in new federal legislation that provided, among other things, for the incorporation of towns and establishment of school districts for white children within incorporated towns. City schools were established specifically for white children, thus further assuring that the federal schools would become exclusively schools for Natives, regardless of the fact that the law in 1884 that established them specified that they were to be without reference to race.

By further urging of settlers, the law of 1900 was subsequently strengthened five years later to assure that white children would have a distinctly different (and, by implication, better) school system. The new law provided

> that the schools specified and provided in the act shall be devoted to the education of white children and children of mixed blood who lead a civilized life. The education of Eskimos and Indians in the District of Alaska shall remain under the direction and control of the [federal] Secretary to the Interior.[15]

Thus, resentment by white settlers against missionary controlled schools and fear that an inferior education was the norm in integrated schools gave rise to a new government policy in 1905 that resulted in a dual system of education. The federal Bureau of Education was responsible only for the education of the Native population and independent city schools became responsible for the education of "white children and children of mixed blood who live civilized lives." Where there was both a Native and a non-Native population in the same town, two government schools, one for Natives, one for whites were maintained alongside each other, a condition that lasted until 1967 when the remaining two schools in a single village were consolidated. Early efforts to change this system, especially if they were efforts to merge schools, often resulted in friction between the two populations and failed. The social/political accommodation of this period, then, created a unique paradox: students in one segment of the population received an education based on the culture of the home; in the other, students received an education alien to the culture of the home.

Although these developments and his advancing years brought the active participation of Reverend Jackson to an end, they did not end his influence or the influence of Protestantism on Alaska Native education. The tradition of the mission schools that required education to be congruent with the American/Protestant ethic prevalent at the time had become well established. Consequently, a philosophy of education that lacked sensitivity to cultural differences and the patrimony of indigenous cultures

15. United States 1905.

instituted in the 1870s was to prevail in many Native classrooms well into the 20th century.

Alaska as a territory of the United States: 1912–1959

The legislation of 1905 that gave birth to a dual system of education failed to provide for local control sufficient to meet the demands of a growing non-Native population. Responding to this condition, Congress extended territorial status to Alaska. Territories are lesser political units than states, but have some of their characteristics, including provisions for a governor appointed by the president and an elected legislature. However, territorial control of education was not among the powers granted in the act of 1912. It was not until 1917 that Congress, in response to a request of the new territorial government, amended the act so that the federal government relinquished responsibility for the education of "white children and children of mixed blood who lead a civilized life." It was made clear in that legislation that nothing in the act was to be construed as transferring schools for Alaska Natives to the territorial government; they remained under the control of the federal Bureau of Education, a unit of the US Interior Department.

The Alaska Territorial Legislature proceeded to establish a Territorial Department of Education, responsible for all education in Alaska other than for schools in the federal system for Native students. The first territorial Commissioner of Education had the job, on the one hand, of developing a system of control over city schools through processes similar to those found in the various states of the United States and, on the other, of performing all of the duties of administrator for the schools under territorial control in rural areas not incorporated as cities, nor a part of the federal system.

Although many of the rural schools in the territorial system were scattered over hundreds of square kilometers in regions with a large population of Native pupils, the programs of instruction made no provision for local conditions or Native cultures. It is ironical that although the federal school system was dedicated to Native education, eventually more Natives were enrolled in territorial/state schools than in the federal systems as new schools were added to the territorial system and the composition of village populations changed.

Growth in the number of schools and students enrolled had been rapid during the first two decades of the 20th century. When the Territorial Department of Education first became organized, there were 46 rural, unincorporated communities with territorial schools that enrolled 1,162 pupils and employed 58 teachers. At the same time, the Bureau of Education operated 71 rural schools with a total enrollment of 3,500 pupils and a faculty of 133 teachers.[16]

Although there were proponents of a single pan-Alaska system of schools for all Alaskans regardless of ethnicity, this idea was not to be realized for many years. The first Alaska Commissioner of Education expressed the view of most non-Native people of that time when in his first official report, he declared,

> There are several objectives to the maintenance of a unified system of schools for white and Native children, the principal ones being the irregularity of the attendance of Natives and their inability to conform to the standard of the whites in the matter of health and sanitation.... The presence of two distinct races of people and the resulting mixing of blood creates difficulties in supervision and administration.... Where the races must mingle, there is usually a certain degrees of friction, the parents of white children often keeping them out of school and securing private teachers in order to avoid the close contact and what they consider the evil resulting therefrom.[17]

In Alaska as a whole there were few events of historic significance during the next two decades. The population had leveled off after economic activity due to the gold rushes at the turn of the century declined, and there was little further commercial development. Reports of the Commissioner of Education reflect the static nature of the population during this period, and there were few refer-

16. US Department of Interior 1918, pp. 11, 74.
17. Alaska 1920, pp. 39, 55.

ences made to the ethnic composition of village schools. Education programs in the territorial schools during the period 1920–40 reflected almost entirely the educational developments and goals of American schools in general.[18] The official territorial courses of study were the same for all schools, from the largest urban district to the smallest rural village.

The Commissioner of Education continued to support the policy that Native education was the responsibility of the federal government, as did the federal Congress, although the number of Natives in territorial schools continued to increase. By 1934, however, enrollment of Native pupils had reached 1,874; approximately one Native pupil out of every three in Alaska was in a nonfederal school. Twenty years later, the territorial government continued to ignore the ethnic composition of its schools.[19]

During these years, while little attention was paid to characteristics of Native cultures in programs of the Territorial Department of Education, the federal government re-examined its policy of cultural assimilation of Native Americans. In the early 1920s there were limited efforts to introduce a few Native cultural elements, such as Native dance and games in the educational program, but these made little impact and by 1926 the federal course of study was the most paternalistic yet. The curriculum syllabuses that year stressed "Health and Sanitation; Agriculture and Industry; the Decencies [so called], Safety, and Comforts of the Home; Healthful Recreation and Amusements; Basic Education and Industrial Schools."[20]

However, a national survey of Indian social and economic conditions initiated by the United States Senate in 1926 found fault with this type of program. Findings of the study, commonly called the Meriam Report, published in 1928, stressed that greater emphasis needed to be put on self-government of Indians, on the need for improved systems of education, and on the need for participation of state and local agencies in Indian affairs. The report

18. Ray 1959, p. 44.
19. For a detailed discussion of curriculum during this period, see Ray 1959, pp. 58–111.
20. US Department of Interior, Bureau of Education 1926, p. 500.

emphasized the need for revised educational programs and stressed as imperative that the Bureau of Indian Affairs broaden its educational programs to reflect Native values.[21]

The most immediate result of the Meriam report in Alaska was realignment of federal responsibility for Native education. To assure that all Native programs were directed through a single federal agency and would be similar to Indian education in other states, Alaska Native affairs were transferred from the Bureau of Education to the Bureau of Indian Affairs. (While agency names and programs at this time usually referred only to Indians, by common agreement, they also applied to Eskimos and Aleuts. Thus, the Bureau of Indian Affairs in reality was concerned with all Native Americans.)

Soon after the transfer of federal schools from the Bureau of Education to the Bureau of Indian Affairs, Franklin D. Roosevelt was elected president. John Collier, who served in his administration from 1934 to 1946, was appointed Commissioner of Indian Affairs. Commissioner Collier, on taking office, declared,

> I conceive that our task is to bring about liberty and positive opportunity for the Indian within an undiminished responsibility by the United States for their welfare.... It means that those Indians whose culture, civic tradition, and inherited institutions are still strong and virile should be encouraged and helped to develop their life in their own patterns, not as segregated minorities but as noble elements in our common life.[22]

A remarkable turn in policy had taken place. Improved conditions in many schools were, however, slow in coming, and did not come at all in others, Collier's policies notwithstanding. By the early 1940s the ill-suited traditional American college preparatory course of study remained in most schools. Just about the time the new policy might have had an effect on the curriculum, World War II intervened and government attention to Native schooling became a low priority. By the end of that decade, there was no semblance of the Collier philosophy remaining in official policy.

21. Meriam 1928.
22. US Department of Interior 1934, p. 129.

The superintendent of the Bureau of Indian Affairs in Alaska in 1949 declared that, in his view,

> at one time our whole emphasis – in fact, when I came here in 1944 – was on an educational program that kept the native child in that community. We have seen the futility of that kind of philosophy, and have completely changed our approach to the education problem. We are now setting up a program that will take the boys and girls out of their community, and we don't care if they ever go back at all. In fact, we urge them not to go back because the communities cannot support them. That is the purpose of Mount Edgecumbe [a BIA residential high school in Alaska] at the present time. Of course, we expect to try and train teachers, and we expect to try and train nurses. We are going to do our best to try and get some dentists, and that kind of professional personnel that is needed back in these communities to help alleviate the conditions that are there. But as far as taking this whole number of boys and girls that come out of these communities and expecting them to go back and live, we do not.[23]

Thus, the policies of the previous decade were reversed. The end result of such vacillation was that pupils could neither succeed economically or socially in the dominant society, should they so choose, nor were they able to preserve or feel comfortable with their Native culture.

In the territorial schools during this same period, policies were also changing, but in just the opposite direction of the federal schools. Whereas the federal government returned to assimilationist policies officials in the territorial school system, for the first time, attempted to get a better understanding of their responsibility to Native students. Faced with increasing instances of strife in the villages because of attempts to integrate Native and white students on the part of some and resistance to this trend on the part of others, the territorial Commissioner of Education requested, in 1943, an opinion from the Alaska Attorney General on the rights of Native children relative to school attendance. The opinion was remarkable for its directness, its unprejudiced view, and its time. In response to the request, the Attorney General wrote,

> Since the question of the right of native children to admittance to the

23. US Department of Interior 1949, in Jenness 1962, p. 59.

> white schools has come up so often in recent years and is again to the fore, it seems proper to deal with the subject at some length, decisively.... The question to be answered is: Is the Territory required to furnish school facilities to children of pure native blood; and failing this, must such children be admitted to white schools when demand for admittance is made?[24]

Following a review of pertinent cases and statutes, the Attorney General concluded that

> the objection raised against the admittance of native children into white schools is not fundamentally their color but rather because, it is said, they are not clean, are afflicted with disease or on account of other objectionable practices or habits. Such objections are not a basis for excluding all native children. The school authorities have ample power to exclude from attendance children of any color who are afflicted with infectious or contagious disease, or who are living under unsanitary conditions or practice filthy or vicious habits. A clean, wistful native child looks just as sweet in the school room as a white child similarly groomed, and therefore he may not be deprived of an education on account of his color alone.[25]

The opinion also directed the Territorial Legislature to provide adequate school facilities for all the youth of the territory and took the position that Native children are entitled to admittance to the white schools of Alaska, regardless of whether or not the federal government also was providing schools.

Although this opinion was enlightened for its time, and may have resolved problems of school choice in some instances, it did not address the question of curriculum choice; few provisions in programs of education took into account Native needs. In the 1954 report of the Alaska Commissioner of Education the territory's programs were described in this way:

> A common program of studies, or course of study, is basic for all Alaska public schools. The standards of instruction in the larger district schools, the larger schools outside districts, the schools on military reservations, and the remote one and two room schools are the same.... In general, the

24. Alaska 1943, p. 1.
25. Ibid., pp. 35–36.

> program of studies ... compares favorably with those which are found in schools throughout the nation.[26]

Despite this condition, a shift away from an ethnocentric, assimilationist approach to Native American schooling had occurred during the 1930s and 1940s. Although it was not sustained in policy, the concept of Native values finding a place in education that had been espoused in the 1930s was given credibility in some governmental and academic circles. In effect, a policy of focusing solely on the cultural principles of the dominant society had begun to give way to the legitimacy of other cultures.

Alaska from statehood to the present

Alaska became a state of the United States in January of 1959. Accordingly, the rules of self-governance changed and Alaskans became legally empowered to make decisions at the state and local level heretofore denied to them. Principles embodied in the state's constitution combined with changes that occurred in the Bureau of Indian Affairs during the previous decade and the civil rights activities that characterized the 1960s were to eventually lead to the development of a decentralized school system in rural Alaska.

The constitution of Alaska simply states as follows:

> SECTION 1. The legislature shall by general law establish and maintain a system of public schools open to all children of the State, and may provide for other public educational institutions. Schools and institutions so established shall be free from sectarian control. No money shall be paid from public funds for the direct benefit of any religious or other private educational institutions.[27]

Soon after statehood there were two reports on rural education, one from the Office of the Governor of Alaska and one from the federal Department of Interior. Each expressed the need to consolidate the federal and state school systems and to change the over-

---

26. Alaska 1954, p. 26.
27. Alaska Constitution, art. VII, sec. 1.

all purposes of education so as to make them more consistent with the needs of the Native population. For the first time in history, the state Department of Education, in its report for the 1965–66 biennium, declared the need for special provisions to accommodate extraordinary conditions in rural Alaska.

At the federal level of government, the Civil Rights Act of 1964 was passed by Congress, and President Lyndon Johnson focused national attention on Indian education when he presented a special message to Congress in which he emphasized the need for an enriched curriculum that included Native culture, teachers trained in the ways of Native cultures and history, and a goal for Indian programs that "ends the old debate about 'termination' of Indian programs and stresses self-determination; a goal that erases old attitudes of paternalism and promotes partnership self-help."[28]

Recognition by national and state offices notwithstanding, of equal importance was the emergence at this time of Alaska Native leadership in educational and political circles. Mr. Emil Notti, first president of the Alaska Federation of Natives, commenting on new program proposals for rural schools declared, "I hope when the decisions are made, I hope we have Native people there because it is their children who are affected.... We have to insist that the Native people are there."[29]

The creation of the Alaska Federation of Natives, a powerful pan-Alaska voice for Native rights established in 1966, and the compelling position expressed by Mr. Notti, introduced a new and indispensable component in the education of Alaska's Native population. It gave rise to a movement in education that is still under way, 25 years later.

Files of the State Department of Education from the mid-1960s onward reveal an increasing number of statements that express dissatisfaction with school programs. Much of this material came from Native leaders and village residents. Up until this time no

---

28. US Congress 1968, p. 5.
29. Conference on Alaska Secondary Education, Transcript of Proceedings, December 1968, on file in the State Department of Education, pp. 51–52.

effective voice of the Native consumer of educational services had been heard. Emergence of the Native population in the movement for improved schools had become the essential ingredient that eventually was to make a difference in schooling.

Patience with the old system was exhausted by the early 1970s. The State Department of Education and the Alaska Legislature endorsed a study done at the University of Alaska to identify ways to provide an alternative system that would be more sensitive to Native educational needs. Findings and recommendations of the study, done cooperatively with the Alaska Federation of Natives, resulted in legislation that created a new administrative structure for schools in rural Alaska.[30]

The system, called Regional Educational Attendance Areas (REAAs), divided rural Alaska into 21 autonomous school districts (now 23 because of 2 recent additions) along lines of regional ethnic and geographic identity, each with its own locally elected school board of directors charged with making local policy. REAAs became operational in 1976.

Initially, some REAA districts got off to an uncertain start, due in large measure to the magnitude of the enterprise and to a combination of inadequate school administrators and inexperienced school board members. As had been anticipated, mistakes were made, but so too were improved programs initiated. A secondary (some might say primary) feature of this situation was the realization of decision-making authority at the local level and its consequential effect on positive self-identity and self-confidence among village residents.

Although the advent of REAAs removed central state control of rural education, many Bureau of Indian Affairs schools were still active, since the legislation creating the REAAs had been silent on the subject of a state–federal school merger. Although there had been several plans over the years to merge BIA schools into the territorial or state system, none had been agreed to. Eventually, it was no single event or plan that brought about the end of Bureau of Indian Affairs schools in Alaska. Rather, it was a culmination of

30. Darnell et al. 1974.

several self-determination efforts by the Native population and federal enabling legislation that made possible the closing of the remaining Bureau of Indian Affairs schools, one by one. The last school administered by the federal government was closed in 1985, one century after the first federal school had been organized and two centuries following the opening of the first Russian school.

Current government and its relationship to education

Just as Alaska has been divided into several regions based on particulars of nature, so too has it been divided politically by man. Accordingly, the Legislature has provided for political subdivisions in the form of cities, boroughs and school districts of various classes, all forms of local government. Provisions for delineating and empowering these divisions bear on the control of educational policy decisions and, consequently, are relative to our discussion. The diverse nature of these provisions, like differences in physical characteristics of the state, influence the lives and cultures of the Native population.

As a state of the United States, Alaska has, except for a few unique provisions of the federal act that established it as a state, the same relationship to the federal government of the United States as any of the other 49 states. Most importantly, in this regard, the Constitution of the United States is the primary controlling authority. However, its own state constitution controls a vast array of activities that enable Alaskans, like citizens of all other states, to enact legislation on an infinite variety of topics, as long as they are not reserved to the federal government by the federal constitution. Education as a function of government, the federal constitution being silent on this subject, is therefore, by default, a function of the state.

In the case of Alaska, as with all other American states except Hawaii, which has a single, state-wide school district, responsibility for daily operations of schools is delegated to local school boards (bodies empowered to make policy affecting the programs of local schools, but within the confines of general state laws and regulations). There are three types of these districts: 1) each first-class city in the unorganized borough is a district;[31] 2) each organized borough, regardless of size, is a borough school district; and 3) the area outside organized boroughs and outside first-class cities (the unorganized borough) is divided into 23 Regional Education Attendance Areas (in 1992). Although each class of school district functions under somewhat different rules, all schools in the state are regarded as a part of the Alaska system of education. In 1992, 54 districts comprised the system as a whole: 16 borough school districts, 18 first-class city school districts, and 23 Regional Education Attendance Areas. Collectively, they are regulated by 350 or so locally elected school board members.[32]

As straightforward as this arrangement may appear, there is a unique relationship between the Native population and the federal government that has complicated it in issues that pertain to education, along with other issues such as those that concern authority in land use and ownership, game management, and judicial procedures; in short, Native sovereignty in general. This topic is treated in greater detail in Chapter 5 in the section on "locus of control."

The Canadian Far North

The early recorded histories of Alaska and the Canadian Far North have much in common, although they did not occur simultaneously. Contact between the Native population and Europeans made at the time of scientific voyages of "discovery," and events

31. The borough is a unique feature of Alaska's local government. Article X of the Alaska Constitution provides for a pattern of local government consisting of cities and organized and unorganized boroughs, but with no other local government entities permitted. The legislature determines the classification of cities and boroughs, prescribes their organization and powers, and allows for the enactment of home rule charters. In short, they are intermediate forms of government between state and local levels. Only those areas with adequate reason for intermediate government have been organized in this way, leaving a large unorganized borough throughout much of rural Alaska. It is in this area that many village schools are located.

32. Alaska 1991, pp. 42–43.

associated with both early and more recent exploitation of natural resources, had the same deleterious effect on the Native populations, although not nearly to the tragic extent experienced by the Aleuts under the hands of the Russians.

The first meeting of Europeans with Canadian Natives came about much earlier than encounters of Europeans with the Alaskan Native population (Bering, 1741). Scholars now consider the Vinland voyages of Norse seamen to North America, about the year 1000, to be the first contact between North American Natives and Europeans. These voyages have now been well authenticated, although details of dates, places and names of the principals continue to be the subject of exploration and study. The Vinland voyages are important because of their early dates, but in themselves had no lasting impact on Native–non-Native relationships.

It was not until the early voyages of Martin Frobisher (1576), John Davis (1585), and William Baffin (1615), names now memorialized on major geographic features of the Eastern Arctic, that the first written knowledge of some features of Inuit culture in Canada became known in Europe. Later, the extensive exploration of central Canada by Samuel Hearne, the first European to stand on the north coast of America, in 1771, added considerably to knowledge about both the Indians and Inuit as well as the land. Nevertheless, it took until the first half of the 19th century, during the early explorations of the British in search of a northwest passage, that the Inuit were made known to the Western world in some detail. The voyage of the Englishman W. E. Parry in 1822–23 to Foxe Basin, especially while in the vicinity of the Inuit settlement of Igloolik, is notable for information that describes Inuit culture of that time.

Just as the distinct cultures of the Indian and Inuit populations were set apart by the tree line, so too did that line shape the nature of early Western exploration and exploitation of the Far North in Canada. Large numbers of fur-bearing animals in the Subarctic boreal forest gave rise to exploration and exploitation by the great fur-trading companies, most notably the Hudson's Bay Company, in the 18th and 19th centuries. Company trading posts established across the country, first from east to west in southern and central Canada, became the principal points of contact between Native populations, especially Indian groups, and Western culture. Not only through the exchange of trade goods was contact expanded, but trading posts also became the locations where religious sects first established missions and eventually schools.

Early travel by Europeans above the tree line was first prompted by the hope of finding a northwest passage or valuable minerals or both, with Frobisher (1576) among the first, as noted above. Others followed over the next two centuries, but it was not until the explorations of the British Navy in the 19th century that the search for a northwest passage became a major undertaking. And it was at this time that American and British whalers began to account for large fleets in Arctic waters.

Later on in the 19th century, more extensive scientific work was carried out to better understand the physical characteristics of the land and the culture, tribal distribution, and living conditions of the Inuit in the central and eastern Canadian Arctic, most notably by the anthropologist Franz Boas. But it was not until well into the 20th century, between 1910 and the late 1930s, that anthropologists such as the American Vilhjalmur Stefansson, the Danes Knud Rasmussen and Kaj Birket-Smith, and the Canadian Diamond Jenness described the Inuit culture in detail in their landmark studies.[33] Nevertheless, contact in these areas was far less frequent and less extensive in scope than in the Subarctic, and it was not until after the Second World War that sustained contact between Western Europeans and Americans and Inuit became routine.[34] Nevertheless, inadequate knowledge of the differences between the Western culture of the school and the culture of the Native population was profound at the time formal education was first introduced and, although to a much lesser extent, remains so today.

---

33. Among the many publications of these men, the following illustrate their work: Stefansson 1921; Rasmussen 1927; Birket-Smith 1971; and Jenness (ed.) 1991.
34. For a more detailed description of the early history of the exploration and exploitation of the Canadian Far North, see Armstrong et al. 1978; Cooke and Holland 1978; and Zaslow 1971.

At the beginning of the 20th century, further developments in the way of mining, most notably the discovery of gold in the Klondike region in the Yukon Territory and copper and nickel in the Eastern Arctic, started a slow but steady influx of non-Natives from the south into the Far North in search of other mineral resources to exploit. Likewise, expansion of the timber industry for wood pulp derived from spruce of the boreal forest became widespread, further altering the population composition and compounding the problems of a stable multicultural population. Just as was the case in the initial development of Native cultures and society, the tree line continues to influence the development and population composition of the region.

Political boundaries in the Canadian Far North have been in flux since it was first occupied by European explorers, exploiters and settlers. The Northwest Territories and Yukon Territory acquired their current political boundaries in 1912, Quebec its first boundaries in 1867 at the time of confederation of the Dominion of Canada, but without its Far North. It was not until 1912 that Arctic Quebec, or Nouveau Quebec as it is sometimes called, that huge, isolated area occupied by the Inuit, was added to the province. The boundaries of Labrador were defined when it became part of Newfoundland in 1949. New boundaries for the Northwest Territories are in store for 1999, at which time Nunavut will become an autonomous territory in the Eastern Arctic, thereby reducing the extent of the Northwest Territories by more than one-third. (The creation of Nunavut as a new territory is covered more fully later on in this chapter.)

Of all the peoples covered in this book, the indigenous peoples in the Central Canadian High Arctic are the most recent to have come under the influence of Western culture, including formal schools. These schools, not unlike the first schools in Alaska, Greenland, and Scandinavia, were established by missionaries. Following that development, mission schools were to remain the sole source of formal education until well into the 1930s, and even then, after the government became active in social affairs in the North, mission schools remained the dominant Western educational influence until the 1950s. Consequently, the nature of schooling reflected the motives and style of most Christian missionaries worldwide during this period. For example, the Church of England's objective in maintaining mission schools, as stated by an early bishop, is typical:

> The Indians in the Yukon Territory and Alaska have only come in contact with civilizing influences at a comparatively recent date. And what are a few years in the progress of a race? The rooting out of old customs, beliefs, the sowing of the seed, and bringing the seed to perfection are all the work of time.[35]

This sentiment (and official policy) prevailed in one form or another until the 1960s, although there were variations on this theme and a few impressive efforts to change it. The efforts of the curriculum committee described in the next chapter is an example of an extraordinary reform movement that was attempted, but tried before its time was ripe.

Intensifying the difficulty to meet the needs of the Native population that education might fulfill was the competition, at times acrimonious, between the Church of England and the Roman Catholics. Unlike missionaries in Alaska, who more or less came to amicable terms in the way they "divided" up Alaska among themselves, competition between Roman Catholics and Anglicans persisted for some time. Richard Finnie described the founding of the first schools this way:

> The Church Missionary Society of the Church of England, in the person of Archdeacon Hunter, and the Oblates, led by Father Grollier, arrived in the Mackenzie Valley almost simultaneously in 1857. An immediate desperate race began between Hunter and Grollier, when each became aware of the other's presence in the valley. Each strove to arrive first in [Native] settlements along the Mackenzie Valley, thereby saving souls from the Devil and from one another.[36]

In this regard, one mission-residence school teacher, while advocating residential schools, went so far as to declare, "Young people in residential schools are far better preserved from sin, and last

35. Carney 1970, cited in Johns 1976.
36. Finnie 1942, cited in Johns 1976, p. 44.

but not least, from their protestant neighbors."[37] This sentiment not only exemplifies religious conviction, it also illustrates the competitive attitude of missionaries that had proliferated worldwide during the latter half of the 19th century. A statement by the first American mission teacher in Alaska, in 1877, in this case a Presbyterian commenting on the Roman Catholics who were at the time "invading our ground," reflects the same type of judgment: "They [the Catholics] at once established a mission. The Indians are so fond of outside display and show that the Romanish Church would suit them in that respect. But we can take courage as we remember that the Lord is on our side."[38]

As in the West, the two or three schools for Inuit in the Eastern Arctic during the early years of formal education were not a concern of the federal government. A policy of benign neglect was to persist for the first half of the 20th century; the few mission schools that did exist were the sole source of formal education and usually only operated for a few years or sporadically as priests/teachers were available. Requests for government financial assistance in the East were generally rejected on the basis that the government believed the people should be left alone to continue their way of life undisturbed.[39]

The same situation prevailed among the Indian population in the Subarctic. Government activities during this time consisted of meager financial assistance to the missions; responsibility for education was seldom acknowledged. Although treaties that had been negotiated between Indian groups and the government spoke to the need for schools, the Department of Indian Affairs did not accept responsibility for Indians outside treaty limits, nor were they responsible for the education of Inuit at that time. Although meager financial assistance was provided to the mis-

---

37. Macpherson 1991, p. 28. It should be noted that this publication is an extensive, well-documented account of the history of education in the Northwest Territories, much of it based on anecdotal records of teachers and administrators from the time schools were first introduced until the present.

38. Jackson 1880, p. 277.

39. Colbourne, Eric, "Introduction to the Baffin Divisional Board." In Farrow and Wilman (eds.) 1989, p. 65.

sions occasionally, neither the Department of Indian Affairs nor the office of the Commissioner of the Northwest Territories saw a need to interfere with the administration or programs of mission schools. Thus, the responsibility for education remained under the control of religious bodies and programs of education reflected their sectarian interests.

The teaching order of Grey Nuns, the common name for the Sisters of Charity of Montreal, instituted the first boarding schools in the Mackenzie Valley in 1867. Thereafter boarding schools became the norm for many years; Church officials saw them "as the only way to properly shelter the children from the disgusting influence of their own home life – that is to say, they were being made over in the image of the missionary."[40] The Superintendent-General of Indian Affairs, E. Dewdney, wrote in 1889, "The superiority of the boarding school system as a means for the enlightenment and elevation, both morally and intellectually, of Indian youth is, I think, unquestionable."[41]

However, during the 1930s, boarding schools for Indians fell from favor and the few day schools of both the Anglicans and Catholics were deemed to be unsuccessful. Accordingly, more attention was directed toward the Inuit farther to north in the western part of the Northwest Territories. And, in 1936, what little interest the dominion government did have in education was transferred from the dominion Department of Indian Affairs to the Northwest Territories and Yukon Services Bureau of Lands, Parks and Forests of the newly created Department of Mines and Resources, and remained there until 1949. Like its predecessor agency, the Department of Mines and Resources was quite willing to let the mission schools continue their role as sole provider of education. However, it was during this period that an important event took place: the Northwest Territories Administration assumed responsibility for schooling among the Inuit population in the Eastern Arctic, although to a remarkably meager extent. School supplies were furnished to a number of mission day

40. Johns 1976, p. 46.
41. Ibid., p. 45.

schools in the northern part of Quebec and support was provided to the school at Fort George, Quebec for indigent Inuit children living there.[42] (Although Quebec is a province, and technically was not under the authority of the Northwest Territories Administration, the Northwest Territories at that time had jurisdiction over all Inuit, regardless of location, and thus had a responsibility in Northern Quebec.)

In short, during the period between the founding of early mission schools until well past the end of World War II, government agencies gave little thought to schooling among the Native population and were content to let missions do as they saw fit. Neither the Northwest Territories Act nor the Indian Act and Regulations, both of which formed the legal basis for the presence of government in education in the Far North, had much effect. Of course, small population numbers, remoteness, and great distances between settlements accounted for much of the insufficiency of school facilities and meagerness of programs that related to the culture and economic condition of the people during this period. But so did lack of concern by government officials for the need to take responsibility to establish government schools among the Native population, especially schools that might accommodate the distinct culture of the people.

An exception to this general situation, one that closely parallels the Alaska experience during the same period, took place on Great Slave Lake in the early 1930s. Mineral discoveries in the region gave rise to a typical all-white school in the then-all-white community of Yellowknife, now the capital of the Northwest Territories. The Roman Catholic bishop for the district failed to respond to a request from the community for a school because of his absence from office for a year. The Anglicans demurred the same request as they were being forced to close schools elsewhere because of insufficient financial resources. As pointed out by Johns,

> in any case, it is doubtful ... whether the community would have accepted a school controlled by either church. Neither would a white population,

42. Ibid., p. 46.

> taught in their southern homes to accept a certain standard of educational preparations, have accepted the programs offered in the missions.
>
> Thus, in 1938, a non-denominational Provisional School Board came into being in Yellowknife ... and the formation of Yellowknife School District Number 1. The effects upon territorial education were more far-reaching than the fact that a school was built. The Yellowknife Public School did not register Indian children from the Yellowknife area.[43]

This development led to the creation of a dual system of education, not unlike the federal-territorial/state dual system in Alaska, although only in a single instance. Nevertheless, the principle and effect were the same. Since the Yellowknife Public School did not register Indian children, Indian children had to attend boarding schools elsewhere. According to Carney,

> by the end of the year [1940], two forms of Territorial schooling were in operation: the first was white-oriented, secular, often segregated, relatively well-funded, almost universal in application, and keeping with the ambitions of the newly arrived; the second was native-oriented, denominational, poorly funded, usually segregated, and of partial application.[44]

Even so, and although "the motivation and the educational practice of the churches have often been criticized," as noted by Macpherson, "it only fair to point out that they assumed control of education by default."[45] This is an argument with some validity. Diamond Jenness, in 1934, observed that

> the early missionaries rapidly took their places alongside the other pioneers of the Arctic. They learned as quickly as possible the Eskimo language in order to perform their religious duties. With that knowledge they became the natives' advisors, not in spiritual matters alone, but in their relations with the traders and other white men who could not understand their tongue. In the absence of government schools, too, they became the educators of the Eskimos – they held classes for the children and taught them to read and write.[46]

43. Ibid., p. 47.
44. Carney 1970, cited in Johns 1976, p. 47.
45. Macpherson 1991, p. 27.
46. Jenness, quoted in Macpherson 1991, p. 27.

But Jenness, writing 30 years later, recalled that some teachers with whom he had visited were of the opinion that the mission schools were "religious kindergartens that hardly deserve the name of schools [and] taught nothing and explained nothing."[47] Both comments probably are correct and speak to the unevenness of school quality and programs.

Emergence of government schools

The indifferent attitude of the government in the early years was to change dramatically in the two decades following World War II, especially in the farthest reaches of the Arctic. The dominion government acknowledged its responsibility to take an active role in the establishment of schools and an agreement was reached in 1955 between the principle agencies responsible for some aspect of education up to that time. The primary purpose of the agreement was to avoid duplication of effort and establish a basis for a unified system of education for the Northwest Territories and those part of Arctic Quebec which were inhabited by Eskimos. In general terms, as described by D.W. Simpson and D.K.F. Wattie of the Department of Northern Affairs, these agreements involved three authorities:

> 1. The Government of the Northwest Territories.
> 2. Two components of the Federal Government of Canada. The Indian Affairs Branch of the Department of Citizenship and Immigration and the Northern Administration Branch, Department of Northern Affairs and Natural Resources.
> 3. The Roman Catholic and Anglican Churches [which] had a vested interest in education because of their earlier missionary activities primarily in the Mackenzie Valley but also in some of the coastal areas of the Arctic.
>
> Prior to this time all three agencies had a marginal involvement in education in the North but in total terms a very small proportion of the population was affected by the total efforts of all three combined.... There was little consistency in attendance patterns and the teaching qualifications were minimal or nonexistent. From the practical standpoint it can be said

47. Jenness 1964, pp. 47, 48.

> that there was virtually no formal education system operating in the Arctic Regions of Canada.[48]

The new Education Division of the Northern Administration Branch of the Department of Northern Affairs and National Resources was established as the agency in charge of administering a unified program of formal schooling. The aim of the school system that emerged was to establish an ethnically integrated educational system that resembled as closely as possible the schools in the south. The cultural characteristics of the population and the physical conditions of the vast environment in which the people lived was not an important consideration. Among a few, however, there was an awareness of the enormity of the undertaking and the need to somehow pay attention, albeit to a limited extent, to the diverse cultural qualities of the people. Simpson and Wattie, at the time the program was being initiated, wrote,

> The primary overall objective of [the Department of Northern Affairs] was to establish an educational system which gives the Eskimo and other northern people equality of opportunity in education with other Canadians. Complicating the achievement of this objective was the presence of a large segment of the population that originated in southern Canada or European countries whose educational standards, traditions and aspirations were linked with southern Canada. It was, therefore, necessary not only to provide educational opportunities similar to those of southern people but also to adapt the content of the curricula to meet the unique developmental needs of people from an entirely different and primitive culture.[49]

Unfortunately, this latter consideration was still based on the concept that schools should be organized around the model of Western school systems in the South. Accordingly, and in spite all its good intentions, a system that inherently was incompatible with traditional Native learning styles and needs. (Efforts to create programs compatible with the needs of the Native people are discussed in Chapter 5.)

---

48. Simpson and Wattie 1968.

49. Ibid., p. 8.

Even after the government took responsibility for education, as recently as 1968 there were 600 Inuit children of school age not attending school because there were still no schools in their communities, and the few boarding schools that had been established were filled to capacity. Nevertheless, notable changes in the social structure of Inuit and Indian communities were taking place during this period. Residence (or boarding) schools were deemed necessary because of the sparseness of population, especially for pupils in the upper grades. This policy notwithstanding, as the system developed, schools were established incrementally in small, individual communities. The social impact of this development soon became obvious. With a trend toward urbanization (a direct result of the permanence of schools and a government housing program started at the same time), the decline of traditional nomadic life style and subsistence economy followed. Children were thrust into a whole new way of life and adults were faced with a new way of organizing social relationships and authority. Schools, especially residence schools, imposed a routine that was based on the clock and calendar and ignored the traditional life style based on natural seasonal rounds. As described by Simpson and Wattie,

> the school schedule itself is a model of routine and teachers are continually emphasizing the importance of regular habits in eating, sleeping, ... cleanliness, clothing, diet and study habits. The large residences operate under modern living conditions and are located in centres with regular services and recreational facilities. Because of the gap in standards between the pupil residence and settlement living some pupils find it difficult to readjust to home conditions. The values acquired by the young people in school and residence sometimes lead to misunderstanding and hostility between Eskimo parents and children. Such conflict is new in Eskimo society as previously children accepted without question the authority of their parents and other adults. Thus the new attitudes of independent thought and action among the young are confusing and disturbing to the older generation.[50]

The partial success of school programs from the perspective of the

50. Ibid., p. 9.

government, especially achieving its goal to Westernize the Native population, brought about an ironical twist to the situation. Adults who had been the recipients of formal schooling during the 1950s and early 1960s had acquired the tools of a literate society, but had witnessed the breakdown of a complex indigenous society at the same time. Although indigenous life style was harsh and lacked many of the physical comforts of Western life, it was stable, its language intricate and highly descriptive, and its art forms complex. Moreover, a confident self-image among people was the norm. As these positive features of society deteriorated, symptoms of societal decline, such as the high incidence of alcoholism and the occurrence of frequent suicides in the population, especially among youth, became commonplace. Increasingly, it came to be realized that several factors associated with increased contact with Western society were to blame as well as the collapse of the traditional economy as a result of ill-advised American and European animal-rights lobby groups. Nevertheless, attempting to cope with formal schooling, centrally designed and controlled, no matter how well intended, was high on the list of causes.

Academics in each of the circumpolar countries during this period started to wonder: could the education system that was in part the cause of social and cultural discord be a source of change that would enable social stability to be restored and positive individual self-images rebuilt? Governments increasingly came to realize that fundamental changes were necessary, although they still failed to understand how to make the right ones. It was the emergence of the Native population at the same time, just as had happened in Alaska, that brought a third and crucial force to bear on the problem.

The awakening of Native activists in the late 1960s and 1970s came to fruition in the decade of 1980s. Curriculum reforms made possible through acquisition of policy-making authority during this period were extraordinary. The resolution in the Legislative Assembly of the Northwest Territories that called for a Special Committee on Education was the initial event that gave the movement momentum (described more fully in Chapter 5). In response to the following motion introduced by Tagak Curley, member of the Legislative Assembly and Inuit leader from the Keewatin district of the central Northwest Territories, the Assembly created the special committee. Charged by the following wording, the resolution called for many changes:

> WHEREAS there are many educational problems faced by people of the Northwest Territories, and particularly with the Natives, including high drop-out rate, poor comprehension, poor parent/teacher relationship, low recruitment of Native teachers and foreign curriculum for northern lifestyle, lack of proper high school facilities, and lack of continuing and special education facilities;
>
> NOW THEREFORE I move that this Assembly establish a special committee on education with support staff to inquire into all aspects of educational policy in the Northwest Territories and an interim report of its findings be tabled during the fall session in 1981 and the final report and recommendations be made by the beginning of 1982 and the size and nomination for membership be made by the striking committee of this Legislature.[51]

Native testimony given to the committee stressed the need for changes that would provide a school system more appropriate to their needs, including control features that gave them a tangible voice in school affairs. The philosophy of the committee reflected this input:

> We can not refuse the challenges posed, but we can say something about the direction in which they may take us. Central to any society's efforts to influence the direction of change is its people's ability to participate in planning processes. And, beyond question, learning is the major factor in a people's ability to participate in such planning. We argue, therefore, that learning is the key to our future.[52]

All through the committee's report, *Learning: Tradition and Change in the Northwest Territories*, the need for community involvement in shaping the schools can be seen as the dominant theme of Native testimony. This concept, coupled with the oft-expressed notion during the hearings that there was no proclivity for gov-

---

51. Northwest Territories Legislative Assembly 1982, p. 6.
52. Ibid., p. 11.

ernment schools to be discontinued, led to several recommendations – recommendations that are still being implemented today. The following are among the most notable:

- The Minister of Education shall delegate the administration of education from Kindergarten to Grade 10 [later changed to Grade 12] to ten divisional boards of education.
- All educational staff working in the communities shall be employees of the divisional board of education.
- Divisional boards of education ... shall have the power to establish their own priorities, programs, and schedules of implementation.
- Each local education authority shall determine the language to be used in its classrooms.
- Recruitment and selection of teachers and principals shall be the responsibility of the divisional boards of education in consultation with the local education authorities.[53]

As much as these recommendations fit the ideal of school reorganization often expressed by indigenous minorities, they did not address the length of time, amount of funds, or detailed planning necessary to implement them. Nor did they address the problems associated with resistance to change implicit in such extreme shifts in policy. Thus, the process of implementation has been slow and at times vexing. But the recommendations did represent a tremendous advance; the principle of self-determination had been recognized. Clearly, the recommendations can be credited with the tremendous advances that have taken place in curriculum development, teacher training, and language development in the Northwest Territories since the report was published. Furthermore, as a result of the report and ensuing legislation, the three school boards in the Eastern Arctic/Nunavut area are now controlled by elected Inuit boards (two have 100 percent Inuit membership), as are the majority of boards in the Northwest Territories.

Contemporary developments notwithstanding, the establishment of Nunavut, a new territory in the Eastern Arctic that is scheduled to become operational in 1999, has the potential to

53. Ibid., pp. 17–21.

stimulate even more profound changes. Approved by public vote and passed into Canadian law in 1993 as an outgrowth a Native land-claims agreement, Nunavut may become the ultimate political solution to Native control of education in the Eastern Arctic. Nunavut, as a new member of Canadian territorial government, will have all of the political responsibilities and authority of any territory irrespective of its ethnic composition. It is not *de jure* Native-specific, but in practice, the population composition of the territory, being more than 85 percent Inuit, confers *de facto* control of all governmental functions to the Native population.

Nunavut will become Canada's third northern territory; formed out of the eastern part of the existing Northwest Territories, it will include principally all the land above the tree line. In size it will be greater than any other province or territory (twice the size of British Columbia), stretching from the northernmost point in Canada, at the top of Ellesmere Island, to the border with Manitoba. With Inuktitut spoken in two out three households, it will become the working language of the government. Furthermore, the land-claims settlement that was part of the act that created the new territory will give the Inuit outright ownership of 18 percent of the land and $1.15 billion with which to generate economic growth and social benefits from it. As pointed out by David F. Pelly,

> For Canada, Nunavut represents a new relationship with an Aboriginal group. For the first time a provincial or territorial government will speak largely on behalf of one group of Native people. While Nunavut will not mean self-government for Inuit in a constitutional sense, it will be self-government in effect because of the Inuit majority.[54]

The significance of Nunavut on schooling in the Eastern Arctic of Canada remains to be seen, but the potential for innovation goes far beyond anything in the past. Nevertheless, much will depend on the goals established for education and the way schooling is finally constituted as a means to reach those goals.

---

54. Pelly 1993.

Scandinavia

Current government and its relationship to education

Politically, Norway, Sweden, and Finland are all social democracies, patterned on Western parliamentary tradition. Each is sovereign and independent of the others, although this has not always been so. While all Scandinavian countries are autonomous and national distinctions well known, their borders are relatively new. The Norwegian–Swedish border dates from the mid-18th century; the Swedish–Finnish frontier was established in 1809 in part, and the remainder in 1826. The border of Finland with Russia was last drawn in 1944, at the time Finland lost to the USSR in World War II.

In all of Scandinavia there are shared cultural characteristics and life styles, especially between Norway and Sweden. In this sense, Finland is the exception. It differs fundamentally in historical and cultural development from Norway and Sweden. While Norway and Sweden were a joint kingdom between 1814 and 1905, Finland was part of the Russian Empire from 1809 to 1917. And while the Finnish language is distinctly different from the other Nordic tongues, it and the Saami language stem from the same Finno-Ugric stock. These differences aside, cooperative commercial and cultural development between the three countries have steadily increased since World War II; a common labor market, a common passport area, and integration of a national health plan have contributed to the furtherance of collective interests among the three countries.[55]

Of all the features common to Nordic countries, the one that may be the most pan-Scandinavian is the international Saami population. Because the Saami are found in all three Nordic countries, and because they have a distinctive culture and language, they share historic indigenous rights. These factors have the potential to work as a positive and unifying force. They also can be the cause of frustrations. Although there are laws that specifically address the needs of the Saami population, such as the interna-

55. Armstrong et al. 1978.

tional treaty discussed below, not all laws are mutually applicable across international boundaries. As a consequence, the ability of the Saami population to function effectively as an international ethnic community is sometimes obstructed by a lack of uniform legal provisions. Schooling falls into this category.

This shortcoming notwithstanding, there is a unique international treaty between Norway, Sweden, and Finland that provides for certain rights over and above the laws of each individual country. Ratified in 1751, the treaty, often called "the Saami Magna Charta," guaranteed the right of the Saami to cross the borders of each country with their reindeer, to hunt, trap, and trade with impunity. However, over the years the force of the treaty has diminished and today only the nomads in Sweden and Norway have, to an uncertain degree, the right to cross each other's borders with their herds.

Although this treaty has lost much of its effectiveness, other efforts to maintain a unified Saami presence compensate for it. Several official agencies and organizations have specific responsibilities for the maintenance of Saami culture and preservation of Saami indigenous rights. Each is related, although in distinctly different ways, to both the Saami and national parliaments. Most prominent among them are Svenska Samernas Riksförbund (Swedish Sami Association), Norske Samers Riksforbund (The National Association of Norwegian Sami), and Norske Reindriftssamers Landsforbund (Sami Reindeer Herders' Association in Norway).

Others that play an important role in a uniform approach to Saami identity include the Nomads Union, the Nordic Saami Council, and the Saami Youth Organization. Moreover, the Saami play an active role in international organizations such as the World Council of Indigenous Peoples (WCIP), Arctic Peoples Conference (APC), International Indigenous Women's Council (IIWC), and UNESCO, all of which have an interest in the human and legal rights of indigenous peoples. In addition to these groups, the Nordic Saami Institute, established in 1973, serves as a research center dedicated to preserving the Saami culture.

Furthermore, there are international laws that protect the legal rights of the Saami in Norway, the only Scandinavian country signatory to these laws at present. Article 27 in the United Nations convention of 1966 pertaining to civil and political rights served as the foundation for a Norwegian act in 1987 in which it is stipulated that Norway will contribute to Saami cultural development. Following this Act, in 1988, the Norwegian Parliament added a provision to the constitution guaranteeing the rights of the Saami to develop their culture and society in their own way. This led to the creation of the Saami Parliament that same year. Enactment of other laws since then to protect the use of the Saami language in the civil service sector, rights to a Saami planned education, and to support Saami language development have been passed.

Based on provisions of the 1966 UN convention, the 76th International Labor Organization (ILO) meeting in Geneva in 1989 affirmed the rights of indigenous peoples in what is termed Convention Number 169. To date, Norway is the only Scandinavian country to ratify this convention. In like manner, the UN Convention on Children's Rights, issued in 1989, influenced the political rights of the Saami in Norway. Most recently the rights of Saami were further strengthened when, in 1992, Norway signed the European Council's charter on the rights of all people to a choice of religion and lesser used languages.

Scandinavian countries are noted for the excellence of their educational systems and the ample way by which they are supported. Schools are open for everyone, have the same high standard in all Nordic countries and graduates have access to the most attractive positions in the society.[56] The general goal for the primary school system is to provide students with the knowledge and skills necessary to succeed in modern society. Collaterally, the home is expected to contribute to the development of the students' personality, especially in terms of responsible citizenship.

School age ranges from nursery pre-school and kindergarten at age 4 and 5 respectively through compulsory secondary or high school to age 16. Further pre-university or college education is offered beyond the compulsory years for students with particu-

56. NORD 1990: 8.

lar vocational or academic interests. All children and youth have the right to attend primary and secondary schools; for those who do not want to attend public schools parents are obliged to give their children the education to which they are entitled through other means.

Systems of education in each of Nordic countries are organized and administered along similar lines. As a means to reach common national goals, school policies are promulgated in each country by the state through ministries of education and administered at the municipal level. Provisions for education prescribed by the state are generally uniform and all-inclusive nation-wide, but with certain exceptions in Norway. In the Norwegian case, where the country has ratified the ILO convention, the right of indigenous minorities to develop their own culture within the framework of the national state has been recognized. Ratification of the ILO convention ostensibly guarantees a Saami voice in education. Generally, this voice is made known through the Saami Education Council, administered in Guovdageaidnu, one of the principal Saami communities, centrally located in Finnmark County of Norway.

Historical perspectives

Just as political relationships and allegiances among countries in Scandinavia have varied historically, so too has education of the Saami varied over the years. For example, from 1350 to 1814 Norway was under the governance of Denmark; from 1814 until 1905, it was ruled by the King of Sweden. In 1905 it became independent as a nation in its own right. Five hundred years ago the Saami were almost the sole inhabitants of the Northern Cap of Scandinavia and the Kola Peninsula, and people learned through the kinship system of education. Thus, during the early period when Denmark was the prevailing power, the Saami population was left much to itself and Western-style formal education was unknown. But as the ruling powers extended their sphere northward in the 17th century, as recounted by the Finnish scholar Karl Nickul,

> a very active colonization of the region was started, gradually the states widened their sovereignty to the northern regions and state frontiers were fixed. When the frontier between Denmark–Norway and Sweden–Finland was determined in 1751, it was stipulated that the Lapps, who were nomads, should still, according to old custom, have the right to move with the reindeer across the frontier and make use of the reindeer pastures in the neighboring country.[57]

During the period of Danish rule Danish authorities decided how the education system was to be constituted and ongoing development was under Danish authority. The year 1589 is generally accepted as the beginning of state-run formal education in Denmark, and thus by default in Norway. Local priests and their assistants were given the responsibility for educating the "common man" in the basic knowledge of Christianity, the primary purpose of schooling at that time.[58] However, in some respects, Norwegians were free to act in educational matters as they wished. During the Norwegian union with Sweden following Danish rule (1814–1905), maintenance and development of the educational system was essentially entrusted to Norway.

Norway

Early education in Norway: The mission period

As was the case in Alaska, Canada, and Greenland, the first to enter the field of formal education in the North were missionaries. In Norway, the missionary Thomas von Westen, in 1716, intensified the work of the Church among the Saami. His purpose was to reinforce the process of Christianizing the Saami by preaching and teaching.[59] The missionaries who joined or followed von Westen were either Danes or Norwegians, but their assistants were young Saami men to whom the missionaries had given a little training so they could serve as teacher aides. Of even greater importance, the Saami aides performed the function of middle-

---

57. Nickul, Karl, "Administrative Situations and the Lapp Population." In Darnell (ed.) 1970, p. 107.
58. Dahl 1957.
59. Hoëm 1989a, pp. 9–16.

men between the people and the missionaries; they knew the land and the people, the missionaries the Bible.

The mission period lasted from 1716 until 1808. During the whole of this period, the goal of the Church was twofold: to provide the Saami with the knowledge they needed to function as what was then considered to be an enlightened person, and to enable them to use the national language to be able to communicate with the majority population. Such a goal was easier stated than carried out, and there was continual vacillation regarding whether or not to use the Saami culture and language as a pedagogical means.[60] As a means to accommodate the use of the Saami language as the language of instruction, Luther's catechism was published in both Danish and Saami in 1728. The first Saami language primer for beginning students was published in 1767. Nevertheless, the success of mission schools was uneven. Generally, the quality of instruction was inadequate, and from the point of view of the Church, the work of the missions was not satisfactory and goals were seldom reached.

By the beginning of the 19th century, the mission period had come to a close in Norway. Government schools became the main agency for formal Saami education, almost 100 years ahead of Alaska and 160 before Canada. The situation in Sweden and Finland has been, to some extent, similar to that in Norway. In the Northwest the Russian Orthodox Church entered the arena from the 16th century and established monasteries in central Saami areas, in Perchenga, and as far west as Neiden in Norway (St. George Chapel).

Introduction of state schools

With the termination of mission schools as the sole providers of formal education and the emergence of government sponsored state schools at the beginning of the 19th century, it became necessary to increase the number of teachers available for schools in the Saami districts. In 1824 the government established a teacher

60. Hoëm 1989b, pp. 159–67.

training college, with special responsibility to educate Saami teachers, at Trondenes. It was the first state-run and -funded teachers college anywhere in Norway. As far-sighted as this movement was for its time (140 years ahead of a similar movement in Alaska and Canada), there were difficulties from the beginning.

The main problem was attracting the number of Saami students necessary for the program to succeed. Various plans were attempted to attract more of them, such as establishing small field-based training units in the principal regions of Saamiland. This technique was later to be used successfully in Alaska, Canada, and Greenland, but in Norway, in spite of its success, it was discontinued after a few years. As a consequence, the teacher training college was attended mostly by Norwegian student teachers. As an outgrowth of this situation it was Norwegian teachers who replaced the Saami teachers who had been installed by the missionaries as they retired. These Norwegian teachers were well educated, but most lacked the qualities of the Saami that had made them so suited to be teachers, namely, familiarity with the land, the language, and the people in general.

To the consternation of Church authorities, Norwegian teachers of this period used the Saami language as far as their ability permitted. To counteract this practice, Church authorities instituted policies to regulate the language of instruction in favor of Norwegian, first in 1862, and then again in 1898, for the last time. These regulations not only made the work of the teachers more difficult, but also had the broad unplanned effect of postponing the Norwegianization of the Saami population. As a consequence, schools became less effective. Church authorities also used economic sanctions to compel the teachers to avoid the use of the Saami language.

Through the efforts of the Norwegian priest, N.V. Stockfleth, there was a reversal of this practice, complete with a resurgence in Saami-specific instruction materials, between 1835 and 1854. But Stockfleth's textbooks, published only in Saami, were contrary to the wishes of the Church. Thus, the policy was changed once again, this time calling for some texts to be published bilingually, with Norwegian and Saami side by side in the same book.

(See Textbook Example 3, pp. 206–207.) This policy prevailed until 1914, but during this period standard Norwegian textbooks used throughout Norway also were introduced in Saami schools. From 1914 to 1960, the bilingual books were discontinued completely, and only Norwegian books were used. From 1960 to the present, the policy has encouraged the development and use of textbooks in the Saami language.

An event in 1902 was especially significant in the historical development of education among the Saami. Although at first it did little for Saami culture, education or Native rights, in that year, the county of Finnmark, the northernmost part of Norway, bordering on Sweden, Finland, Russia, and the Arctic Ocean, was established as a separate school district with its own director of schools. The purpose of the Norwegian government in so doing was to improve education in this remote and sparsely populated section of the country; for the Saami it meant another incremental step toward Norwegian enculturation and the further loss of Saami culture. Through this act, national policy mandated that all schools be exactly the same, with similar programs and equal standards throughout the country. Schools were to be organized in like manner in Saamiland as the rest of the country, with uniform curricula and pedagogical techniques. In Finnmark, because of the sparseness of the population over such a large area, boarding schools were established, as they have been elsewhere in the Far North, as one of the means to accommodate this policy. Several boarding schools were built between the beginning of the 20th century and 1960, some of which are still in use.

Toward a Saami educational system in Norway

Early this century, three leading Saami, all teachers, made Saami schooling a national issue: Anders Larsen (1870–1949), also editor of a Saami newspaper; Isak Saba (1875–1921), also a member of the Norwegian Parliament; and Per Fokstad (1890–1973). All three advocated a system of education based on the Saami culture and run by Saami teachers with authority to make policy. In spite of these pioneering efforts at school reform, little change resulted from the effort. Nor did ostensibly important governmental committees in the 1920s, '40s, and '50s, constituted to bring about improved learning conditions, contribute to significant changes; little in school programs could be identified with Saami culture and ethnic status.

As improvements were made to the national education system during this period, they were expected to be uniform throughout the country and therefore did not account for the presence of the Saami as a viable indigenous minority in Norwegian society. Even though Norwegian law specified that all children were to be taught in their mother tongue, Saami children continued to be taught in Norwegian. This left responsibility for coping with linguistically mixed schools to those teachers who, because they had no formal training, were unable to comply with the requirement.

In some case this gave pupils who were fluent in both Norwegian and Saami a place of special importance in the classroom when the teacher could speak only Norwegian. Pupils would act as "middlemen" between the teacher and the students and thus were as much in control of the classroom as the teacher. Paradoxically, in those few cases where the teacher was a Saami, instruction would be carried out in the fashion of a typical Norwegian classroom, following the official syllabi with no particular reference to Saami culture or learning style.

Following World War II and until the 1960s, several committees were at work dealing with the Saami situation in general, but to little avail. Although there had been interest shown in the need to accommodate Saami needs in schooling in a manner more appropriate to their culture, there had been little research on the effects schooling of this nature had on students. However, a study in the 1960s confirmed what was generally believed: school performance among the Saami students differed appreciably from that of Norwegians. At all levels, Saami students were significantly below the norm in school performance.[61]

During the 1960s national school programs were expanded to

61. Hoëm 1976a.

cover nine years of basic education throughout Norway, and, for the first time in the history of the modernization of the primary school, Saami schools exceeded the attendance requirements of the rest of the nation. As early as 1965 the nine-year school was established in the municipalities of Nesseby, Tana, and Polmak in Finnmark County. In Guovdageaidnu, in 1967, the use of the Saami language as the language of instruction was initiated; furthermore, it was introduced as a basic subject for those not fluent in the language.

Two years later a law was enacted that gave legal status to Saami primary schools that promoted Saami language and culture. Although this development had a positive effect on student performance, it was not to the extent desired. In 1976, as a result of general development and Saami political activism, an event of importance to the expansion of compulsory schooling through the ninth year took place: The first Saami Board of Education, with headquarters in Guovdageaidnu, was authorized by the Ministry of Education. This board, with the Saami teacher Edel Haetta Eriksen as director, was given the authority necessary to influence the direction of future schooling.

At the same that a Saami-specific curriculum was being improved through initiatives of the board, a department for Saami teacher training was established at the Alta Teacher Training College. In 1987, by an act of the Norwegian Parliament, the Saami Cultural College, located at Guovdageaidnu, was created. Responsibility for Saami teacher training was then moved from Alta to the new college.

These events, and the creation of the Saami Parliament in 1990, which put the responsibility for the education of the Saami in Norway in Saami hands, at least in name if not entirely in fact, are the most recent developments tending toward a Saami system of education. Assessing the extent to which they are working has become one of the current topics now being debated in Norwegian Saamiland.

Sweden

As mentioned above, it is thought that the Northern Cap of Scandinavia has been populated for over 10,000 years, the first people having settled there at the close of the last ice age. Still, it is hard to say exactly when the Saami became settled in the northern part of Sweden, which continues to be called Lappland. It is well documented, nevertheless, that they were well established there during the Middle Ages.

Throughout the centuries, interaction between the Saami and the Swedes brought the Saami into contact with Christianity. But it was not until 1598 that a more systematic upbringing in Christianity was organized through the Church. Interestingly, parishioners were examined as to the extent of their understanding of Christianity by the priests at the local markets when they came to trade.[62]

By 1603, the Swedish King decided that churches were to be established in Lappland. In the first half of the 17th century, six were built. From the beginning, differences between the language of the priests and the Saami were a hindrance to their work; priests spoke Swedish, the Saami their own language. To overcome this barrier to communication, a school for the Saami was established at Lycksele in 1632. According to Israel Ruong, noted Saami scholar and authority on Saami culture, the school was a remarkable success.[63] Nevertheless, its primary purpose was the study of theology and it did not endure for long; few parents were willing to send their children to the school.[64]

The period of ecclesiastical expansion in the first half of the 17th century was followed in the second half with widespread colonization of the North of Sweden. Government exploitation of mineral resources in the central portion of Lappland motivated an influx of Swedes to settle in the North.

At first, intensified efforts of the Church and the government's

62. Henrysson et al. 1993.
63. Ruong, Israel, "Lapp Schools, Teacher Education and Trans-Cultural Studies." In Darnell (ed.) 1972, pp. 328–29.
64. Henrysson et al. 1993, p. 6.

effort to encourage colonization in Lappland had little effect on Saami beliefs, language, or society. Nor was literacy much improved during this period. Since the attempts to Christianize and educate the Saami were unsuccessful, the need for improvement was debated in the Swedish Parliament. As a consequence, it was decided, in 1723, to built a government school at each of the seven main churches in Swedish Lappland. Teachers were required to be qualified both in Christianity and the Saami language, although instruction could be offered in either Saami or Swedish. Pupils were expected to be enlightened in the way of the Christian faith and to be able to read. The more gifted students were given opportunities to learn to write and to understand arithmetic. When graduated from school after two years, it was expected that successful students would spread their knowledge among those who had not attended school.

The program was successful enough that some parents started to send their children to school again. However, the effect on the graduates in their home community was unanticipated. Church authorities decided that to improve education among the Saami, gifted students should be trained as catechists. These catechists were then supposed to work as teachers or preachers in Saami communities. Nevertheless, some parents remained reluctant to send their children to school. As a consequence, children of the Swedish settlers replaced Saami pupils and thereby filled the ranks of catechists. These problems notwithstanding, expanded efforts by the schools, both government and mission, were increasingly effective; by the end of the 18th century, probably half of the Saami population was able to read simple texts.[65] This situation lasted until the end of the 19th century, although the number of government schools fluctuated over the years. By the late 1800s, many Saami children were in attendance at either government or mission schools.

---

65. Ibid., p. 18.

The Swedish school reform movement

Although the number of children in schools had increased appreciably by the turn of the 20th century, there was growing dissatisfaction with the quality of Saami schooling. Olof Bergquist, a leading bishop of the time, was given the responsibility to account for the state of education and devise a means for its improvement. The goal of the bishop was to provide all Saami with an education at such a level and of sufficient standard as to make it possible for them to remain nomads and retain Saami cultural characteristics while simultaneously becoming literate.

The plan suggested by the bishop was to develop a school system in accordance with Saami culture and society. Use of the Saami language, therefore, was an essential element of the plan, together with learning about Christianity and acquiring reading skills. The plan was accepted by the Swedish Parliament and initiated in 1913. The first three years of the program required that pupils be taught during the summer in traditional Saami tents and turf huts while following the migration of the reindeer herds. The last three years of a six-year program were given in stationary schools at church sites. Housing of the pupils was provided in local Saami homes or in special wooden huts erected for the school children, the precursor of standard residence schools.

Bishop Bergquist's plan remained the fundamental approach to Saami education until 1950, although it came under sever criticism from the Saami from the beginning. They claimed that the school was an inappropriate way to achieve a satisfactory standard of education, and an inadequate means to maintain and develop Saami culture. Nor did it provide the pupils with suitable health care. On the other hand, the merit of this type of school arrangement was that it made it possible to give all Saami children some formal education.[66]

Following World War II, yet another educational reform movement was undertaken in Sweden to refashion the entire national education system, including Saami education. Two important

66. Henrysson et al. 1993, p. 26.

recommendations concerning the Saami were proposed during this period, the first in 1960, the second in 1973.

The 1960 reform brought the education system in the Saami area more in line with the education system in Sweden in general, thereby expanding compulsory schooling to nine years of instruction. Additionally, Saami were given the option to choose between the nation-wide school system or a system that was somewhat modified to reflect the Saami culture. To accommodate this option, some schools were established for only Saami children. Called Nomad Schools, the curriculum in these schools was the standard Swedish program, but with additional lessons in Saami culture and language. The Nomad Schools covered the first six years of instruction. For grades seven to nine there was one school erected for Saami students in which advanced syllabuses contained standard Swedish lessons, augmented with instruction in the Saami language.

Although the efforts at reform in the 1960s recognized the need for Saaminess in the Nomad Schools, both the generally slow development of Saami society and the weak position of the Saami culture and language remained a concern of the Saami people. Thus, and in keeping with the worldwide movement for more tangible recognition of the schooling needs of indigenous minorities, yet another reform act was instituted in 1973. Programs defined in this act came under the more direct influence of Saami groups. Nevertheless, only a few of the changes placed greater emphasis on Saami culture and language. Despite this effort, and although renamed The Saami School, most schools continue to offer, for the most part, the standard Swedish programs of instruction and await the next "reform act."

Finland

It is believed that Saami occupied all of present-day Finland in the first century. Soon thereafter, Finns began to enter the country, first in the southwest, but progressively northward since that time. In the early years of settlement, as the Finns proceeded to populate the country they cleared the forests to make way for the cultivation of fields, thereby requiring the Saami, who depended on the forests for subsistence hunting, to move ever northward. Moreover, this development produced extensive intermarriage between Finns and Saami, with the result that traditional Saami lands came into the hands of Finns through family inheritances.[67]

Historically, from the time of the Renaissance until 1808, Finland was a part of Sweden. But in 1808, Sweden relinquished Finland to Russia after losing a war with the latter in that year. Thus, the history of education among the Saami in Finland until 1809 is much the same as the history of education of the Saami in Sweden. However, although Finland and Sweden had a common history for many years, and the political standing of Finnish and Swedish Saami are similar, Finnish Saami may have undergone more rapid cultural changes than Swedish Saami, in part because it was not until 1917 that Finland declared itself independent of Russia.

Finnish Saami, like the Saami of Norway but unlike the those of Sweden, experienced extensive losses and relocation during World War II. Much of their territory was ravaged by the German army in its retreat from the Russian front. As devastating as this period was on Saami families and life style, ironically it had a positive long-range effect. Relocation of Finnish Saami to Sweden for security reasons gave rise to closer contact with Swedish Saami and, consequently, a better understanding of mutual problems, including a closer feeling of solidarity – a feeling that persists today. Furthermore, wartime tribulations of the Saami resulted in a more sympathetic attitude toward minorities by Finns in general, just as there developed a feeling of greater humanity among Norwegians toward minority groups in Norway for the same reason.[68]

These developments aroused an interest in improved education resulting in a government commission in the 1960s that, similar to comparable groups elsewhere in the Far North, recommended new school policies that recognized the importance of indigenous

67. Vorren and Manker 1962, pp. 165–66.
68. Ibid., p. 167.

cultures and the need for their support. This brought about recommendations for the production of Saami-specific textbooks, better trained teachers, and greater use of the Saami language in Finnish schools, either as a language of instruction or as cultural enrichment as a second language.

As well-intended as these recommendations were, however, they were not implemented to the extent required to give them permanence in school policy. Until quite recently, most of the movement for Saami culture as a consideration in schools has been replaced by a national program of universal instruction for all students in Finland, regardless of patrimony. Developments in 1994, however, may portend a change in attitude toward Saami culture in the schools and society in general. Increased interest in research on Saami affairs at the universities of Turku and Helsinki has the potential to lead to improved school programs. Requests for Saami language course work have led to course offerings in a few schools. For the first time the Saami have gained the right to use their own language in public meetings and before government authorities. Moreover, permission to develop localized curricula in some instances has been granted by the Ministry of Education, indicating a slight trend toward devolution of authority in school matters. On a more contentious note, there is now a national debate on whether to transfer responsibility for education from the Ministry of Education to direct control by the Parliament, a controversial issue that has yet to be resolved.

As mentioned in Chapter 3, it is estimated that today there are approximately 4,000 people in Finland who might call themselves Saami. However, because of the methods of census taking used to determine that number – that is, reliance on the use of the Saami language in the home to determine ethnic identity – an exact count of their numbers is not known. Some authorities put the figure as low as 2,500, others as high as 7,000. As in the other Nordic countries, industrial development and expansion of Western culture in the North of Finland have greatly modified the culture and social characteristics of Finnish Saami in recent years. Because of extensive in-migration of Finns to the north of the country, the "Finnicization" of Finnish Saami may be more complete than the nationalization of Saami in Norway and Sweden. Furthermore, Finnish Saami, more than any others, have been increasingly unable to preserve their Native language, in part because it marginally resembles Finnish and in particular because of extensive interaction with the majority population.

Summary

Although there are differences between the three Saami national groups, the similarities are far more widespread than are the differences. In each Scandinavian country, policies have vacillated between the obliteration of Saami culture to strengthening it, thereby frustrating the means to foster a stable society. Moreover, the struggle for identity and the right of self-determination among the Saami as a whole is similar to the indigenous peoples in the Far North areas of other countries. Their mutual histories exemplify subjugation and colonization by those who came to save souls, to trade, or to exploit the natural resources. As elsewhere in the Far North, it has only been during the past 25 years, the period of the worldwide movement for self-determination among indigenous peoples, that marked progress can be identified. One reason why their struggle has taken so long, and continues even today, has been described by Meriot:

> Merchants, officials and missionaries all acted in the interests of so callcd higher powers, without always realizing that their methods of civilization and government were sometimes unsuited to the old Saami world. The end result was that from the middle of the eighteenth century, this world started to decline and disintegrate; poverty increased, the social system and traditional beliefs weakened and disappeared, a tendency to withdraw into themselves and distrust others increased, and while lip service was paid to the new religion and socio-political structures imposed on them, the people gained nothing from them to replenish their vital resources. Only after the religious revival ... in the middle of the nineteenth century and with the struggle for ethnic identity at the end of the twentieth century, is it possible to see these people of northern Europe for what they are and would like to become.[69]

---

69. Meriot 1984, p. 383.

Broadly speaking, it can be seen that the assertiveness of contemporary Saami peoples throughout all of Scandinavia today has the potential to bring about more favorable attention to their needs in official circles than in previous years. Although many Saami educational needs have not been met, and these are sometimes rejected as unattainable by some observers, their struggle for an ethnic identity through schooling continues to acquire credibility.

Greenland

Historical highlights

From the first Eskimo migration across North America to Greenland, approximately four thousand years ago, until the 18th century, Greenland society was monoculturally Eskimoan and isolated from the influences of other peoples. Except for the possibility that there was a slight residual influence on Eskimo culture that can be attributed to the short-lived presence of early Norse settlers, no outside influences were present. Prior to the arrival of permanent European settlers in 1721, Greenland was one of the most solitary locations on earth. Harsh physical characteristics in part account for this condition, but so does the general history of Western expansion worldwide which was slow to turn in a northward direction.

One thousand years have passed since the first Europeans attempted to settle Greenland. Eric the Red, a Norse adventurer who had come from Iceland, landed on the southwest coast of Greenland in what is thought to be the year 982. Acting on his advice that Greenland held promise as a colony, Icelanders formed the nucleus of the first population to settle Greenland from the East, 3,000 years after the first immigrants, Eskimoan peoples who were precursors to today's Inuit Greenlanders, had come from the West. The Norse colony, established in what was then the uninhabited, "temperate," southwest corner of the island, prospered for the first two centuries of its existence. By the 13th century, however, Thule-culture Eskimos from the North (or Skrailings, as they were then known) were increasingly encountering

Norse settlers during their travels to the south. It has been well established that during these encounters the two groups often were hostile toward each other. It is thought that this unfavorable relationship and a change in the climate resulting in more severe living conditions for the settlers may account for the disappearance of the colony. The exact cause remains a mystery. It is known, however, that when the English explorer Martin Frobisher visited the site in 1578, only Native Greenlanders were in residence and no traces of living Norsemen were found.[70]

During the time of the first Norse attempts at colonization, Greenland was affiliated with Norway and was a bishopric of the Roman Catholic Church under the jurisdiction of the archbishop of Trondheim from 1126 until 1536. This manifestation gave rise in Greenland to the Danish–Norwegian mode of policy making and implementation. After 1536 it became exclusively Danish and, furthermore, Roman Catholicism was replaced by Lutheran Protestantism. During the middle of the period the Norse colony disappeared. The importance of the period rests on a concept that grew out of it and became an abiding force in future years: to the Danish–Norwegian government, Greenlanders were considered to be subjects of the king.[71]

With the advent of extensive exploration and whaling by Europeans in the 17th century following Frobisher's voyage, and the opening of whaling along the Greenland coast, casual trade was opened with the Greenlanders and the process of assimilation to Western culture was initiated. Thus it was that at Nuuk (known by its Danish name, Godthaab, for many years), the first permanent European settlement was establish by the Norwegian missionary Hans Egede in 1721. Even though Egede was Norwegian, because Norway was a part of the kingdom of Denmark at the time, the Danish king, Frederik IV, claimed Greenland as a colony of Denmark.

Subsequently, Egede had no doubt that Greenland was a possession of the Danish–Norwegian king, and since the king had

70. Armstrong et al. 1978, p. 170.
71. Gad, Finn, "Danish Greenland Policies." In Washburn (vol. ed.) 1988, p. 110.

obligations as a Christian toward all inhabitants in his domain, Egede had responsibility as a missionary to civilize the Natives as well as any Norsemen who happened to be on hand.[72]

When the Danish colonization of Greenland was initiated it can be said that the country was in a pristine state, that is, it was both pure and primitive, and the Native population was living in equilibrium with available resources to the best advantage that their limited material culture allowed. This is not to say that life was easy or ideal; but neither was it uncultured and untamed. The Danes found a people living a subsistence life style in a land with little vegetation, extremely cold and long winters, and with no knowledge of the comforts found in Western civilization. They were well adapted to their environment, however, with special skills for survival developed over a long history. But opportunities to develop their material culture beyond those things necessary for survival were limited. Archaeological evidence suggests that life was extremely arduous and exacting at times. Small population numbers and scattered settlement concentrations were controlled by the level of available food, all of which was acquired by hunting and fishing.

The first Western teachers in Greenland, as in the rest of the Far North, were missionaries arrived there first of all to save the souls of the unenlightened. When Hans Egede came to Greenland in 1721, he believed he was going to meet the descendants of the Norsemen who had preceded him by several hundred years. It was they that he had decided to convert to the Lutheran Church. Egede, therefore, was completely unprepared for the challenges he faced when encountering an exotic, indigenous population with a culture and language completely unknown to him.

Surprisingly, mission efforts succeeded quickly, undermining the shamanistic religious concepts of the Greenlanders by substituting Christian ones. Success (in terms of missionary goals) was due in part because the Lutheran Church was motivated by the presence of Moravian missionaries who, at first, presented a threat to the pre-eminence of Egede's efforts. Similar to provisions

72. Ibid., p. 111.

that established Den kongelige grønlandske Handel (KGH), a colonial-style trading company given exclusive rights to trade in Greenland by the king as a means to force out other Europeans who were moving in with the same profit motives as the Danes, the Lutheran Church was given a monopoly as a means to force out other denominations.[73]

This religious monopoly was to have a lasting effect on the nature of Greenlandic society. As pointed out by Gad,

> in accordance with Lutheran doctrine, the service was conducted in the mother tongue, which was a dialect of west Greenlandic Eskimo. The missionaries had to learn this language, which required extensive study. A language system was soon created for Greenlanders, and books were printed using it. Since in Lutheran belief each individual made his own decisions about the fundamental doctrine of the faith, a more general education had to be provided him. Greenlanders, therefore, learned early to read and write.[74]

This tenet of the Lutheran Church, along with general Danish–Norwegian social liberalism and egalitarianism, account in large measure for the major differences between the development of education in Greenland and North America. In this case, Egede's adherence to the doctrine of his Church eventually accrued to the benefit of Greenlandic education. His first project was to learn the Native language and to become acquainted with the people. It appears that he never mastered the language completely, but even with his somewhat unsophisticated use of it, he made a few textbooks in Greenlandic that enabled him to teach from the written Bible.[75] In effect, a pedagogical precedence had been set.

The first Greenlandic primer was published in 1739, although it was for the most part a catechism used in the training of reading and spelling. As a means to initiate a system of education, Egede attempted to establish schools where the new KGH trading centers were being established. The first two schools opened in 1740, but it was not possible to sustain them, primarily because of the

73. Ibid.
74. Ibid.
75. Larsen 1977, p. 8.

inadequate education and training given to the local Inuit as teachers. These schools were discontinued after only eight years.

The principal deterrent to successful mission work during the early years was due to inadequately prepared teachers. In an attempt to correct this shortcoming, as early as 1724, two Greenlanders were sent to Denmark to improve their education and ability as teachers, an event that became a routine practice that endures today. Also, as a means to increase the number of partially literate teachers, a group of young inmates of an orphanage in Copenhagen were sent to Greenland as catechists during this period

For the remainder of the century, the main thrust of the education system was to Christianize the population. Accordingly, most of the work of teaching fell to priests and catechists, the overwhelming majority of them Danes. Results of their work varied in quality from place to place, but overall there was an increase in the number of Greenlanders who knew the fundamentals of reading and writing. Despite this, the number of priests assigned to Greenland was reduced from ten to five in 1792. Mitigating this reduction in force, however, was an increase in the number of Greenlanders trained as teachers.[76]

By the end of the 18th century, Danish sovereignty over much of Greenland was assured. But it was not until 1921 that Danish rule was extended to the Far North in the Thule area. Regardless of the boundaries of administrative responsibility, missionary suppression of Inuit customs and religious beliefs was largely completed by the end of the 18th century. As a result of this development, Native leaders in positions of authority were replaced by missionaries and traders. This substantially contributed to a breakdown of Native social structure. Native religious beliefs and social institutions were vanquished in part, but also persisted in other, albeit covert, ways. This development had debilitating consequences on the society, vestiges of which remain today. As pointed out by Armstrong, Rogers and Rowley,

76. Ibid., p. 11.

> the social anarchy that resulted from Egede's destruction of native leadership had far-reaching effects and did much to neutralize the well-meaning efforts of the Danish administrators. The sudden substitution of rules of conduct based on a different culture, under different conditions, in a different land, for the norms that had evolved over the centuries in response to the special conditions in Greenland, could only lead to confusion and demoralization.[77]

Moreover, natural resources were not as rich as first hoped, and much of the trade with Native Greenlanders was monopolized by whalers and other independent traders. With this condition apparent, and the breakdown in Native society the motivating reason, the Danish government moved to take control of all trade and management of social affairs. Greenland thereby became an authentic colony, with Denmark in complete control of an artificial economy and social structure. The most far-reaching consequence of this act was to isolate Greenlanders from the rest of the world. Outsiders were permitted to visit only with permission from the Danish government, professedly to protect Native Greenlanders from undesirable influence from the outside world so as to preserve the Greenland culture and secure a harmonic development.[78] As a result, Greenland remained a closed country until the Second World War. The Danes did not allow free passage of people to or from the country unless they had specific purposes in keeping with prevailing policies of the time. There was neither free trade nor casual travel in or out of the country.

The declared long-term objective of the Danish government was to enable Greenlanders to eventually attain a standard of living with elements of Western culture that would make it possible for them to become part of the rest of the world on economic and social parity. However, this policy proved to be highly paternalistic and, for Greenlanders, socially debilitating. While Native subsistence economy was encouraged, it was only done so to provide temporary relief until the population as a whole could be prepared,

77. Armstrong et al. 1978, p. 172.
78. Bornemann, Claus, "Economic Development in Greenland and Its Relationship to Education." In Darnell (ed.) 1970, p. 213.

albeit slowly, to enter Western society. With education programs caught in the middle of this policy, the social experiment that was to characterize Greenland until contemporary times spawned controversy surrounding the goals of education advanced by Denmark, and the pedagogical means to achieve them, for decades.

At the start of the 19th century, the general impression of Church authorities was that the Greenlanders had been Christianized.[79] As Danish interests in Greenland expanded, a government commission with the mandate to closely examine Denmark's policies in Greenland was appointed in 1835. Empowered to investigate all aspects of Danish colonial rule, educational policy was one of the topics explored by the commission. Recommendations of the commission in this regard advised that education be provided in a more profound and culturally cogent way than previously considered. Consequently, bilingual textbooks in arithmetic were published, and the teaching of Danish strengthened. Compared with the education system in Denmark at this time Greenland was far behind in the ways of Western education, but there was more progress in improving schools than during previous periods.

Most notable, improvements in teacher training grew out of the commission's work. Lack of qualified teachers had been a constant weakness in the system up until this time. As a consequence, two teacher training colleges were established in 1847, one in Nuuk and the other in Ilullissat (Jakobshavn). The college in Nuuk has prospered and continues to prepare teachers today; the college in Ilullissat was closed after a few years.[80]

The establishment of teacher colleges may be the most significant event in the early history of education in Greenland. By arranging for Greenlanders to be teachers a sense of value was placed on the capability and culture of the indigenous people, considerations that were not recognized in Alaska and Canada until well into the following century. Having said this, however, a constant shortage of Greenlandic teachers was always a concern even though a core of Greenlandic teachers endured, thereby

79. Berliner 1987, p. 176.
80. Berthelsen, C., "School and Education." In Hetling et al. (eds.) 1975, pp. 213–29.

affirming the value of the concept. Since there never were enough Greenlandic teachers, by the end of the century, priests sent out from Denmark increasingly had to rely on Danish trained catechists.

Nevertheless, and on a more positive note, during the last half of the 19th century, there was a considerable shift in the opinion among Danes concerning the potential of Greenlandic culture. From almost complete denial in the early years of Danish settlement, a romantic notion of Greenlandic culture came about resulting in both the culture and language occupying a more visible place in the curriculum.

By the end of the 19th century, until which there had been an almost complete lack of knowledge about Greenland in Denmark, legislators were becoming more conscious of needs of the people in the colony. Accordingly, in 1905, the first law concerning schooling in Greenland was enacted by the Parliament. The purpose of the law was to provide the means for the schools to become more closely integrated into the existing educational system in Denmark. This was in keeping with a growing interest among the "educated elite" in Greenland to strengthen the Danish language and culture in the schools. As a consequence, many average members of Greenland society at large were exposed to this concept for the first time.[81] Furthermore, another consequence of this act, according to Berthelsen, was a strengthening of the scope of the teacher training college in Nuuk.[82] Although there was a tendency to bring the schools more in line with Danish traditions during this period as a result of the law, a heterogeneous school program, Greenlandic and Danish, continued to be the dominant trait in schooling.[83]

Twenty years later, in 1925, the act was updated on the supposition that there was a need to continue to keep Greenland up to date with new school trends in Denmark and to give Danish culture an even more prominent place in Greenland schools. Further

81. Berliner 1987, pp. 87, 193–204.
82. Berthelsen, in Hetling et al. (eds.) 1975, p. 214.
83. Larsen 1977, p. 37.

accentuating a Danish presence in the schools, the Danish language was introduced as a school subject in 1926. These acts notwithstanding, at the same time there was a tendency to retain some of the old Greenlandic culture which society was slowly abandoning, giving the schools a bicultural quality.

With the advent of World War II, the policy of keeping Greenland isolated from the rest of the world became a moot point. That policy, invoked at the time Greenland was officially made a colony, was intended to allow time for Greenlanders to acquire sufficient multicultural sophistication to gradually become assimilated into Western society and establish communication with the rest of the world. Although prompted by good intentions, this was a paternalistic policy with no design for the indigenous population to bridge the gap that separated it from the rest of the world. Without direct contact with the outer world, it placed a responsibility on the school system that was impossible to fulfill. But World War II changed all that. Because of the strategic location Greenland occupied during the war, accompanied by the construction of American military bases there, interest in Greenland was generated in the rest of the world. Exposure of Greenlanders to the outer world, and the outer world to Greenland, meant that it could no longer be kept isolated.

Furthermore, following the war, the deplorable social conditions that had developed as a result of Danish social and economic policy came to the attention of the Danish government when, in 1948, the Danish prime minister, Hans Hedtoft, visited Greenland. The plight of the population, as evidenced by dire social and health conditions, prompted the prime minister to establish a commission to deal with the problems. The report of the commission gave rise to a number of reforms that were to follow during the next decade. Most notably, in 1953 colonial status was abolished and travel between Greenland and Denmark (as well as the rest of world) was opened. With the end of colonial status Greenland became a county of Denmark and all Greenlanders became full citizens of Denmark. In particular, this development led to large numbers of Greenlanders traveling to Denmark for various types of specialized schooling, including graduate school at the

University of Copenhagen. It also resulted in a large increase in the number of Danes traveling to Greenland in various official capacities as a means to modernize and rebuild the society in the style of Western Europe.

This had the effect of accelerating the integration of the Greenland schools into the Danish system, although not at the expense of losing Greenlandic as the mother tongue. The general goal remained that Greenlandic as an indigenous language should remain viable and that Greenland was to be a bilingual country.

With the country opening up, yet another change in the system, even more extreme than earlier changes, was enacted by the Danish Parliament. Included in the new legislation were the means to carry out the development of Greenland society along the lines of Western, essentially Danish, society. To the educational system this meant separating the Church from the school; the school was to function on its own, but increasingly in accordance with the design of the educational system in Denmark. This meant that the Greenland schools were to embody the textbooks, teacher training programs, and structure of Danish schools as the ideal model. By default, this arrangement required a preponderance of teachers from Denmark.

As well intended as the Danish reformers of the 1950s were, because of the previous geographical isolation, incompatibility of the people with many aspects of Danish culture, and physical characteristics of the land, the reforms did not extinguish the differences in the quality of education among the various regions of Greenland, nor the gap in quality between schools in Denmark and Greenland. The schools continued to struggle with multiple problems of finding a balance between local cultural needs and an education with the mechanism to enable the population to undergo industrialization, modernization, and cultural replacement, goals that may or may not have been in the best interests of the people at the time.

The contemporary Greenlander Ingmar Egede, having been born and reared into the Greenlandic Inuit society as well as having been formally educated at the University of Copenhagen, and who for many years was head of the Greenland Teacher's Training

College in Nuuk (Grønlands Seminarian), is uniquely qualified to address problems of schooling in Greenland. He has captured the essence of the problem of achieving a balance in life style between traditional Greenlandic culture and the culture of Denmark and the Western world during the post-war period in the article "Educational Problems in Greenland," written for the Danish periodical *Pedagogik* in 1976. Because the article describes so well the situation in Greenland prior to the advent of Home Rule (as well as today in many respects), an extensive portion of the article follows:

> In 1953, in the name of equal rights, Greenland's status as a colony was abolished. Now some years later, one might ask: "Equal rights to what and on what basis?"
>
> In connection with new political ideas [based on a constitution that provided for a democracy, a liberal economy, and the western educational system and administration] and consequent economic opportunities, a virtual migration from Denmark to Greenland was initiated. About 20 percent of Greenland's inhabitants are Danes born outside Greenland. The duration of the stay of the individual Dane is on average 3 to 4 years. Thus one might note that the number of adult Danes, who lived in Greenland during the last 20 years [1956–76], is considerably higher than the number of Greenlanders who today are more than 15 years old. What the influence of this has been, one can only guess at.
>
> During the last 30 years [1946–76] the original population has doubled. Today more people live in the urban communities alone than the whole of Greenland in 1960. Economic activities and the way of life have altered radically, and the Eskimo/Greenlandic cultural heritage has been considered restraining and hampering baggage on the way into the new age, both politically and administratively. The premises on which planning and development rest are West European; and the pillars of the functions in the society are Danes, except for a few Greenlanders, who culturally have taken the plunge. The ordinary Greenlander stands alienated and has become an economic, social and cultural minority in his own country.
>
> In the long run this situation is unacceptable. However, the question is whether the Greenlander has to adapt himself to the society as it is, or the structures of the society have to adapt to him. [Realistically] neither of these alternatives is possible ... The solution must be found through an analysis of what we Greenlanders want to retain, develop, or reject – from both cultures....
>
> Today the Greenlandic school is a product of circumstances that made

legislators, educators, and parents disregard the fact that two cultures exist side by side in Greenland. One of the cultures is dominant, because it has defined the political ideology of the development, and has controlled the means of production, the means of communication, the educational institutions, and the administrative machinery. The other culture has been neglected, is dying and has been devaluated.

When an effort is made to describe the educational problems in Greenland it becomes necessary to describe some aspect of the background of the indigenous culture. The original Greenlandic communities were small – in the literal sense of the word. A settlement of 3–4 families was nothing exceptional, and it was considered a large settlement if 20–30 families were living at the same place. Because of the location of animals which constituted the sole basis for the Greenlander's livelihood, the settlements were distinct places scattered along a vast coastline. For this reason they seldom saw people from outside. And when it happened, it was usually from the nearest settlements....

While growing up, the children were in constant contact with the grown-ups in the family. Apart from the children and parents, the grandparents often lived in the house too; frequently there was also an aunt or uncle, who had not married yet.

Any sign of undesirable behavior was noted by others and checked in the beginning stage, among other things by people's astonishment. It was seldom that unacceptable ways of behavior became habitual, the social control was too close and tangible for that to happen.

It was difficult to distinguish between play and training for adulthood. By taking part in the daily life of the family, the children learned the necessary skills as they gradually developed the ability to master them.

During the evenings and the period of bad weather, when the men were at home, they spent their time making or repairing their hunting tools. On these occasions the hunters told about their confrontations with weather, ice, sea, and especially with the game. Whereas all the other experiences belonged to the collective world, the hunters experienced these confrontations in loneliness. Through the tales the hunters shared each other's experiences, and the boys were introduced to the kind of life that lay ahead of them.

In the static community, experience and age were important to a degree which is about to be forgotten in a dynamic community. The older one grew, the more variations one had seen of the pattern which is followed by the different years and the lives of the individuals. Seen from outside, one day resembled the next, just as each year could give the same impression. But remote and incomprehensible forces altered the weather and the migration routes of the hunter's game. Only tradition and the old people would then know what to do....

[Today] many young people have during the time they grew up and

> received their education gained insight into their own situation and have had an opportunity to analyze this situation. For many of them this brings about a feeling of frustration and powerlessness, which to a great extent is unbearable. This in turn leads many of them to excessive alcohol consumption. Many grow apathetic and neglect their education, if they do not give up. Threats of suicides and fulfillments of the threats become more and more common.[84]

It was into a society constituted along lines described by Egede that Danish authorities set about to remake in their own image in Greenland. Efforts to develop an education system that would accomplish goals laid out in the 1950s continues today, although the advent of home rule government opened a new period of Greenland history and opportunity to develop a system of education by the people themselves. Home rule for Greenland, attained in May 1979, was the culmination of years of Native assertiveness and advocacy for the right of self-determination. Thus, home rule provided local responsibility for many governmental functions that previously had been carried out through Danish authority, primarily by the Ministry for Greenland in Copenhagen. It did not, however, mean complete autonomy for Greenland, especially in the realms of military defense and provisions for foreign trade. However, education, which had been one of the most contentious issues leading up to home rule, became a local responsibility through a new education act appended to provisions for home rule that assured local control of schooling. As expected, this development aroused fervent public debate as to what education should include and how it should be delivered.[85] Moreover, the act provided that the language of instruction was to be Greenlandic and new subjects dealing with Greenlandic cultural characteristics were to be developed.

Even though home rule has given Greenlanders local control of schooling, the present approach to education remains much the same as it was prior to 1979, that is, the tradition established in 1721 of slow evolution of the education system rather than radi-

84. Egede 1976.
85. Berliner 1987, pp. 221–30.

cal revolution prevails. Programs continue to be developed that tend toward the Greenlandification of education that reflect the basic values and culture of Greenland on the one hand, but also are flexible enough to meet fluctuating needs of a qualified labor force and general Westernization of pupils on the other. These have required an extensive expansion of the system since, as Karl Kristian Olsen, Director of Culture, Education and Church for Greenland, has pointed out:

> [The] post-colonial evolution of political reality has given rise to a pattern of pedagogical development concerning instruction in the public schools in which teachers, students and parents have obtained extended ownership of the institution through participation in the planning, implementation and evaluating of the learning process.[86]

This statement from Greenland serves to describe the most recent political developments in all of the countries covered in this book. Although it shows that there has been remarkable progress at the highest policy level, student performance remains abysmally low and problems of providing an appropriate and adequate education at the school level are still to be resolved. Accordingly, in the following chapter we examine current issues faced by those who work for a better system in the future.

86. Olsen 1993.

Photographs

Hundreds of pictures dating from the late 19th century have been saved in the archives of governments, universities, and private organizations. We have not tried to present a representative sample of everything that is available for this would require a book of its own. Nor have we made an attempt to present a collection that represents all of the various categories of pictures available. We have, however, selected a few as a means to further illustrate our theme and to give a feeling, no matter how incomplete, of what schools historically looked like, and how they compare with schools today. Even more importantly, they demonstrate the commonalty of schooling experiences throughout the Far North.

Group I: Early schools, pupils, and teachers

1. Teachers and pupils, Presbyterian Mission School, Sitka, Alaska. Included in the picture are former US vice president Adlai E. Stevenson and former Alaska governor James Sheakley. Source: Senate Document No. 111, 54th Congress, 1st Session, *Report on Introduction of Domestic Reindeer into Alaska*, by Sheldon Jackson, Washington, DC, 1895.

2. Eskimo families on the Kuskokwim River, Alaska, 1886 (from photographs by Messrs. Harmann and Weinland). Source: *Report of Education in Alaska*, by Sheldon Jackson, Washington, DC, Government Printing Office, 1886. Under the first picture was the caption "Uncivilized" and under the second "Civilized," illustrating a strategy whereby photographs were contrived to generate financial support for mission and government schools.

3. Saami teacher, a member of a well-known family from the Southern Saami District, c. 1900. Source: Norsk Folkemuseum, Billedsamlingen.

4. Group picture of an American government school for Saami children. The children were members of Saami families who were engaged to teach Alaska Eskimos the art of reindeer husbandry. Descendants of these immigrants still live along the Norton Sound coast today. Source: *Ninth Annual Report on Introduction of Domestic Reindeer Into Alaska*, by Sheldon Jackson, 1899, Washington, DC, Government Printing Office, 1900.

5. Eskimo children posed for group school picture, Unalakleet, Alaska. Source: *Ninth Annual Report on Introduction of Domestic Reindeer into Alaska*, by Sheldon Jackson, 1899, Washington, DC, Government Printing Office, 1900.

6. Saami children pulling latrine wastes for disposal with Norwegian teacher directing the exercise, at Lakselv Skoleinternat (Boarding School), c. 1914. Source: Arkiv, Finnmarksbiblioteket, Vadsø, Norway.

7. US government school for Natives, Nome, Alaska, c. 1915. The school was located some distance from the Nome city school for "White" children. Source: Alaska State Library, Early Prints Collection No. 01-3293.

8. Saami children, early 1900s. Source: Norsk Folkemuseum, Billedsamlingen.

Group II: Examples of pedagogical styles from turn of the 20th century to today

9. Typical one-room school, Golovin, Alaska, c. 1900. Source: Alaska State Library, Photo Number PCA 307-22, from the collection of Daniel S. Neuman.

10, 11, and 12. Ordinary classroom situations, from reading and writing to mathematics and gymnastics, in Greenland in the early 1920s. Source: Nunatta Katersugaasivia Allagaateqarfialu (Greenland National Museum and Archives), Nuuk, Greenland.

13. Bilingual reading class, Kárášjohka, Finnmark, Norway, late 1950s. Source: Norsk Folkemuseum, Billedsamlingen.

14. Inuttitut programmed computer with syllabics, Eastern Canadian Arctic, 1987. Source: Culture and Communications, Government of the Northwest Territories, Yellowknife. Photo by Tessa Macintosh.

15 and 16. Baker Lake, 1987. Contemporary pedagogical techniques in language arts and science. Source: Culture and Communications, Government of the Northwest Territories, Yellowknife.

Mary Had a Little Lamb

17. Sir John Franklin High School, Iqaluit. Contemporary pedagogical techniques in language, arts, and science. Source: Culture and Communications, Government of the Northwest Territories, Yellowknife.

Group III: Leisure-time activities

18. Saami children at recess at the Guovdageaidnu Boarding School, c. 1930. The school was destroyed in World War II. Source: Norsk Folkemuseum, Billedsamlingen.

19. Saami boys preparing their footwear, Guovdageaidnu Boarding School, c. 1930. Source: Norsk Folkemuseum, Billedsamlingen.

20. Saami children on their own. Source: Norsk Folkemuseum, Billedsamlingen.

21. Saami children having their supper at the boarding school at Guovdageaidnu, early 1960s. Source: Arkivet, Finnmarksbiblioteket, Vadsø, Norway.

22. Greenlander string orchestra from the early 1920s. Source: Nunatta Katersugaasivia Allagaateqarfialu (Greenland National Museum and Archives), Nuuk, Greenland.

23. Improvised football, Tusarvik School, Repulse Bay, Northwest Territories, 1992. Source: Culture and Communications, Government of the Northwest Territories, Yellowknife. Photo by Tessa Macintosh.

24. Bull session, Kivalliq Hall, Rankin Inlet, 1988. Source: Culture and Communications, Government of the Northwest Territories, Yellowknife. Photo by Tessa Macintosh.

Chapter 5

Contemporary Issues

In this chapter we examine the topics most frequently at issue in the education programs offered to the peoples of the Far North of the Circumpolar countries. These include organizational structure of the school, locus of control, the curriculum, language of instruction, professional development of teachers, and pupil performance. These topics, combined with the previous chapter on schooling in historical perspective, provide the basis for our conclusions that follow in Part Three.

Before proceeding, however, it should be pointed out that dividing these topics into specific categories creates an artificial structure that tends to oversimplify the situation. In real life there are multiple variations in the way the topics we cover interrelate/interact to form a whole, namely the school. This means there will be a certain amount of overflow of subject matter as each topic is discussed. Of greater importance, it means that each topic should not be thought of in isolation from the others since they mutually influence each other.

Organizational structure of the schools

As noted in the chapter on the historical development of schooling, in some locations in Alaska and Canada provisions for schooling are fairly recent. Such is not the case in Greenland and Scandinavia. Accordingly, we draw first on the Scandinavian experience to illustrate our perception of the reason that school structure has been a problem and why there is a need to restructure schooling to better fit Native needs.

It has only been in this century that there has not been a prominent presence of the Church in formal schooling in Scandinavia. This means that formal education during the Roman Catholic era, from the end of the 9th century until the first half of the 16th, was part of an international establishment organized to serve the purposes of the Holy See. With the introduction of the Protestant Church in the first half of the 16th century, formal education continued to be an important responsibility of the Church, but with the added dimension of a notable alliance with the Crown and the national culture.

In either case, Roman Catholic or Protestant, from the very beginning, education was initiated and organized as a bureaucratic hierarchy as part of an enterprise whose presuppositions and main goals were decidedly outside the local community. So, too, was this the case in Greenland, and although the Church was not instrumental in setting organizational precedents in Alaska and Canada until late in the 19th century, its effectiveness in establishing a similar structure with the same goals was no less than that in Scandinavia and Greenland.

Because of its inadequacies, however, the concept of bureaucratic hierarchies is being increasingly challenged by educational theorists. Nevertheless, the hierarchical, bureaucratic model, the way most school systems are structured, persists everywhere as the norm. It follows, therefore, that this model is the school structure invariably clung to in the Far North. This system, with its pyramidal tiers of authority, often described as the "factory" or "top-down" model of school organization, is based on the concept that authority and decisions flow downward from the top. Authority to make policy originates with legislative bodies and ministries, passes through middle management and supervisors (superintendents and principals) with the advice of educational specialists, and only then finally to classroom teachers. At the lowest level, the base of the pyramid, where teachers and students come in contact with the system and each other, little is left to be decided. Although it is as this level that local conditions are best known, options for adapting to local conditions are the most limited. As a consequence, hierarchical bureaucracies are notoriously fraught with shortcomings regardless of where they are found, but all the more so in the Far North where such a structure lacks congruence with the way indigenous societies have traditionally organized themselves, and their ways of passing on important skills and information, their knowledge. This disparity is the root cause of many points at issue in Far Northern schools.

The American critic of contemporary schooling in the United States, Theodore Sizer, has identified several reasons why the hierarchical system causes problems: ignorance of local conditions; excessive dependency on specific quantifiable school data that misrepresents or distorts the unquantifiable character and qualities of learning; norms based on central tendencies that lead to excessively rigid expectations of everyone; high levels of specificity at the expense of students who do not stand out; irrelevant, entrenched regulations promulgated far from the people they regulate; and the tendency of bureaucracies to stifle initiatives at their base.[1]

Furthermore, members of a special school improvement project in the United States (Quality Education for Minorities Project) concluded their work in part with this summary:

> Factory model schools teach students to memorize through drill and practice rather than through the use of knowledge and skills to solve problems, innovate, and learn. The factory model treats students as objects to be acted on rather than as active participants in their own learning.... the factory model ignores individual differences by assuming that there is one best way to learn and teach. It assumes that management's responsibility is to understand what is best for the system and impose it through bureaucracies on teachers and students.[2]

This description of the factory model, and Sizer's list of shortcomings that characterize schools organized under a hierarchical structure, reflect a situation in the Far North as it is now, and has been since the beginning of formal schooling. In the light of what

1. Sizer 1985, pp. 206–9.
2. Quality Education for Minorities Project 1990.

we now know about indigenous societies, it is remarkable that some school officials continue to persist in defending policies that confer so much authority in bodies located at great distances from the operational level. The result of this arrangement is that those with the least authority have the greatest day-to-day exposure to and comprehension of the problems of schooling, while those with the greatest authority are the farthest removed from the scene of the problems. Moreover, this situation even creates unnecessary problems at the local level. More often than not, subject matter is neatly packaged as courses containing specific bodies of knowledge that are often trite or irrelevant, and which are expected to be rote learned (often at mediocre levels of mindfulness) and at rigidly prescribed times in the students lives.

This typically Western way of organizing the delivery of education services is the antithesis of the typical social structure of indigenous peoples. As pointed out by the Native scholar Oscar Kawagley, "the Western educational system has made an attempt to impose a mechanistic and linear world view into contexts previously guided by the typically cyclic world views of indigenous people."[3]

The factory model of school organization found in most schools in the Far North derives from this mechanistic and linear world view. Where authority in Western schools is hierarchical or vertical, and bodies of knowledge compartmentalized, the authority of those responsible for learning in traditional indigenous societies is horizontal and communal. In indigenous societies bodies of knowledge derive from, and are analogous to, that part of nature from which they come. Each body of knowledge contributes to the survival of the society. Persons with a specific body of traditional knowledge, regardless of their position in society, are responsible for holistically carrying forward knowledge that integrates all other dimensions and relationships. Such knowledge is concrete and immediately operational.

Historically, indigenous societies have looked upon knowledge in the context of the role it plays in their relationship to nature as

---

3. Kawagley 1993, pp. 116–17.

a whole, while formal knowledge in Western society is abstract and general. Thus, knowledge of Western society has to be made tangible and specific before it becomes operational. It may or may not be understood or appreciated at the time it is taught (if ever) as having a relationship to the whole. Consequently, the Western school model superimposed on Native societies unfamiliar with or not yet accustomed to Western culture often has been only marginally productive at its best and devastating at its worst.

Although this is the case, those responsible for organizing schools are not necessarily to be faulted for want of trying to improve them. In recent times, governments responsible for education in the Far North have not shirked from a perceived moral responsibility to improve the economic and cultural life of indigenous peoples. But given the social structure in which they operate and their background in philosophical and pedagogical training, it is not surprising that they doggedly stick to the only system they know. Their efforts over time have been in accordance with the standards and norms of pedagogical science accepted most everywhere in the Western world. Given a willingness to cooperate in recent years, it is unfortunate, then, that the Western model has not been questioned more forcefully.

Increasingly outspoken Native discontent in the 1960s and 1970s drew attention to the organizational structure of schools and cast doubt on it as the most appropriate way to systematize formal learning in small indigenous societies. Increasingly in Native circles, it has come to be realized that the way schools have been organized for so long is incompatible with Native organizational systems and life styles. Likewise, in Western society there is a growing awareness among scholars that students everywhere learn in different ways due in part to cultural orientation, thus calling into question the hierarchical system of school organization. When applied to cross-cultural or multicultural situations in the Far North, where the very nature of Native societies does not correspond to the structure of the large urban societies for which the hierarchical model was developed, restructuring becomes imperative.

Our account of this topic thus far may make this issue appear deceptively simple. But the question of school structure is not a choice between traditional Native ways or Western ways. It would be naive to assume that all Native cultures remain unaltered or at the same stage of social development. Of course, they are not. As mentioned earlier, Native societies in the Far North are constantly exposed to and are implementing new ideas and technology and weighing value systems, both from within their own societies and from without. There is much in Western knowledge, especially technical knowledge, desired by members of Native societies that may best be learned through ways other than traditional Native approaches.

It is inevitable, therefore, that there comes a time when the organizational system of education in Far Northern societies must become more broadly constituted. That is, it needs a wider scope that will enable it to incorporate Western thought more than traditional Native systems can accommodate. If individuals in Native societies are to acquire new skills that will enable them to compete successfully in the western economic system and enjoy the enrichment afforded by familiarity with elements of cultures other than their own, the scope of their education must be broadened. However, those responsible for providing systems of formal education must come to realize that the factory model as a way to organize schools is not necessarily appropriate in Native societies. The problem today, then, is not necessarily how to sustain or revitalize the structure of education in the traditional Native mode, nor is it to cling to the factory model in the hope that it will eventually prove to be right. The problem is how to utilize the best features of all possible structures in innovative ways that fit a large variety of independent situations in accordance with local needs which are culture-specific.

Answers to three pertinent questions may help resolve this problem.

1. What alternatives are there to either Western or traditional Native style school structure that will better enable schools to meet the needs of societies in transition?
2. Can formal education be organized in such a way that educa-

tion programs can be made to fit the contemporary structure of Native societies and still fulfill those broad purposes mutually agreed to by the providers of educational services and those being served?

3. At what stage of societal development are some aspects of Native social structure an appropriate model for school organization and when is Western-style education or an improved variation of it appropriate for schools in Native communities?

Contemporary problems in schooling that can be attributed to the ways schools are organized are not unique to the Far North. Since much of Western society is in transition, as is Native society, answers to the first question may apply as much to Western society as to Native societies. Accordingly, we can first turn to scholars who recently have addressed this topic in Western education in general. One of the notions most frequently advocated for school improvement by this group is the need for flexibility in all aspects of the educational enterprise, school structure in particular. Moreover, as suggested in the American report *Education that Works: National Goals for the Education of Minorities and How to Achieve Them,* schools should be restructured as centers of inquiry and reflection, and that school-based planning with shared governance for decision making at the local level holds the most promise to enable schools to adapt to changing world conditions.[4] During the past few years numerous books and articles by academics have been devoted to these themes. Typical among them, Joseph Murphy in his book *Restructuring Schools* succinctly points out that

> schools that are engaged in reforming delivery systems have ... shown considerable flexibility in the ways they organize students for learning. In the best of these, "students are arranged in a variety of ways for various activities and skills throughout the day resulting in alternative grouping patterns for different students and subjects" (McCarthy and Peterson).[5] At least six different threads are evident in the tapestry of flexible organizational arrangements:

---

4. Quality Education for Minorities Project 1990.
5. McCarthy and Peterson 1989.

flexible use of space,
less regimented scheduling patterns within classes,
nontraditional grouping patterns within classes,
more flexible instructional arrangements,
less emphasis on self-contained classrooms,
less use of age grouping patterns.[6]

The extent to which these criteria for organizing schools for more effective education resemble the structure of learning systems in traditional Native societies is striking. The remarkable feature of Murphy's list is how little it would need to be changed to describe the traditional organization of education in Native societies where learning takes place through the activities of members of the Native community in the context of the kinship system. Other than the fact that "teachers" in the traditional Native society come from many quarters of the community dependent on specialties and levels of expertise, and depending on their role in society, all of the steps in this list describe closely a way of learning that has been in practice for centuries in Native societies.

Theodore Sizer's commentary on reforms in school structure in *Horace's Compromise,* cited above, is similar. He suggests personalization and flexibility of learning as a theme for improved structure, a concept that is basic to traditional Native education:

> Personalization of learning and instruction requires a flexible school structure. A flexible structure implies a *simple structure.* A school day segmented into seven or eight time units, each with its own set of imperatives, is almost impossible to bend ... [and] a fractionated and specialized set of subjects distorts knowledge for young minds.[7]

As is the case with Murphy's criteria for improving school structure, Sizer's observations speak to a form of school structure that could well have been drawn from a study of the personalized, flexible learning environment of traditional Native life style.

Practical suggestions such as these notwithstanding, at the mere mention of restructuring, many school officials become

6. Murphy 1991, p. 67.
7. Sizer 1985, pp. 216–17.

defensive and intransigent. The issue instantly becomes polarized and ideological, paralyzing imagination.[8] Historically in the Far North it has been this trait that has limited innovative thinking, thinking that may have the potential to enable schools to become more congruent with traditional Native learning style.

Moreover, even when Native leaders themselves point out the need for better schools, only occasionally do they question the validity of the hierarchical school structure. This is not surprising, given that the factory model of schooling is the only one to which they have been exposed. Without objection, it is generally accepted as the only way schools can be organized. However, Native leaders who have been the exception to this generalization, and have spoken out on the subject, have done so with rare insight. Jan Henry Keskitalo, a Saami teacher and scholar who was raised in the traditional Saami culture and is now head of the Saami Cultural College (Saami Allaskuvla), is one such spokesperson. He commented on structure the following way:

> The basic principle of education of any people is that education has to be planned and organized in and through the language and the culture of the group. This principle may be demonstrated by analyzing the connections between education and society. Each society, separately, has its own practical and theoretical knowledge, just as its members have specific norms or behavior and values....
>
> In less complex societies, cultural habits are shared and are common to a greater part of the society's members than in more complex societies. Knowledge, habits of behavior, and value norms are more static, while in highly differentiated societies they are of a more dynamic character.
>
> In low-specialized societies, shared cultural values are transmitted from one generation to the next basically through informal learning, through socialization, through self-experience, and by limitation of situations where there is interaction between different generations. In a more industrialized and complex society, which is rapidly evolving in Samiland, values are transmitted through learning in more formalized situations.... The formal educational system is, then, an instrument of socialization. Its task is basically to act as a catalyst, transferring cultural heritage into terms of common knowledge and passing on only a sample of cultural values from one generation to another. The educational system has taken

8. Ibid., p. 218.

over the role of raising the new generation; it prepares the pupils to be members of the future society at the same time it qualifies the pupils to be professionals and to take part in further education.

Since different societies have to solve different problems, they need different educational systems. In a multicultural society, this fact has to be taken into consideration. If, then, the system is planned without taking this into consideration, it means that the school will not meet the needs of different sub-societies. Among these sub-societies, indigenous people constitute a group with specific needs, particularly with regard to an educational system structured to solve problems connected with the maintenance of their cultural heritage and values and the transmission of these to future generations. Of course, other groups also could take up this position, but we are talking in terms of the ethnic heritage of groups outside any kind of formal constitutional nationality as these are defined by western societies....

Besides the transformation of values taking place in the educational system mentioned above, the system also has a hidden society, in terms of what it reflects through its reorganization, its values, its choice of goals and methods, and its decisions regarding equipment and teacher qualifications.

These are integrated into the system itself and are easily transferred to new systems or to systems undergoing a change.... This does not mean that the school is unable to exist as an institution for learning particular subjects in any particular context. But if the school is seen to have a special role in terms of transferring cultural values, these facts have to be taken into consideration.

Otherwise, we are talking about an educational system reflecting maladjusted relationships of power between states and indigenous people. The child will experience the school as a meaningful situation only to the degree there is a significant relationship between the child's cultural values, represented by the local school. This does not mean that school has to transfer the culture of the home only. It also has to impart necessary knowledge needed in the future society. We need, however, to stress what kind of identity the school must reflect. For people in the Saami areas, the educational system has to be based on and has to be an integrated part of the Saami culture.[9]

Keskitalo's appraisal of the situation applies just as well to the needs and perceptions of other indigenous peoples throughout the Far North as it does to the Saami of whom he writes.

9. Keskitalo, Jan Henry, "Education and the Native Saamis." In Demmert (ed.) 1986, pp. 12–14.

Thus, answers to the questions that define this issue interestingly are found in both the traditional Native structure of education and in contemporary theories advanced by scholars in Western education. Flexibility in organization and involvement of a broad cross-section of community members are the means to improved school structure in both instances. Recommendations made by scholars for restructured schools in Western societies in general contain many of the elements consistently found in traditional Native education. Conversely, many aspects of the traditional way of organizing Native education are comparable with the thinking of modern theorists on school reform in Western societies.

It follows, therefore, that if flexibility and local involvement are the means to better schools, no one system of organization can be prescribed or mandated as a panacea that would lead to more sensitively constituted schools. By definition, flexibility is an antonym of uniformity. The need for flexible structures, programs, and goals tailored to individual circumstances speaks to the need for local involvement. It is not an oversimplification to say that answers to the questions posed under this topic are ultimately the responsibility of those people working at the local level. However, adoption of this thesis does not guarantee that the answers will be sufficient in scope or adequate in quality to guarantee more effective schools. That will depend on who has the authority to decide answers to any number of questions in need of daily consideration. This contingency leads directly to the next issue, locus of control, a topic that often is one of the most worrisome among central government departmental authorities.

Locus of control

Locus of control, that place where school governance is carried out, as an issue, is closely related to school structure, each merging into the other in the daily operation of schools. The conflict over control in the Far North in its most basic form is not much different from anywhere else in the Western world. In the simplest of terms it revolves around who decides what should be taught and how. The extent to which a given body or individual can control educational processes and make these decisions, in any school or school system, is dependent on the power and capacity to make adequate policy decisions. Typically this power is acquired through legislated authority (usually in statute), by having access to sufficient funds to exercise that authority and by superior knowledge of the subject being governed. The structure of the school, on the other hand, is the organizational environment of the school, that is, the setting in which operational decisions are made, leadership exercised, and routine tasks carried out.[10]

Locus of control as a topic at issue, like organizational structure, is not confined to schools in the Far North; it has become a contentious topic in many school systems worldwide. John E. Chubb of the Brookings Institute, writing on the school improvement movement in the United States, has explained the importance of the interrelationships of organizational structure and locus of control in schools that might apply anywhere:

> [The] institutional structure and character [of schools] is shaped by their environment – by their relationship with parents, of course, but more pertinently by the way they are controlled.... Those organizational qualities that we consider to be essential ingredients of an effective school – such things as academically focused objectives, [and] pedagogically strong principals ... do not flourish without the willingness of authorities to delegate meaningful control over school policy, personnel, and practice to the school itself. Efforts to improve the performance of schools without changing the way they are organized or the controls they respond to will therefore probably meet with no more than modest success.[11]

Although spoken in broad terms, these points are especially appropriate to schools for indigenous minorities, those in the Far North in particular. From the Native perspective, Mary Simon, at the time President of the Inuit Circumpolar Conference, came to the same conclusion and carried this concept one step farther by introducing the need for commitment and responsibility:

> The success of Native education is directly related to the amount of com-

10. Alaska 1991, p. 61.
11. Chubb 1988, p. 29.

> munity control and involvement there is in the school system. Only when Native people feel a part of that system, that they have a stake in it, will they assume responsibility in a meaningful way and become committed to its success.[12]

The logic of these points notwithstanding, there are practical problems to overcome before Native control at the local level will be fully realized.

In Chapter 4 it was shown that the movement for devolution of control from large, central bureaucracies to local indigenous groups and the school itself started to gain momentum in the late 1960s. Control of the policies and processes of education was identified at that time as one of the crucial means to advance the nativistic movement for self-determination in all fields of Native interests. And control of the policy-making process in education was seen as an essential procedure necessary to influence the fundamental nature of the school system.

Since that time, governments in each of the Circumpolar countries have made a conscious, although at times inconsistent, effort to correct this deficiency. In Alaska, it was through a legislative act that established Native controlled school boards in rural Regional Education Attendance Areas, but not until many village residents had clearly expressed dissatisfaction with what was being taught and how. The factors in contention at that time (1974) were primarily the inadequate extent of local participation, policy making, and power in educational processes.[13] In the Northwest Territories, it was through the creation of local school boards authorized over time through federal and territorial legislative bodies, especially the Northwest Territories Legislative Assembly's Special Committee on Education in 1982, co-chaired by Tagak Curley, Inuit member of the Assembly.

In Arctic Quebec, constructive changes came about quite differently as the result of the James Bay Agreement and establishment of Kativik School Board. The James Bay Agreement grew out of economic developments in northern Quebec that were col-

12. Simon 1989, p. 62.
13. Darnell et al. 1974, p. 7.

liding with orderly political development. Signed in 1975 by the governments of Quebec and Canada, and by the Grand Council of the Cree of James Bay and the Northern Quebec Inuit Association, the agreement was designed to settle Native land claims and allow for the orderly development of the huge northern portion of Quebec. A section of the agreement provided for the creation of Kativik School Board, a totally Inuit controlled body which assumed full responsibility for schooling. The board is notable for its autonomy and extraordinary powers such as authority to design its own curriculum, determine its own calendar, decide on the languages of instruction and methods of training of its teachers.[14]

In the Yukon Territory, after many years of indifference to educational needs of a small Native population, there is now a concerted effort under way to undo this neglect.

We have touched on Labrador only lightly, in part because there is little to report in contemporary times. Nevertheless, Northern Labrador is very much a part of the Arctic with miles of unbroken tundra and frozen seas along its shores. And although the Native population is small, about 1,000 Inuit and 1,000 Indians in all of Labrador have experienced many of the same problems as other peoples of the Far North. The first schools were established by Moravian missionaries in 1771, at about the same time that Moravians first went into Greenland. As elsewhere, education was an integral part of religious conversion. At first, instruction was limited to the scriptures, but was expanded early on to include the basics. Most notable during the early years, actually until permanent non-Native settlers arrived, Inuttitut was the language of instruction. In Greenland the Moravians had become familiar with the problems of education among the Inuit. There they had studied the Greenlandic language and translated parts of the New Testament into the West Greenlandic dialect, which differed very little from the dialect spoken in Labrador. Similar to the work of Danish missionaries in Greenland, the German Moravians utilized the Inuit language extensively in their

14. Cram 1985, pp. 217–18.

schools. This feature of Moravian schools resulted in the schools being well received by the Inuit population and, according to Jenness, by 1884 all Inuit along the Atlantic coast of Labrador could read and write their own language, although the education imparted by the Moravians was not profound, if judged by European standards.[15]

With the arrival of the settlers the issue of monolingualism versus bilingualism became a problem, as elsewhere in the Far North. This situation continued up until Newfoundland became a province of Canada in 1949, at which time the character of education was replaced by a broad, secular, integrative program. With this new system based on the curriculum of schools in the rest of Newfoundland sensitivity to much of the Native culture was lost with the result that by the mid-1960s many parents argued that their children received an education of little value and urged a return to the teaching of Native languages and cultural skills.[16] Only in the most recent times have education officials recognized the need to accommodate the unique nature of the indigenous population of Labrador, and locus of control may now be acquiring momentum as an issue there.

While locus of control in the various political units of Canada has taken slightly different forms, so too is this the case in Greenland and Scandinavia. In Greenland soon after a home rule government was conceded by the Danish Parliament in 1979, control over schools was given to Greenlanders. In the Scandinavian countries recent changes in laws affecting the relationship between the Saami population and state governments have improved, although not uniformly so among all countries. This can be attributed in part to the long history of education being a direct concern of the Crown and the Church. From the time of the first rudimentary form of education in Scandinavia was initiated, the King and his officials exercised control over schools until the middle of the 19th century. At that time municipalities were

15. Jenness 1965, pp. 38–40.
16. Kennedy, J.C., "Northern Labrador: An Ethnohistorical Account." In Paine (ed.) 1977.

established, thereby creating the potential for local communities to exercise direct control in community matters. From then on, the Saami were able to take part in municipal governance. This they did, but not intrinsically as representatives of the Saami people. Instead, they participated as members of the different political parties, with full rights as citizens to take part in affairs of local governance, not as members of an ethnic minority.

Although these developments moved the Saami closer to self-determination, they did not do so completely. Schooling in Scandinavia remains the ultimate responsibility of the central state government. For example, teachers are appointed by local authorities, but the appointment has to be approved by officials of the state. The same provision applies to policies that affect the daily operation of the school as well as other aspects of municipal government.

For many years after municipal governments were established teachers of Norwegian descent or local Norwegian residents dominated the governance over the education system. It was not until after World War II that the Saami saw an advantage in exercising their potential for substantive power to control schools and other local matters. As long as the school was perceived to be more of a hindrance to their well-being as a people, they did not take part in the operation of the system at all. But as soon as education was seen as a means to an end and could be constituted for their welfare, individual Saami willingly took part in the governance of the schools.

This is essentially the situation in both Finland and Sweden today, and illustrates a type of local control that may or may not be Native control, depending on the extent to which there is Native participation. In Norway the process may be tending toward an absolute Native-controlled system. This is possible because the Saami population has been formally recognized by the Norwegian government as the rightful indigenous peoples in their traditional districts. This affords an opportunity to develop a distinctive Saami system, should it be decided that such a system would be desirable. At the macrolevel the topic is being now debated with opinions varying between those who speak in favor of cultural autonomy and those who endorse assimilation into the majority society.

At the local or microlevel concerns are of another type. There are problems getting parents to become involved in the various boards and committees in which they are obliged to participate in order to exercise control over programs such as health and social services. In the typical Saami family today both parents are wage earners with little time left for involvement in school affairs, thereby further complicating the problem. This limitation notwithstanding, women are increasingly more motivated to be involved in schooling policy and there is a tendency for this interest to strengthen a Saami presence in the schools. Offsetting this trend, however, is a tendency on the part of men to dominate in public life where they may discourage increased Saami participation in school affairs.

Aspects of this issue such as these are part of what may be called the political dimension of education. As such they are fraught with all the shortcomings associated with political decision making in any field of public endeavor, as well as its strengths and potential to eventually set things right. Unrealistically, local control has been held out as the panacea for all the social ills of Native society. Examples of political naivete and abuse of power are found alongside the best of political motivation and accomplishment.

In indigenous societies where education was an informal process based on the kinship system there was no need for the complexities of formal education. Abstruse laws, inflated teacher certification requirements, curriculum guidelines, and testing criteria bear little resemblance to the informality of flexible Native learning styles. Thus, once authority for making decisions is devolved to local communities, a period of transition during which time the rules of procedure are learned and responsibility is accepted is necessary. It is regrettable that this period has often been characterized by local residents unfamiliar with and uncertain of their authority and responsibility, thereby becoming victims of misguided advice. In some communities this situation has given rise to serious abuses of trust. In the most unfortunate circumstances local control has created opportunities for unprincipled administrators to take advantage of the trust placed in them by credulous members of Native boards of education.

Experience in Alaska following decentralization of state and federal school schools systems, where the legal means for self-determination in rural school governance was first enacted into law, illustrates some of the problems associated with devolution of authority. As discussed in Chapter 4, the Alaska State Legislature decentralized the state-controlled rural school system in 1975. Twenty-one Regional Educational Attendance Areas (REAAs) were created. Although these regions, or "districts" as they are now more commonly called, were the result of devolution of authority, villages within their boundaries were not necessarily locally or Native controlled. This was because of the huge size of most of the districts, each with many small villages under their jurisdiction. These districts were, however, independent of the previous centrally controlled state and federal systems. Individual village schools were more or less locally controlled, depending on the extent to which they were required to defer to central regional office policies.

A few years after the rural districts were created by the legislature, a study was undertaken at the University of Alaska Fairbanks to examine their characteristics. Published in 1984, a report describing this study, "Patterns of Control in Rural Alaska Education," identified the complexities of the problems of devolution of authority and some of its shortcomings as well as an evaluation of its effectiveness. Although the study was Alaska-specific, findings from the investigation speak to aspects of devolution of authority that may have bearing in all Far Northern schools.

The researchers who carried out this study were primarily concerned with patterns of control and the advantages and disadvantages of schooling that is controlled locally. They found in districts with 100 percent localized control

> advisory boards and administrators [that] work together to develop school programs and determine school routines [and] suggested that localization of control was dependent on several conditions, including a stable local administrator who *shares* influences with the school board,

> has a positive orientation toward the local community, and a respect for community values;
> local boards or committees that represent major community interests, including factions;
> stability (low turnover) on the local board,
> district-level communication processes
> and a district superintendent who personally supports the ideology of local control.[17]

Localization of control was clearly found to be dependent on regional as well as local factors. The attitude and values of district superintendents appeared to be singularly important in the decentralization process. Unfortunately, it was found that only two-fifths of the total number of rural districts in Alaska had truly localized schools, the ultimate goal of the decentralization movement.[18]

Among the remaining districts, 36 percent were termed "Mixed control schools," that is, they were in a range part way between local and total regional control. Regionally controlled districts were found in the remaining 24 percent of the districts. In the mixed control group it was found that there was a far greater degree of teacher, administrator and community dissatisfaction that seemed to be associated with higher turnover rates. Conflict and tension associated with mixed control schools had an adverse effect on school climate, student adaptation and parent satisfaction. Regionally controlled schools, where policy is set by the district office, lacked systematic local input. Furthermore, decisions affecting staffing of schools and the curriculum were found to be district-wide functions under the direction of the regional office.[19]

Problems attributed to implementing the REAA system as a whole were found to include

> ambiguity regarding the objectives of decentralization and the level to which decentralization was to occur;...
> lack of participation by rural residents ... that would influence the design of the new system;...

---

17. McBeath et al. 1984, pp. 4, 5.
18. Ibid.
19. Ibid., p. 6.

> lack of expertise in the state administration and within districts to ... plan new schools and programs;
> lack of training of administrators and teachers;... insufficient training and preparation, at the community level, regarding powers and responsibilities of local boards; [and]
> lack of evaluation procedure, or any means of determining whether districts and schools were performing adequately.[20]

These problems notwithstanding, substantial decision-making authority was transferred downward to rural Alaskan communities. A pattern of successful and not so successful districts has now emerged into almost routine predictability. This suggests that all societies contemplating decentralization of decision-making authority, or now engaged in the process, can profit from the experience of the various Native boards that first implemented the REAA system of rural school districts.

For Native societies eventually to succeed in remaking the school systems where they live, they must understand the nuances of Western political processes, processes that should reflect the best of democratic principles, but at times fail to do so. Ideally, decisions affecting the character of the school should be representative of the majority will of the people affected by the decisions. More precisely, the right to participate in determining the form, choosing the officials, making the regulations, and carrying out the functions of education should be invested in the people who constitute the system. However, the right to participate often is not sufficient to bring about the necessary levels of committed Native participants. There is a need for provisions that enable local governing groups to be trained or educated in the processes of school governance, a need that should be met by central governmental bodies as their contribution to devolution of decision-making authority. Where these provisions have not been made, experience has shown that local control is apt to be subverted, sometimes simply because of ineptitude, but often tragically because of unscrupulous school administrators who do not truly accept the right of indigenous peoples to control their own

20. Ibid., p. 7.

affairs, taking advantage of the trusting nature of village and settlement populations. Without an adequate understanding of the political dimension of school governance, such as was provided by the Baffin Region Education Society (later to become the Baffin Divisional Board) in the mid-1980s, the likelihood of sought-after local considerations finding their way into the education system is unlikely.

The curriculum

Broadly speaking, until the last decade or two, the history of curriculum development in schools for the Native population had been the history of curriculum development in each of the nation states of which they are a part. Except for a few worthy attempts to the contrary, described below, there had been little or no attention given to curricula that specifically took the Native population into consideration. Similar to issues related to organizational structure and locus of control, the curriculum had typically reflected the dominant values of the majority society. It has only been in recent years, years in which there have been major changes in the Native society, that the minority culture has had an influence on the curriculum. But this trend has not been without problems.

Alaska

The curriculum adopted for the education of Alaska Natives early in the history of schooling closely mirrors the prevailing attitudes of the people of the United States toward education. As described in the chapter on historical perspectives, it can be seen that the tendency was for the curriculum to adhere to uniform national goals of education. There were notable exceptions, however, exceptions that prepared the way for the major efforts for change initiated in the 1960s and carried forward to the present time.

In the United States the proposals of Lewis Meriam in the 1920s and John Collier in the mid-1930s, as mentioned in Chapter 4, were the first to have a tangible influence on curriculum reform during that period. Also in the mid-1930s, H. Dewey Anderson and Walter Eells of Stanford University, after the first comprehensive study specifically undertaken by university researchers to examine Alaskan Native education, concluded that the subject-centered, formal curriculum, extensively copied from the public schools in the United States, was an "inept patchwork of various American textbooks quite unsuited to the Eskimo environment."[21] They urged that the standard American curriculum be modified in favor of one that included features of the indigenous culture. Five years after Anderson and Eells published their conclusions, Charles Reed of Teachers College, Columbia University, concluded from his investigations that the Alaska curriculum in Native schools was "especially unsuited to the needs of Native children, who constitute a large majority of rural schools."[22]

In spite of these scientifically derived findings, the Territorial Department of Education issued a uniform, Alaska-wide curriculum in 1941, the same year that Reed published his findings. That curriculum, drawn exclusively from the dominant American culture, mandated a highly detailed, standard American course of study without reference to Alaska's unique multicultural circumstances. Without dissension it became the standard course of study in all schools, city and Native village alike, for the next 20 years.

It was 18 years after Reed reported his findings before the next major study on Native education took place. The University of Alaska scholar Charles K. Ray found that little had changed since Reed's time. The need for change had been interrupted by World War II and by the post-war immigration of settlers more disposed to conservative views in regard to schools than those of behavioral scientists. In his report, *A Program of Education for Alaska Natives,* Ray emphasized the need for new curricula based on materials appropriate to the cultural environment of the Native population.[23]

---

21. Anderson and Eells 1935.
22. Reed, Charles F., cited in Ray 1959.
23. Ibid.

Ray's work, and a political climate conducive to change made possible by statehood for Alaska in 1959, prompted several calls for curriculum reform. The federal Department of Interior and the Office of the Governor of Alaska jointly issued a report in 1962 in which it was recognized that provisions had to made for the special needs of the Native population.[24] This was followed in 1966 by a statement from the Bureau of Indian Affairs in which it was declared that Native education often failed, in part, because "the curriculum has frequently remained a result of current educational practices as found throughout the public schools system throughout the United States."[25]

Independent of government initiatives such as these, Native organizations were making their interest in the curriculum known. This was to have two effects. It brought the politicians of the day into the process of curriculum reform and it introduced the common-sense approach of traditional Native learning style into the schools. Up until this time, regardless of the good intentions and at times genuine understanding of the need for reform on the part of a few education officials, programs in the schools changed little. But by the late 1960s that situation started to change. Native leaders acting through their state-wide associations and Native members of the legislature were increasingly asserting their right to have a voice in school affairs in more forceful and articulate ways. For example, in 1968 the *Christian Science Monitor* reported the following:

> During a recent Bureau of Indian Affairs conference, an Alaska Native rose and spoke: I've been reading Kierkegaard. (You could hear a pin drop.) He says there are three basic fears that confront man – marriage, God, and death. I want to add a fourth fear – change. To BIA personnel, no word could strike more deeply.[26]

The change most often called for by Native leaders centered on the need for new curricula, curricula that would be derived from

24. US Department of Interior 1962.
25. Tiffany 1966.
26. Hendrick 1968, p. 1.

Native control of educational policy. Two important conclusions may be drawn from a review of the historical roots of Native discontent that motivated Native assertiveness in Alaska. In a study done at the University of Alaska Fairbanks, Darnell, Hecht, and Orvik reported that, first, the prevailing attitudes of policy makers over the years had vacillated between the promotion of programs leading to the assimilation of the Native population into the dominant society and the promotion of programs leading to the retention of Native cultural heritage. Such ambivalence had promoted confusion in the mind of the education consumer as to the goals of education and has contributed to the erosion of his self-confidence in making his wishes known. Second, that from the very beginning members of the dominant Western society had developed education programs in Alaska under the premise that they knew what was best for Native education without affording Native people a major share in the decision making. Programs have been developed for, rather than with, Native people.[27]

The Alaska State Commissioner of Education in a letter to the US Office of Education in support of federal financial assistance, sensing the tone of Native pressure, opined that "it is a well accepted fact that it is not the [Native] student who has failed in the school setting, but the fact that the program provided has been inadequate."[28] Two years later the Alaska Governor's Commission on Cross-cultural Education documented the need for curriculum reform in their report, *Time for Change in the Education of Alaska Natives.*[29] Even the President of the United States, Lyndon Johnson, in 1968, called for the creation of a model school community for Native Americans, a school community that would "have the finest teachers familiar with Indian history, culture and language ... [and] feature an enriched curriculum."[30] Following President Johnson's lead, the United States Senate passed a resolution calling for "long term general, vocational, technical and professional education [for Indians and

27. Darnell et al. 1974, p. 7.
28. Alaska 1968.
29. Ray et al. 1971.
30. US Congress 1968.

Alaska Natives] ... so that they may share fully in our society." In 1970, not to be outdone by Congress, the Alaska legislature called upon the state Department of Education "to intensify its programs to develop culturally relevant programs for the Native pupils in the state, to encourage the teaching of Native studies to all pupils regardless of cultural or ethnic background, and to encourage these programs throughout ... the state."[31]

Attention at the highest levels of government added a note of credibility to the statements being made by Native leaders and groups. Since those calls for attention to the specialized needs of the Native population there have been innumerable curriculum improvement initiatives; many innovative projects and instructional materials have addressed Native interests. However, it is not surprising that they comprise a mixed bag of successes and failures. Because there are several Native cultures and a small population in some ethnic groups, many programs have been short lived for want of funds or creative ideas. Others were initiated only in response to political pressure and were not worthy of a sustained life. Those with substance that have made a positive difference have usually been developed locally in rural school districts with school board members, administrators, and teachers especially sensitive to village culture and the practical problems of cross-cultural schooling. In these cases improved curricula reflect a sense, or feeling, for culture in the context of village life while taking into account the needs of people growing up in a rapidly changing social and economic structure.

Canada

Curriculum development in the early years of formal schooling in Canada is representative of early curriculum development in much of the rest of the Far North. Norman Macpherson, in his history of education in the Northwest Territories, pointed out that,

---

31. Alaska 1969.

> from the day the first federal teacher rang the first school bell at Tuktoyaktuk in 1947, teachers and administrators both realized the Northern schools in this unique Northern environment demanded a uniquely Northern curriculum, and also that the ideal Northern education would begin with instruction in the student's native tongue. A NANA [Native and Northern Affairs] directive from 1952, 'Education in the Eskimo Territory' suggests that: "careful study based on the experiences of those in the field concerning the needs of the Eskimo will be necessary in arriving at a sound form of curriculum.... Every effort should be put forth to have the Eskimos retain their native abilities."[32]

Positions such as this in the early days of formal education in the Canadian Far North, and a keen sense of awareness by some teachers in the field notwithstanding, recommendations calling for a Native-centered curriculum had little impact in the field and had no influence in central offices in Ottawa whatsoever. Instead, the official curriculum of the province of Alberta, closest to the particular region of the Northwest Territories, was adopted for the schools of the Northwest Territories. In defense of central government personnel of that time, since alternatives to the standard curriculum simply did not exist there were no other options. As pointed out by Gordon Robertson, Commissioner of the Northwest Territories, 1953–63,

> it is true that the curriculum was not closely connected to native cultures or native circumstances, but again there was no alternative. The whole staff in the education division and in the schools had to be established by using people qualified for the tasks. They had to learn about northern circumstances and only after that would it be possible to devise a curriculum related to the north and the native peoples.[33]

Nor were the parents of the children at that period of history in a position to offer alternatives to the curriculum of standard Western schooling. This is not because they lacked knowledge that would have been of value in the curriculum, but because they lacked an understanding of the nature of Western schooling that they suddenly were obliged to accept. The concept of Western

32. Macpherson 1991, p. 287.
33. Ibid.

schooling could not have been more foreign or formidable to them. Furthermore, they had yet to learn the nuances of Western culture and, therefore, how to assert themselves in Western society. Native assertiveness and involvement in devising a curriculum for Northern schools was 30 years in the future. Moreover, except for a few social scientists, notably anthropologists, the North had not yet been discovered by the research community. Thus, although there was recognition on the part of some of those closest to the problems of everyday school life that Native knowledge, interests, and abilities were valuable and should be integrated into the curriculum, what happened was that

> Dick and Jane was to be the text. "The problem of developing the curriculum for Eskimo schools is probably the most complex in the whole field of Canadian education," the Chief of Education for the Northern Affairs told the first NWTTA [Northwest Territories Teachers Conference] in 1953. Meanwhile, teachers in the region were using the Alberta curriculum, and students were learning to read with 'Dick and Jane'.... In the early years of northern education there was little choice.[34]

However, by the late 1960s, at the time the government of the Northwest Territories in Yellowknife overtook responsibility for education from the Department of Northern Affairs in Ottawa, a Curriculum Services Division was established in the department. In recognition of the inadequacy of existing programs, a policy that called for the development of a curriculum that more closely related to the needs of Native children was adopted. An internal departmental study was undertaken to review the curriculum and policies then in place to ascertain what changes were necessary to keep the department's program abreast of the needs of the territory and to improve efficiency.

The initial plan for a "Northernized" curriculum was to involve central staff personnel in extensive field travel and consultation at school sites. At first, little thought had been given to Native involvement in the project, but that changed as the project became one of the most controversial in the history of Northwest

---

34. Ibid.

Territories education. After extensive input from the field, including Native involvement, the Chief of Curriculum Services, Dr. Paul Robinson, and project personnel developed three principles that became the basic rationale for their recommendations:

1. The child should be taught in his own language during the early years at school, and Native languages should be a part of the curriculum throughout the school year.
2. Schools should reflect the culture of their communities both in curriculum and learning materials.
3. A parent should have a dominant voice in determining the education of his child.

These concepts were so radical and futuristic that they even came to the attention of the National Council of Teachers of English (USA). In summarizing their analysis of the curriculum guides developed around these principles, it was noted that the program was expected to 1) develop from the child's characteristics; 2) teach English, when it is not the mother tongue, as a second language; 3) reflect the pluralistic cultures of the region on an equal basis; 4) allow students to choose freely their life patterns; 5) regard basic English as superfluous; 6) allow students to progress at their own rate through the curriculum; 7) not use standardized tests; 8) use heterogeneous grouping; 9) emphasize learning in general more than specific subjects; 10) recognize that communication is the heart of the curriculum; and 11) keep accurate records of students' progress.[35]

As practical as they now seem, the curriculum guides that grew out of Robinson's work were considered revolutionary and soon became highly controversial. In a letter to the professional staff, the Director of Education, B.C. Gillie, declared that "it may well be that a minority of personnel will not feel comfortable working within a system having these expectations. If this assumption proves correct for you, then the time is ripe to make your

---

35. *Reading and Communication Skills*, National Council of Teachers of English, Urbana, Ill. Cited in Macpherson 1991, p. 290.

plans regarding the next school year."[36] The teaching topics and methods suggested in the guides were well received by many teachers, reluctantly accepted by some and outwardly rejected by others. A number of more traditional teachers, unable to compromise their belief in the standard Alberta curriculum then in use, and sensing the turmoil that was to follow, did just as the director suggested: they left the North the following June.

The *Calgary Herald,* on November 11, 1972, opened its story on the subject with the following statement:

> A radical new curriculum introduced into Northwest Territories schools last year has triggered a flurry of international interest and excitement among educators.... Paul Robinson led seven assistants a year ago in developing a curriculum for Northwest Territories classrooms that has as an ultimate goal the junking of many traditional concepts of education developed in southern Canada.... Mr. Robinson threw out most of the reading texts prepared in the south for white pupils. In their place he created a hand-made reading program drawing extensively on the cultural and historic background of the North.[37]

In glowing terms, the paper went on to report accolades from a broad cross-section of educators in Canada and the United States. Requests for samples of the materials developed for the new curriculum came from many corners of the world. But criticism soon followed. The unusually heavy faultfinding of the program by conservative forces, popular acclaim notwithstanding, and the controversial personality of the curriculum chief, coupled with his frequent deprecatory remarks concerning his detractors, brought an untimely end to his service to the Northwest Territories. He resigned under pressure in 1974. Nevertheless, the curriculum debate generated by Robinson's work was not to be resolved for years. It was not until the emergence of influential Native voices in the early 1980s that brought the debate full circle with a call for the same kinds of reforms that had been advocated in the *Survey of Education* initiated in 1969.

It is ironic that the features of the Robinson curriculum, open-

36. Ibid., p. 290.
37. Ibid., p. 291.

endedness and flexibility, are the ones that education reform advocates most often urge today, yet were, in some measure, the reasons why Robinson was compelled to resign after four years in the office. Departmental documents from the time reveal that, as Chief of the Curriculum Service, Mr. Robinson was "original and dedicated to improved education for the Native population, his ultimate goal." In official circles he was praised for "a sound and progressive philosophy of education and introduced many valuable ideas and innovative practices." Conversely, in those same circles, he was reviled, castigated and denounced for being intransigent and contemptuous toward all who opposed him.[38] But in retrospect, personality problems aside, his ideas were 20 years before their time. Many of the principles he espoused for curriculum development were to become those advocated by Native reformers in the 1980s.

The awakening of Native activists in the 1960s and 1970s came to fruition in the decade of 1980s. Curriculum reforms made possible through acquisition of policy-making authority during this period were extraordinary. The resolution in the Legislative Assembly of the Northwest Territories authored by Tagak Curley, an Inuit member of the Northwest Territories Legislative Assembly, that called for a Special Committee on Education, and the Education Act of 1983 that followed the committee's work, were the critical events that gave momentum to the movement.

The first Inuit-controlled education system to come into existence in the Northwest Territories as a consequence of this act came under the jurisdiction of the Baffin Divisional Board of Education in 1985. Located in the Eastern Canadian Arctic, it is illustrative of the vastness that characterizes so much of the Canadian Arctic. The jurisdiction of this board extends a distance of 4,800 km (3,000 miles) from Grise Fjord on Ellesmere Island to Sanikiluaq on the southern shores of Hudson Bay. Extension of the perennial debate about the content of the curriculum, especially as it focuses on the balance between cultural continuity and

---

38. Ibid.

cultural replacement, has become more intense as an outgrowth of this board's existence. Although arguments in favor of one position or the other may not differ more than in the past, for the first time the arguments are being debated by the people themselves. Their goals have been described by the superintendent of the district in this way:

> The Board's mission, then, is to ensure our own cultural survival and to ensure that the children in our schools today are prepared to take on the responsibilities of our society in the future; responsibilities which at present are undertaken by others but which Inuit are rapidly assuming. In realizing that mission, we are confident that we can make the right decisions and for the first time we have the opportunity to do so. We had been told so many times in the past that others had to make those decisions for us. You will, therefore, excuse us if we make a few mistakes along the way.[39]

With the board's jurisdiction spread over such a huge area it might be thought that the district can not be called a unit of local control. However, the make-up of the board gives local control. Each community in the region elects a Community Education Council and the chairperson of each council is also, automatically, a member of the divisional board and represents his/her community. The divisional board concept, therefore, effectively gives both local and larger regional control.[40] Since membership of the board is largely Inuit in composition, it is also a good example of Native control. And herein lies a problem in governance as well as in curriculum development. The board, in its eagerness to remake the schools, has identified a set of goals that are ambitious in the extreme. Among them are the following:

> We expect children to develop the skills in reading, writing, mathematics and in other areas which they need in order to continue further training or in order to take advantage of the opportunities in our society.
>
> We expect that children will discover their natural, human and social worlds – that they will have knowledge of the land, the sea, the community, and knowledge of our social customs.

39. Colbourne, Eric, "Introduction to the Baffin Divisional Board." In Farrow and Wilman (eds.) 1989, p. 69.
40. Wilman, David, personal communication, 1995.

> We expect that children will develop a thorough knowledge of their language and culture – that they will come to understand the past and present realities of our society.
>
> We expect that our children, while retaining their own language and other skills to enable them to function effectively in Canadian society.[41]

Developing a strong Inuit identity, developing competency in Inuktitut, preparing students to function in the English language, developing basic academic skills, promoting a strong personal value system, and preparing students for college or university level training, all declared objectives of the board, speak to the hope of overcoming the shortcomings of schooling in the past. However, of concern, they illustrate the inherent danger of overloading the curriculum with such ambitious designs. This is a danger seen in all countries in the Far North as Native control becomes the norm. How best to find a balance between what is realistically achievable and formidable expectations has become an important consideration in the development of the emerging curricula.

The Dene-based curriculum in all schools located among the five Dene Indian tribes in the western Northwest Territories is an example of recent efforts to include Native knowledge in the schools with an expanded curriculum imposed by the necessity of adjusting to a multicultural society. Based on a curriculum derived from a Dene world view and way of learning it incorporates what it means to be Dene into daily activities and lessons. Dene Kede, the formal name for the curriculum, "integrally involves the community and the administrators, not just the teachers. [Based on involvement of elders and other community members,] it defines the relationship of academic subjects to the Dene perspective rather than sprinkling Dene culture into academic subjects."[42] Since Dene Kede is a community-based curriculum, the limit to which it is used is determined by the community and the teachers; thus its content will depend on the characteristics of each school's local needs.

---

41. Colbourne, op. cit., p. 73.
42. Education and Resources Group 1994.

Reporting on the development of curricula for the schools of the Northwest Territories at length is not to single out the Canadian experience as exceptional. Rather, it reveals a history of gradual curriculum development that is characteristic of similar progress in all of the Circumpolar countries. Although particulars in each country have been different, the sequence of events is typical. The most significant phenomenon throughout this process has been the emergence of Native influence in the development of unique programs that depart from the status quo.

Scandinavia

Curriculum development in Scandinavia was tied to the Church until recent times; thus it was inclined toward cultural replacement derived from a conservative philosophy that denied Native cultural values. At the time the development of curricula for schools in the Scandinavian Far North was begun, the indigenous cultures and languages were seldom included as fundamental parts of the content of education. When they were made a peripheral part of the curriculum it usually was to provide a means to remedy local instructional problems or as token recognition of the nature of the society the school served.

In Norway, for example, during the first half of the 20th century, local school boards developed curricula in accordance with standard rules prescribed by the central government. This procedure changed when a new national law defining the content of compulsory primary schooling was promulgated in 1936, and further refined in 1939 when a standard national curriculum was issued by the Parliament. The right of Saami children to be taught in their mother tongue was included in the law of 1936, but not a single paragraph specifying the right of Saami children to a culture-specific education was mentioned in the plan of 1939.

This deficiency was corrected in the standard curriculum issued in 1972 when a section concerning the education of the Saami was included in the law that drew attention to their specialized needs. The most significant developments along these lines, however, did not occur until 1987, at which time the

Norwegian Parliament delivered a comprehensive plan for Saami education. It had taken a prolonged effort to reach this level of recognition. Persons prominent in the early movement for recognition were Anders Larsen, Isak Saba, Per Fokstad, and in more recent times, Edel Haetta Eriksen. Important national committees appointed by the Parliament, such as Den parlamentariske skolekommisjonen av 1922, Samordningsnemda for skoleverket av 1947, and Komiteen til å utrede samesporsmål av 1956, were instrumental in the movement. The most significant event to influence curriculum development in recent times was the founding of the Saami Education Council in Guovdageaidnu in 1976. Recognized as the turning point in curriculum development, the work of this council was instrumental in establishing a Saami-specific cultural foundation for schooling. From that time on, development of the curriculum for Saami schools has been under the direct influence of the Saami.[43]

In Sweden and Finland the curriculum evolved along lines similar to those in Norway, although the circumstance were somewhat different. In the early part of the 18th century (1723), a decree by the king reinforced a policy that supported the tradition that the Saami language should be central to the language of instruction and the curriculum. The Church strengthened this position in 1735 with its own regulation, promulgated to assure that Saami educational needs would be addressed at the regional level. However, in a letter from the king in 1818 it can be seen that a tendency to emphasize the standard Swedish curriculum in the schools for the Saami was the prevailing policy. This trend was reversed in the school reform act of 1846 in which a curriculum with a greater amount of Saami culture was reintroduced.

At the turn of the 20th century, through the work of Bishop Olof Bergqvist, the Church undertook the task of examining and improving the curriculum of Saami schools. Bergqvist suggested the whole school system be based on the Saami culture. Although the curriculum he suggested was specifically designed for the Saami, it was strongly opposed by them. In 1918, at a meeting of

43. Hoëm 1989b, pp. 159–66.

Saami leaders, including Torkel Thomasson and Gustav Park, schools for the Saami were characterized as inferior to the Swedish system and it was recommended that the curriculum be replaced. Despite resistance among the Saami to the special cultural provisions in the curriculum on the grounds that they were inadequate and inexact, they endured until 1957. At that time the Swedish system of traveling schools, Nomadskolutredningen, with a revised, non-Saami-oriented curriculum, was initiated. From 1957 until 1971 the curriculum of the Nomadskola was the same as in all other schools in Sweden. A shift in emphasis came again in 1971 when the report of a special committee on Saami affairs in general, the Sameutredning, was issued. As a consequence of this report, Saami language and culture in the curriculum were strengthened.[44]

Although there were shifts in policy that reflected the ongoing debate between cultural retention in the schools versus cultural assimilation as in all other countries of the Far North, the Swedish experience stands out because of its Saami-Nomad schools. By use of traveling schools, a particular form of Saami traditional life style was recognized as a having value in the education system and served to preserve customs that otherwise might have been lost.

The Scandinavian experience is illustrative of a perennial, basic problem in curriculum policy similar to the Baffin Education Board's very ambitious expectations described above: the large number of subjects in the curriculum. A need to have school programs based on the national culture and language, on the one hand, and elements of the culture of the ethnic minority, on the other, can result in inadequate coverage in both subject areas. In Norway the most frequent ways to avoid this problem have been to ignore the minority culture entirely or, conversely, to develop a curriculum based exclusively on it. For example, attempts to provide classes consisting of pupils with different degrees of connectedness to Norwegian and Saami culture have been made. Other efforts have been to differentiate between pupils who are truly bilingual in Saami and Norwegian, and monolingual pupils.

44. Henrysson 1993.

Likewise, the necessary extent of language capability and professional knowledge of Norwegian and Saami teachers is now being discussed. And yet another way has been to develop textbooks in two languages. These efforts notwithstanding, so far school authorities, teachers, and the Saami in general have been frustrated in their attempts to find a way to combine the two options in a balanced way.

These arrangements draw attention to the different methods of instruction for different subjects and grade levels as well as cultural and language differences of the pupils, further complicating the problem of deciding on curriculum content. Closely related to this problem is the contentious question of the pedagogical meaning of the concepts of "mother tongue" and "first language" instruction. The answer to this question has a direct bearing on how courses will be developed, including their content, scope, and sequence, as well as deciding what kinds of backgrounds teachers should have. In short there are implications for every aspect of education in the answer.

Equally important to achieving an understanding of the issues in curriculum development is an answer to the most basic question of all, a question that is asked in Scandinavia and all other Polar countries as well: What is Saami (or indigenous) knowledge? From an insider's perspective, it can be asserted that the knowledge Saami people currently use and continue to master is traditional Saami wisdom and understanding. Conversely it can be argued with equal conviction that little of the body of knowledge that the Saami now use and are dependent on in contemporary society is related to earlier traditional Saami learning and understanding. A case can be made for both positions, but depending on the direction school curricula and programs are to take the outcome of the debate will be dramatically different. Today that debate is, in principle, the same as that which has taken place throughout the centuries. However, a development in contemporary times represents a major departure from the past: the Saami people themselves are driving the debate and giving it more expression than ever before, as are most indigenous groups discussed in this text.

Greenland

Greenland has inherited both its political and educational systems from Denmark as well as having come under the influence of other Scandinavian countries. As a consequence, Greenland faces the same challenges as do the Saami and both are now developing their own political and educational future.

When Hans Egede landed in Greenland in 1721, he brought with him not only the desire to Christianize the population but also the instrument for doing so: the Danish system for managing political and religious matters. From the earliest times, therefore, missionary activities took place in trading centers and the homes of Greenlanders, as well as in church. The language of communication was a combination of Greenlandic and Danish. The content of the curriculum was almost exclusively the teaching of Christianity; the method of teaching was rote learning.

It is important to note, therefore, that from the very beginning of the missionary period, unlike in Alaska and Canada, both the Greenlandic language and culture played a central role in these activities. Thus a tradition in the methods of education among Greenlanders was Native oriented, but the goal of this approach, as in all the Far North, was to bring about a religious and cultural shift among the people.[45]

As early as between 1752 and 1760, the missionary Bruun, working in Nuuk, gave lessons in Danish. The missionary Glahn, who was assigned to Greenland from 1763 to 1769, introduced the system of peer teaching where the most able students instructed the others. But no official positions on education were taken in Denmark until 1835 when a commission was appointed to give a broad overview of Danish–Greenlandic politics. Among those things covered was the content of the curriculum then in use. It was recommended that the subjects of reading, writing, mathematics and even health care be introduced. The commission also considered the degree to which instruction should be secularized compared with the extent to which the cultural con-

45. Berliner 1971, pp. 170–76.

text in which the children lived should be the schools' point of departure. The potential worth of textbooks in Greenlandic was discussed as well as the possibility of giving classes in the Danish language. Suggestions made by the commission were accepted by the king in 1844. The trend set by the commission established the character of the schools for the rest of the 19th century and made Danish officials more sensitive to the culture of Greenland.

The first law that was specifically drawn for Greenland was passed by the Danish Parliament in 1905. It was concerned primarily with the Church and the educational system. Specifically, it provided that classes should be given in religion, Greenlandic, arithmetic, writing, and a moderate amount of geography and history. Later on music and gymnastics were introduced. The most significant development brought about by the law was the introduction of Danish as a standard subject in the curriculum. Although the law was definite about the subjects that were to be covered, in reality there were many differences in the curriculum among the schools. This was due to the extensive diversity of the qualifications and interests of the teachers, and the gap in quality and content between the schools in the larger population centers and schools in remote places of the country.[46]

Danish attention to Greenland had grown by 1920, the year in which a special commission was established to recommend a comprehensive position on Greenlandic society. The commission, with membership from both Greenland and Denmark, set forth its recommendations which were put into law by an act of the Danish Parliament in 1925. Included in the act were provisions that established a modern school system by Danish standards, including compulsory school attendance for pupils between the ages of 7 and 14 and obligatory study of the Danish language as a subject. Following this trend, a few years later, it was mandated that Danish be the language of instruction. Also during this period formal Danish school examinations (the standard exams taken by all Danes) were made mandatory. Strengthening of school laws notwithstanding, diversity in quality and subjects

46. Larsen 1976, pp. 36–39.

offered among the various schools and communities continued to be a problem, due mostly to differences in teacher competency.

The advent of home rule for Greenland in 1979 created the opportunity for changes in the curriculum once again, but this time it was in the hands of Greenlanders. Greenlanders had acquired the responsibility and opportunity to develop a modern educational system with a curriculum that was intended to modernize Greenland along lines determined by Greenlanders themselves. The reaction against excessive Danish presence in the curriculum that acquired momentum in 1979, and the means to foster a distinctly Greenlandic persona in the schools, continue today. As elsewhere in the North, that quest has its problems, but in Greenland they take on a dimension unlike other regions of the North.

Curriculum issues summarized

Looking back at the development of curricula in each country, it can be concluded that contemporary problems growing out of the need for improved curricula are much the same throughout the Far North. Mary Simon, former president of the Inuit Circumpolar Conference, summed up the basic issue when she declared,

> It is important that northern education systems be able to adapt to changing circumstances in circumpolar regions. Within such a framework, students should be taught the attitudes, skills and knowledge necessary to achieve success both in subsistence and wage economies.[47]

Simon's contention reflects a recurring theme in many of our observations – the need for flexibility in the ways schools are constituted, but also the problem of overloading the curriculum. But certainly flexibility is the key to the goal put forward by Simon. This suggests that there are essential, universal aspects of any curriculum that need to be included in the school program. It also means, however, that when programs of instruction are decided the curriculum needs to reflect the cultural, economic and geo-

47. Simon 1989, p. 46.

graphic circumstances of the society in which the school functions.

It is generally accepted in Native communities that students need to be taught in a way that will enable them to succeed in two worlds, Western society in general and the traditional Native society into which they are born. Or if the latter is not possible because the Native society is no longer viable, respect for what that society once was becomes an equally important part of the curriculum. Unfortunately, programs of education drawn from Western schooling, although adjusted to accommodate this need in a few places in the past few years, essentially continue only to favor skill development related to wage economies and Western life styles.

Karla Williamson, a Native Greenlander and Canadian scholar, explains the consequences and potential of the Western curriculum (and thereby speaks to the essence of the main issue in curriculum development in each of the countries we cover) as follows:

> It is interesting to note that school often is seen as a learning institution which, for some reason or another, is lagging behind the progress of industrial society. However, in the Arctic the school has been too futuristic. Futuristic in unrealistic ways when utilizing curricula which have all been geared towards preparation for life in industrialized society. So far the industrial way of life has not been realized by any means and so many of the graduates of the school system are left in limbo. Such a factor has caused a conflict of values and understandings between generations.... [However], the school system, having been blamed for its failure to adapt to the needs of Inuit, has nevertheless been seen as a system needed to help Inuit in the unavoidable process of changing their society....
>
> It is true that Inuit do not wish to return to their traditional patterns of life. On the contrary, they do wish to be seen as a valid culture, participating and contributing to the contemporary way of life in their particular countries.... So, seeing the great potential which the school system can offer in overcoming the loss of pride and self-sufficiency, Inuit push for education. Inuit, like other peoples in developing countries and the fourth world, are willing to learn the other culture of the school because they feel this could be achieved without the loss of human resources and talents they possess as the heritage of their culture.[48]

---

48. Williamson, Karla Jessen, "Cultural Discontinuity among Inuit as Exhibited in Their Concepts of Human Existence and Having Children." In Farrow and Wilman (eds.) 1989, pp. 165–67.

Achieving this end will require an open-ended process in curriculum development. As times change, needs of students will change. More specifically, the most pressing issue today, posed as a question, is this: Can education systems create the means for acquisition of improved economic and social opportunities by northern Natives without destroying their rights to retain their preferred cultural characteristics? All curricula designed in and for the Far North need to be developed with this question in mind. This will require taking into account the obligations it implies while being aware of the risk of being ineffective because of overly ambitious attempts to do too much at once.

Language of instruction

> Languages bear within them the biases of their originators – their attitudes and values. So that if young people grow up speaking and learning in the language of their ancestors, then certain central components of their cultural heritage are absorbed by them automatically. If, on the other hand, a language emanating from some other culture becomes the primary language of young people, then their most important link with their own cultural past is broken, their cultural identity begins to weaken, and ultimately, perhaps, the attitudes and values cherished for many generations by their people are supplanted by those of the alien culture by which the language was imposed.[49]

Of all human traits, none is more human than language. Moreover, among indigenous minorities the proper use of Native languages in school is the most emotional issue in education. It is also the most political.

At the time formal schooling was introduced in each of the Circumpolar countries, there were no standardized orthographies for Native languages (with the exception of the very successful development of syllabics in the Canadian Far North) and few speakers of Western languages among the indigenous populations. This was but a small problem for the first teachers since the aim in most schools was to eradicate Native language and cultur-

49. Vaudrin, Bill, cited in Barnhardt (ed.) 1977, p. 135.

al identity. Exceptions to this policy can be found in each country, as noted below, but extinction of Native languages was the intent more often than not. To accomplish this, at times excessive measures were used, including punishment of students when a Native language was spoken at school. In Alaska the official position by which Native languages were to be eliminated was stated by high government officials in their instructions to missions schools under contract to provide education to the Native population in 1888:

> The Board of Home Missions has informed us that government contracts for educating Indian pupils provide for the ordinary branches of English education to be taught, and no books in any Indian language shall be used or instruction given in that language to Indian pupils.... this rule will be strictly enforced in all government Indian [and Eskimo] schools. The Commissioner of Indian Affairs urges, and very forcibly too, that instruction in their vernacular is not only of no use to them but is detrimental to their speedy education and civilization.[50]

Cases of harsh punishment as a means to eradicate Native languages have been documented in all countries that we cover. Certainly, criticism of extreme measures to enforce language policies in the early years is valid, but it needs to be kept in mind that most teachers took their assignments because they were motivated to help develop the children, not destroy them. What they were doing was trying to improve what was a desperate situation, and doing their best according to what was right in their time. Of course, such practices are no longer tolerated, both because classroom management practices have changed and because they are now recognized as being morally wrong. Nevertheless, although extreme measures to repress Native languages are now prohibited, survival of many Native languages is in doubt, and retaining language competency by many individual Native residents is often a problem.

---

50. From an article in the newspaper *North Star*, published in Sitka, Alas., 1888. Cited in MacLean 1990.

Alaska

Among the peoples of the Far North there are many languages, some with several dialects. However, compared with the number of individual Native speakers at the time of contact with Western society (when 100 percent of all of an indigenous group would have spoken its language), the percentage of Natives who speak the language of their culture is now dramatically reduced. Furthermore, the percentage continues to decline. According to the eminent Alaskan linguist Michael Krauss, it is expected that in Alaska all 15 Indian languages, the Aleut language, and both Eskimo languages will be extinct by the middle of the 21st century. The only possible exceptions will be Central Eskimo Yup'ik and Siberian Eskimo Yup'ik dialects.[51]

Among the four broad classifications of Alaska Natives, there are 20 language groups. Five are found in the Eskimo–Aleut family where there are two branches; Aleutian Aleut is one and Eskimo the other. One language, Aleut, is found in the Aleutian Aleut branch and four languages are found in the Eskimo family. The Eskimo component of the Eskimo–Aleut group primarily is located on the north, west, and southwest coasts and adjoining coastal plains and St. Lawrence Island. The Aleut portion is found on the Aleutian Chain. Within the Indian population there are three language families: Tsimshian, Haida, and Athapaskan–Eyak–Tlingit, collectively containing 15 distinct languages. The Athapaskan groups occupy the interior of Alaska, extending on into Canada and a portion of coastal South-Central Alaska, mostly along Cook Inlet. Tlingit, Haida, and Tsimshian language speakers are located in Southeast Alaska.[52]

Although education for the Native population during the Russian period is not noted for humanitarian motives, the work of the Russian priest Veniaminov stands out as both innovative and benevolent. His use of bilingual instructional materials marked the beginning of contemporary language programs. As a mission-

51. Krauss 1980.
52. Ibid.

ary, however, he was most interested in spreading the work of his church. To this end he developed the first orthographies of the Aleut and Tlingit languages. His translations of the books of the Bible into Aleut and Tlingit in the 1830s were instrumental in teaching the first Natives to learn to read while at the same time converting them to Christianity (see Textbook Example 1, pp. 198–99).

The precedence set by Veniaminov, however, was not long lived. By the time Alaska became a possession of the United States in 1867, the concept of extinguishing the cultures of Native North Americans was the convention of the day. Nonetheless, as pointed out in the chapter on the historical development of education in Alaska, there were periods when awareness of Native culture and the need to make it part of the curriculum surfaced. The most notable effort along these lines occurred during the 1930s when the director of the Bureau of Indian Affairs, John Collier, attempted to install practices that recognized the rightness of using Native languages in the schools, both for their pedagogical advantages and to foster a feeling of cultural self-worth among the students. But it was not until the late 1960s and the civil rights movement of that period that a concerted effort to instill respect for Native languages became widespread.

Alaska became the first state in the United States to recognize the worth of bilingualism in statute. The Alaska State Legislature, in 1972, enacted a law which provided that

> [any] school which is attended by at least 15 pupils whose primary language is other than English shall have at least one teacher who is fluent in the native language of the area where the school is located. Written and other educational materials, when language is a factor, shall be presented in the language native to the area.[53]

As progressive as the law is, it failed to prescribe the means to carry out its provisions. These were left to the state Department of Education, the University of Alaska, and local school districts. In many if not most cases, this oversight resulted in lack of resources,

53. Alaska 1972.

especially personnel familiar with Native languages and the money required to implement the mandate. As a consequence of this condition, the status of Native languages as a worthwhile subject of study remains low. Few school boards give much support to Native languages and there is lack of commitment and enthusiasm for Native languages as languages of instruction, or for their study.[54]

One positive note, however, was creation of the Alaska Native Language Center at the University of Alaska Fairbanks at the same time as the passage of the Bilingual Education Act. Since its creation, this unit has produced a wealth of orthographic material, instructional materials and specialists in Native languages. Today it stands as a leading institution among linguists everywhere.

In spite of the bilingual education law and current state regulations that require all school districts to provide bilingual programs for all students who are "limited English proficient," the number of Alaska Native students who speak their Native language has continued to decline. This is thought to be the result, at least in part, of low esteem of Native languages held by many school officials, even in the light of convincing evidence that student performance is enhanced when exposed to bilingual instruction in a well-planned and sequenced curriculum.

Canada

The linguistic distribution of the Native peoples of Canada is far-reaching. Use of the Eskimoan language of the Inuit, Inuktitut, extends all the way in the west from the northern edge of the eastern border of Alaska to Newfoundland. While there are regional differences in the language across such a vast distance, it is essentially one language from coast to coast. Canadian Indians, however, are represented by several groups. In the western Subarctic region, living close to and south of the tree line, there are 15 Athapaskan tribes spread out from the Alaska border to Hudson

54. MacLean 1990.

Bay speaking regional differences of Athapaskan. According to Krauss and Golla,

> attempts to classify the Athapaskan language into historically meaningful linguistic subgroups have not met with success. The effort has been hampered to some extent by the lack of good comparative data, but the principal difficulty arises from the fact that Athapaskan linguistic relationship, especially in the subarctic, cannot be adequately described in terms of discrete family-tree branches.[55]

However, of the 23 languages recognized as Athapaskan geographical subdivisions, 5 are found in Canada: Han and Kutchin, which are also found in the eastern interior of Alaska (Tuchone); Slavey-Hare; Dogrib; and Chipewyan.[56] There are others, but these are located too far south to be considered Subarctic in the way we have defined that term. A concise distinction between Canadian Athapaskan language groups continues to be a problem for linguists and is beyond the scope of this book. What is important to our subject is that the reality of Native language use in multicultural classrooms in this part of Canada is extremely complex. Except in a few cases where exemplary efforts have been made to develop orthographies and subsequent bilingual instructional materials, the problems of multiple languages are almost insurmountable.

In Canada, Inuktitut (the most common term for a variety of Inuit–Inupiaq dialects) is now taught and used in many of the schools with an Inuit population. It is well developed in written form and is transmitted electronically with ease. Inuit leaders promote the language as a means to maintain and enhance Inuit patrimony. Nevertheless, the relative number of Inuktitut speakers is declining. Linguists give it no more than 50 years before becoming extinct, except for possibly a few individuals who may deliberately keep it alive as a curiosity.[57] However, this may be an overly pessimistic forecast (Krauss believes that Inuktitut is one of

55. Krauss, Michael E., and Victor E. Golla, "Northern Athabaskan Languages." In Helm (ed.) 1981, p. 68.
56. Ibid.
57. Tschanz 1980.

the few aboriginal languages that can survive), especially in the Eastern Arctic where the creation of Nunavut as a new autonomous territory of Canada is expected to put a renewed emphasis on the importance of Native culture. Furthermore, in Alaska Native languages are more at risk because of a political distaste for bilingualism among a large conservative element of the non-Native population. Historically Canadians have had a more tolerant attitude toward diversity in language use.

Indian languages in the Canadian North may be even more at risk than Inuktitut, primarily because their numbers are greater, their speakers are less isolated, few people can write them with any degree of facility, and standard orthographies are only recently developed. Programs such as Dene Kede described in the section above on Native curricula in Canada may sustain some Indian languages for a longer time than without, but current trends do not bode well for their extended life.

Scandinavia

The origin of the Saami language is obscure, but it is related to Finnish and closer to it than are other Baltic languages. Proto-finnic and proto-samic, it is thought, separated between 1,000 B.C. and 500 B.C. Of the seven different Saami dialects found in Saamiland today, the dominant language is North Saami or Mountain Saami as it is often called. This is the form of the Saami language spoken by approximately 80 percent of the Saami population. It has four dialects. The remainder of Saami speakers are distributed among the South Saami with two dialects, the Lule Saami with three, the Inari Saami, the Skolt Saami with two dialects, the Kildin Saami and Turja Saami.[58]

Similar to predictions made for the future of Native languages in North America, survival of the Saami language is in doubt, but possibly not as much so as Native languages in North America. In Scandinavia the future of the Saami language depends on political and legal considerations as much as popular usage. It may be

58. Aikio 1991.

most at risk in Finland where there no longer is a legal ethnic Saami identity. There, ethnic status is tied to linguistic criteria. "A person is a Saami if he/she speaks or has spoken Saami as his first language or at least one of his/her parents or grandparents spoke it."[59] In Norway the same linguistic criteria apply, although, as specified in an act of Parliament in 1987, a Saami is also one who subjectively identifies himself as a Saami (in addition to being able to speak the Saami language). In this case there is the additional standard that a person simply sees himself or herself as a Saami or had parents or grandparents who spoke Saami. Swedish law is much the same as the Norwegian.

Historically in Scandinavia there have been several episodes, both favorable and unfavorable, in the use of the Saami language as the medium of instruction. Throughout Saamiland, the introduction of the Lutheran Protestant Church meant that Latin was replaced by the national languages of the majority populations as the language used in religious services. This meant that for the majority, the National mother tongue was given the predominant position. For the minority population, the Saami, this made little difference; a new unfamiliar language had taken the place of an earlier unfamiliar language.

However, during the mission period when the Church tried to "get in touch with the souls of individual Saami," it was the policy to try to use the Saami's mother tongue as a means of communication and transformation of Saami beliefs to that of the Church. So too was that the case when the Church established more comprehensive schooling among the Saami. The mother tongue and fragments of Saami culture were used as pedagogical tools (see Textbook Example 2, pp. 200–205). But those efforts were far from adequate due to the complexities of the language and the small number of people with the qualifications necessary to do this work.

Although the language of the Saami people has an extensive vocabulary and is very expressive, as school programs became

59. Kleivan, Inge, "Monolingualism, Bilingualism, or Multilingualism in the Arctic?" In Lyck (ed.) 1992, p. 271.

complex and comprehensive it was obvious that it had to become even more complex and inclusive to handle new concepts and technology. Moreover, the existence of several dialects compounded the problems of developing broad-based instructional programs in a similar fashion as elsewhere in the Far North.

The use of Native languages in Sweden is a good example of how these problems complicate attempts to develop a lasting and appropriate language policy. As early as 1619 the first two books in the Saami language had been published in Sweden. One was a handbook for use in the Church and one a basic reading primer. Since then there has been ongoing publication of schoolbooks in Saami. In the first instance, books in Saami were of poor quality. But by 1743 and 1744 an important conference on the standardization and development of a written Saami language was undertaken. The southern Saami dialect was adopted as the standard from which the written language was developed. This caused difficulties for the northern Saami, whose dialects differed from those in the south. For example, should the Saami in Finland, at the time part of Sweden, use the Finnish language and then the standardized Saami language from the south, or get by with no Saami written material?[60]

In Norway there has been a constant conflict between those who believed that the Saami should be educated in a humanistic way by using the Native language as the language of instruction and those who argued that Norwegian was the only realistic approach.[61] But in reality the only consideration officially given to use of the Saami language was based on the regulations pertaining to language of instruction issued by the Ministry of Education in 1870, 1880, and 1898. As a consequence, little consideration was given to the Saami language between 1870 and 1945. Following World War II, however, a remarkable shift took place, not only in support of the Saami language as a language of instruction, but in support of Saami culture as a valuable component of the school program. This is not to say that Saami in

60. Forsgren, in Henrysson 1993, pp. 31–52.
61. Hoëm 1976a.

the schools became institutionalized or endorsed by all. Nevertheless, a trend had set in, and in light of previous attitudes, that in itself was remarkable.

It was not until 1948 that the written Saami language in Sweden was standardized on the basis of the northern Saami dialect. This standard orthography was developed through a joint effort of linguists in Sweden and Norway. By 1979, use of the written northern dialect was widespread in the northern counties of Finland, Sweden, and Norway. Whereas there has been serious debate concerning the value of the use of Native languages elsewhere, in Sweden the value of the Saami language in school has seldom been doubted. Despite this near universal opinion there has always been a critical lack of priests, teachers, and civil servants qualified to use the Saami language in their work. Similarly, a general lack of textbooks in Saami persists as a problem.

To overcome these shortcomings and meet the needs of modern society, the Nordic Saami Council set up a committee to construct new words based on Saami linguistics in the 1960s. But because the difference in dialects continued to cause difficulties of uniformity, and the complexities of the language are not readily adaptable to contemporary technology, the work has gone slowly. Nor has the policy of promoting the Saami language been universally accepted by the Saami themselves. Where Saami is endangered or has become the second language, parents want school instruction to be carried out in Saami as a means to conserve it. Where Saami is still the first language, parents want instruction to be in the majority national language thereby enabling their children to compete economically and socially in the larger society. Adding to this dilemma, some parents have tried to sustain the language through the home, but because their knowledge of it often is inadequate, it becomes even more difficult for the school to correct errors.

Asta Balto, who did not learn to read and write her Native Saami until age 30 and who, at the time of writing the following was director of the Saami Education Council, has summarized the Saami language situation in Norway this way:

> From 1870's until the last World War, the authorities tried to "Norwegianize" the Sami people in a very harsh way, and the Sami language was absolutely forbidden at school. This hundred years of convincing the Sami people that their language and culture were worthless has been effective. Many of the Sami parents are still believing that being Sami, speaking the Sami language, is identical with defeat, poverty and contempt.
>
> Only slowly mistrust and misunderstanding seem to be disappearing. Therefore some Sami parents choose Norwegian as the first language for their [child's language of study at school], even if the child speaks Sami and does not understand Norwegian. On the other hand there are Sami people who have learned only the Norwegian language in their childhood and now feel that they have lost their identity both for themselves, and even for their descendants. Now they choose the Sami language as the first language for their child. The Norwegian school law allows the parents to do this.[62]

Greenland

Just as the Saami are seeking the best way to handle the Native language as an issue, so too are Greenlanders looking for the best way consistent with available resources. The importance of Greenlandic in schooling and society at large has fluctuated over the years depending on the political climate of the day and the level of importance give to language by education officials. The present practice of publishing official documents in both Greenlandic and Danish is indicative of the current high level of importance given the topic of language use.

The level of importance now given to Greenlandic notwithstanding, Ingmar Egede, in a paper written in 1976, has concisely described the problems of schooling in Greenland that, for many years, were a result of language differences between the majority culture of students, Greenlanders, and the majority culture of teachers, Danes. Several years have passed since the paper was written, but the conditions and dilemma described by Egede, although not as acute today, persist.

62. Balto 1990.

> If a brief description of the characteristics of the Eskimo/Greenlandic language is to be given, one will have to distinguish between the language used to describe the collective world and the language employed to describe the world of the individual hunter. The former is an implicit language, containing a rather small vocabulary and its function is to eliminate misunderstandings and to express wishes and feelings which are closely related to an actual situation. The language of the hunters' tales, on the other hand, is differently developed and varied; and its function is to introduce a world where even the smallest details are described to ensure that the listener fully understands the overall picture.
>
> The daily life of a few people with many common experiences resulted in the development of a language which built on the familiarity of the experiences. To a great extent, the language became retrospective and reliant on implications whose most distinguished functions are to serve as tools of ideas and planning. A prerequisite for this is knowledge about cause and effect in a world which can be influenced....
>
> [Consequently] for many [school] children the linguistic problem means that important aspects of their development become subjected to wide-spread neglect. The result is that throughout years at school, a lagging behind in skills and knowledge gradually is built up as a consequence of half understood and half learned knowledge, a difficulty which cannot be corrected later on.
>
> What perhaps is worse is that many children and young people interpret the Greenlandic language's position in the school as an indication that language and consequently also the way of life connected with it are inferior.... For many years there have been incalculable linguistic barriers between the pupils and majority of the teachers [although to a lesser extent today than when Egede's article was written]. Because of this one can only speculate on how diffuse many Greenlandic children's experiences are of themselves, of their parents, of their teachers, yes and of their environment.[63]

This problem notwithstanding, the language situation in Greenland is more favorable than in other Northern countries, in part because of the early development of a Greenlandic orthography and use of the language in the first missions schools, and partly because there is only one Native language. Furthermore, in recent times, Greenlandic (the term often used for the Inuit language of Greenland) has acquired legal status. Also, the population composition lends itself to a more favorable climate for Greenlandic

63. Egede 1976, pp. 4, 5, 11.

language development. Of the 55,533 residents of Greenland accounted for in 1991, 46,691 were born in Greenland and 8,842 were born elsewhere. These figures are fairly representative of the proportional mix of the Greenlandic-Danish population. Among these two groups, individuals born in Greenland speak Greenlandic, many of whom are bilingual. Of the others, essentially Danes, most speak only Danish.

Both Greenlandic and Danish are referred to as official languages in the act that established Greenland's home-rule status. Greenlandic is designated the first language, but Danish is a mandatory subject in the schools. And because of the large number of Danes in Greenland, many in the government, Danish prevails in many circles, especially among the more affluent and the social elite. However, both languages must be spoken in institutions that offer public services. Of equal importance is a recent act of the Greenland Parliament in which it became mandatory in 1994 for all non-Greenlandic-speaking children to be integrated into the Greenlandic-speaking classes of the *folkeskole* (the primary and lower secondary school).[64]

Even with these developments in mind it should be pointed out that the Danish way of life, the Danish language, and the Danish education system have a high status in Greenland. Realistically, but paradoxically to many Greenlandic traditionalists, the Danish language is considered the most important key to education, to better financial conditions, and to greater social possibilities. Such developments and perspectives may be indicators of the prospect for a limited life of indigenous languages in the North, even in Greenland, where the best chance for the survival of a Northern Native language is found.

Issues in language of instruction

The most enduring issue concerned with the language of instruction is the meaning of bilingual education as a pedagogical technique and its value. The issue is often debated as much from an

---

64. Kleivan, Inge, in Lyck (ed.) 1992, p. 274.

emotional angle as from scientific findings. One reason for this is the many ways that bilingual education has been defined. Furthermore, before the various aspects of bilingual education can be discussed properly and applied to school policy and programs, the bilingual status of the population must be considered.

A simple definition specifies that a person is considered to be bilingual when capable of using two or more languages interchangeably on a routine basis. The number of Northern Natives considered to be bilingual by this definition is constantly declining. Hence, bilingual education is apt to be doubted as a viable way to teach because the life expectancy of the minority language is in doubt. For example, in Alaska, Krauss classified Alaska villages according to their numbers of Native-language speakers in three ranks: fluent Native-language-only speakers, bilingual speakers, and fluent English-only speakers. He calls fluent Native-language speakers "Monolingual Native." In this case the Native language predominates in all age groups, including all or many children. "Bilingual" persons are those who reside where speakers of Native languages are located but where there is constant contact and communication with English speakers and where there are few or no Native-language speakers under 10 years of age. The third category, "Monolingual English," applies to places where Native languages are seldom, if ever, used and there are no Native speakers under the age of 30 years. In the 1970s there were 36 villages in the Monolingual-Native-only classification, 47 in the Bilingual group, and 109 in the English-only category. In the first category, 31 of the villages were Eskimo–Aleut and 5 were Athapascan. In the second, the Bilingual group, 40 were Eskimo–Aleut and 7 Athapascan. Among the Monolingual-English-only category, 54 were Eskimo–Aleut, 39 Athapascan, 1 Tsimshian, 2 Haida, and 13 Tlingit.[65]

Figures in these classifications, while different today than when first described in the 1970s (there are now more people in the third category, at the expense of the other two), emphasize by the sheer weight of their numbers the complexity of the language

65. Krauss 1980.

situation and thereby the difficulty encountered in developing and providing bilingual education. In short, they define the issue of feasibility.

Bilingual education has been described in different ways, often to fit a particular program or political point of view. For our purpose we prefer the simple definition that specifies that "bilingual education is instruction in two languages and the use of those two languages as mediums of instruction for any part or all of the school curriculum."[66] However, in a subject as complex as bilingual education, general definitions are inadequate. James Orvik has pointed out that

> the central limitation of all widely used definitions of bilingual education lies in their not properly accounting for cases where the children possess the residual effects of an indigenous language but are not able to speak it.[67]

This situation is the norm more than the exception throughout the North, village English described below being one example. It means that when programs in bilingual education are being considered, the bilingual condition of the student, the community, and the school must be considered. Because of the nature of the bilingual environment in which many Native children grow up, early language development is problematic. As Marjut Aikio, linguist who studied language shift in Saami villages, has pointed out,

> the deciding factor is whether a child's bilingualism takes an additive or a subtractive turn. Additive bilingualism means that the speaker acquires a new language, while the former stays vital.[68]

In most cases where the indigenous language increasingly is accorded a lower status because of heightened contact with the Western world, bilingualism tends to be subtractive. According to Aikio, the students' first language,

---

66. US Office of Education 1967, p. 1.
67. Orvik, James M., "Definitions of Bilingual Education in Alaska." In Barnhardt (ed.) 1977, p. 145.
68. Aikio 1991.

> which has a lower status, declines as they become proficient in the second language.... Balanced bilingualism [on the other hand] is not only additive but also parallel by nature, which means that the semantic systems of the two languages are kept apart.[69]

This condition illustrates the interrelations and complexity of this topic. Even with recent advances in the development of new instructional materials in Norway, for example, there is an ongoing debate concerning fluctuating standards for written Saami and their consequences for learning the Saami language. Moreover, there is controversy as to the best way to teach the language to pupils with diverse aptitudes for language. These discussions lead to arguments as to the kind of professional knowledge teachers should be able to demonstrate and to the ways in which classrooms can be organized and constituted at different ability levels. The whole body of pedagogical knowledge related to language instruction is currently being questioned in search of more suitable methods of instruction. The most recent and successful efforts to advance the use of Saami as the language of instruction can be seen in the work of the Saami Education Council and the Saami Cultural College, both located at Guovdageaidnu.

A growing controversy stems from what some teachers believe is the need to recognize the difference between the use of a language as a tool of communication and the study of a language as an academic exercise. As a tool of communication it is important how one performs in the use of a language, that is, how well one can be understood by others. As a student of a language it is important to conform to the standards and canons of the language as established by authorities on the language. The two requirements, performance and conformance are not necessarily the same, especially in Native village schools. Where the Native language and the national language have intermingled to form a compound language with characteristics of each, communication can still be adequate, indeed, at times, highly descriptive. However, when conformity is demanded in the classroom but only performance is required, conflict between teacher and pupil is likely.

---

69. Ibid.

One example of a performance language (or possibly a dialect in the making), "village English" incorporates several linguistic aspects of a Native language into what was English. Although this situation is not well understood and there is disagreement as to the extent it is a problem, it has become an issue. Students using village English may be either monolingual or bilingual English speakers, but their manner of speaking retains some of the grammatical structure and intonation of their Native language. When teachers fail to accept this form, or "corruption" of English, as a valid form of communication and insist on "proper" or classroom English, a practical form of communication is denied. As a consequence students may be made to feel inferior and, failing to see the cause of their frustration, reject schooling in general. The complexity of this type of situation has been pointed out by Ron Mackay and Lawrence Myles, who reported on a survey on Indian education in Ontario that relates to this issue and the situation in the Far North:

> [An] area of concern cited by Native and non-Native educators was some students' use out of school of non-standard English. The sociolinguistics background to this is complex, but the fact is that many Ontario Native children come to school with little previous exposure to the academic English commonly used in textbooks and classrooms. Insensitivity by the school community to the students' variety of English and their need for time, possibly unacknowledged by some teachers, to master the new idiom may further undermine these Native students' already fragile sense of identity and self-esteem. Any obstacle to students' mastery of the language and literacy skills required for acceptable school performance will tend to deflect them away from success.[70]

As Native languages continue to decline in use, but without "proper" national languages replacing them, this situation may continue to increase as an issue in need of attention.

The ultimate dilemma under the topic of language of instruction stems from the ever-declining numbers of Native or "lesser used" languages. It is estimated that of the 6,000 viable lan-

70. Mackay, Ron, and Lawrence Myles, "A Major Challenge for the Education System: Aboriginal Retention and Dropout." In Battiste and Barman (eds.) 1995.

guages in use in the world today, half will be extinct by the end of the 21st century. Considering the current status of the indigenous languages in the Far North, it is reasonable to expect that they all will be among the 3,000 no longer in use at that time, with perhaps one or two exceptions (Greenland and Eastern Canadian Arctic Inuktitut). It is this situation that introduces the most abstract issue in Native education.

It is frequently said by indigenous peoples that no component of their culture is more important to them than their language. It is this aspect of their persona that distinguishes them from others as much or more than any other. For most it is indeed an integral component of self-identity. In recent years the emotional force of this fact has enabled Native groups to successfully lobby for laws to protect their rights to maintain their language and to have it made a part of formal schooling. Given their human rights to an inherited language and the legal means to its use it can be argued that there should no longer be opposition to bilingual schooling. And it should be added to this argument that recent improvements in pedagogical techniques, such as total immersion Native-language teaching, have shown that Native-language use need not decline and may even be revived.

From another perspectives, however, given the current condition of most Native languages, that is, their declining use, the large numbers of dialects, their small numbers of speakers, the few teachers prepared to teach in a Native language, and the inadequacies of the language in contemporary Western society, how can it be practicable, indeed feasible, to offer bilingual programs as a means to perpetuate a little-known language on a sustainable basis? From the pragmatic point of view of those who oppose bilingual schooling, the answer most often given is that it is not. It is because of this answer that adequate appropriations for additional linguistic work and development of learning materials are often rejected by those with funding authority. And in part it is because of this that school district officials are less supportive of bilingual programs, notwithstanding the advantage they offer in pedagogical and psychological benefits to their students.

There is no satisfactory solution to the dilemma these two conflicting points of view give rise to. Some argue that to insist on new and more elaborate bilingual programs in light of the status of Native languages is folly. Others argue that to disallow the human rights of any people to retain their patrimonial identity through language lacks compassion and denies the schools a proven pedagogical technique. Thus, the topic remains at issue and the debate goes on.

Textbook Examples: Bilingual/Monolingual Language of Instruction

ТУМА́НИНЪ АГУ́ГУМЪ

ІИСУ́СЪ ХРИСТУ́САМЪ

ТУНУСАЧХИ́САГИНЪ

АПУ́СТУЛАМЪ МАТѲЕ́ЯКЪ

ИЛАХТА́ГАНЪ А́ЛУХТАСАКА́ҔИНЪ.

Ка́мга-тукку́мъ Іоа́ннъ Веніами́новъ ила́хта́ганъ Каса́камъ тунуганъ ку́гинъ Уна́нгамъ тунуганъ и́линъ 1828 тулмачи́салинъ, ка́юхъ 1836 слю́лаганъ и́лянъ атхагу́сака́ҥинъ;

Та́га Ка́мга-тукку́мъ Іа́ковъ Нецвѣтовъ илахта́ганъ атхагусагуса́линъ ка́юхъ Ни́гугимъ, ту́нумъ инакахта́ матана́ганъ, а́данги́нъ канчима́дусигинъ итха́ҥинъ.

1. Title pages from the Gospel according to St. Matthew in Aleut and Russian devised by the Russian priest Ivan Veniaminov in 1828 and 1836 after development of an orthography for the Aleut language.

ГОСПОДА НАШЕГО

ІИСУСА ХРИСТА

ЕВАНГЕЛІЕ,

НАПИСАННОЕ

АПОСТОЛОМЪ МАТѲЕЕМЪ.

Съ Русскаго языка на Алеутско-Лисьевской перевелъ Священникъ Іоаннъ Веніаминовъ 1828 года, и въ 1836 году исправилъ;

а Священникъ Іаковъ Нецвѣтовъ разсматривая его окончательно, своими поясненіями сдѣлалъ понятнымъ и для Атхинцовъ, имѣющихъ свое нарѣчіе.

2. First pages of an ABC and reader in Saami, 1837.

Abes

ja

Låkkam-girje.

Kristianiast, 1837.

K. Gröndahl lut prenttijuvvum.

a	a,	k	k,
o	o,	d	d,
u	u,	d^e	đ,
e	e,	t	t,
i	i,	$t^e h$	ŧ,
aa	å,	l	l,
æ	æ,	n	n,
b	b,	ngh	ŋ, (engh)
f	f,	r	r,
m	m,	s	s, (es)
p	p,	sj shj	š, (eshj)
v	v,	z dz	ʒ, (eds)
h	h,	zhj dzhj	ǯ, (edshj)
j	j, (jod)	z tz	c, (tse)
g	g,	zhj tzhj	č (tshje)
g^e	ǥ,		

I.

a, o, u, e, i, å, æ.

---

b, f, m, p, v, h, j, g, g̶, k, d,
đ, t, ŧ, l, n, ŋ, r, s, s̑, ʒ, ʒ̑, c, c̑,

A, O, U, E, I, Å, Æ.

B, F, M, P, V, H, J, G, K, D,
T, L, N, R, S, S̑, C, C̑.

1.

A, ad, ađ, at, aŧ, ag, an, aŋ, ar,
as, as̑, aʒ, aʒ̑, ac, ac̑.
O, ob, om, ok, ol.
Å, åb, åf, åg, åm, år.
E, ep, el, em, es, es̑.

1 *

4

Æ, æp, æl, æm, æs.
U, us, us̑, uʒ, uʒ̑, uc, uc̑.
I, ib, il, ir, is, is̑.

2.

B, ba, bo, bå. P, pa, po, på.
V, va, vu, vå. F, fa, fu, få.
M, mo, mu, mi. H, ha, hu, hæ.
J, ja, jo, jå. K, ko, kæ, ki.
G, ga, go, gå,

3.

D, de, di, då, dæ.
T, te, ti, tå, tu.
L, la, lo, lå, le, læ.
N, na, nu, nå, no.
R, ra, ro, rå, re, ræ.

4.

S, su, so, så, sa.
S̑, s̑u, s̑o, s̑å, s̑a.
ʒ, ʒa, ʒo, ʒå. ʒ̑, ʒ̑a, ʒ̑o, ʒ̑å.

5

C, ca, co, cå, cu.
C̄, c̄a, c̄o, c̄å, c̄u.

1.

Gi, go, mi, min, di, din, si, sin, da, dal, dat, jå, jåk, læ, læk, læm, lut, mån, dån, sån, has, hæg, gam, gåv, rav.

2.

A, al, ald; a, av, avl, lavl; l, la, lav, lavl. G, ga, gam; g, ga, gas, gast; a, as, ast, gast. I, il, ilv, gilv; g, gi, gil, gilv. M, mo, mof, moft; o, of, oft, moft. N, nu, nuf, nuft; u, uf, uft, nuft. Å, år, årg, fårg; f, få, får, fårg. U, ur, urd, jurd; j, ju, jur, jurd.

Ib-mel, Ac̄-c̄e, Æd-ne.
Æd-ne, Ac̄-c̄e, Ib-mel.

Dr. M. Luther

ucca

Katekismusaš,

oktanaga

Manai-oapa guoratallamin

ja

Kristalaš gačaldagai ja vastadusaiguim sigjidi, guđek mannek Hærra bævđdai,

ja

Sentensaiguim Ibmel sanest.

Asatuvvum oappagirje.

Ođđasist samas jorggali J. A. Friis.

Dat girje maksa loge ænkel.

Kristianiast dam jage 1860.

Prentijuvvum Brøgger & Christie lutte.

3. Title pages of a bilingual catechism in Saami and Norwegian, 1860.

Dr. M. Luthers
lille
Katechismus,
med
Børnelærdoms Visitats
og
christelige Spørgsmaal og Svar for dem,
som gaae til Guds Bord,
samt
Sententser af Guds Ord.

Autoriseret Udgave.

Denne Bog koster 10 Skilling.

Christiania 1860.

Trykt hos Brøgger & Christie.

a-tâ-ta o-ĸar-poĸ: pi-ta, i-ma o-ĸa-rit:
ag-pap pa-pê. nâ-me pi-ta sa-per-poĸ.
i-ma o-ĸar-poĸ: á-va-va-vé. ã-ma â-ne
o-ĸar-poĸ: á-ma-ma-mé.

sungiusautit:

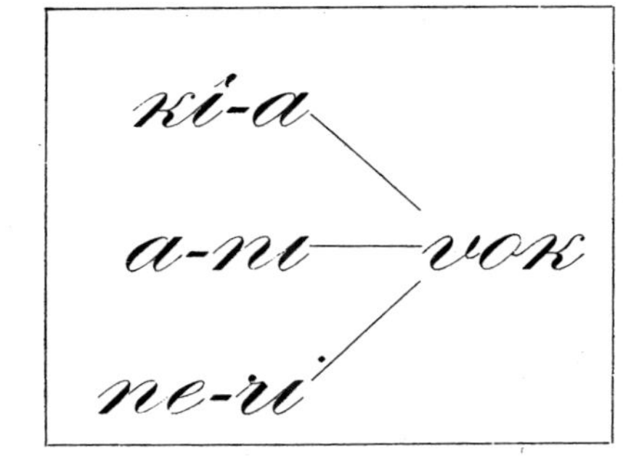

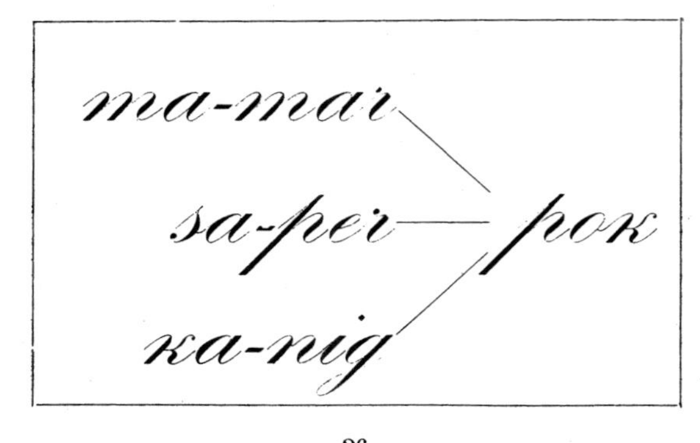

26

4. Sample pages of a monolingual Greenlandic ABC, 1946.

â-ne i-ser-poĸ. pi-ta su-le nâ-me. mér-ĸat i-la-gai. ki-si-á-ne er-nī-naĸ a-nâ-ná-ta a-nger-dlar-ĸu-vá. pî-ta a-nger-dlar-poĸ. i-ser-poĸ. ig-dlup i-lu-a ki-ak. a-nâ-na kâ-gi-li-or-poĸ. â-ne pi-ko-re. a-ná-na-ne i-ki-or-pá. pi-ta, ting-mi-at pé-ruk. a-tu-a-gaĸ u-na ti-gûk. u-na a-tu-a-ruk:

mā-na tá-ssa

u-ki-or-mat a-pi-voĸ.

<u>***sungiusautit:***</u>

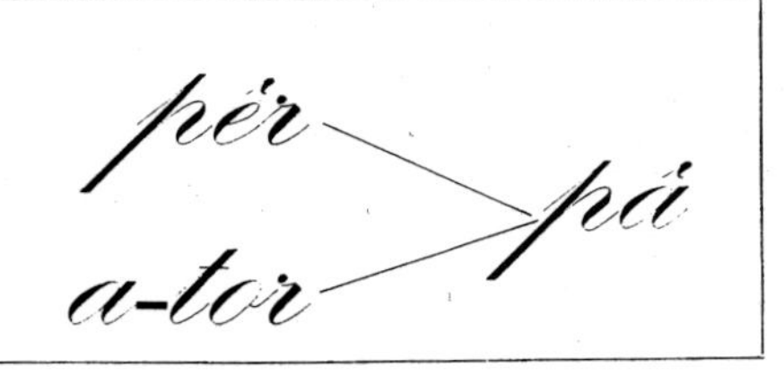

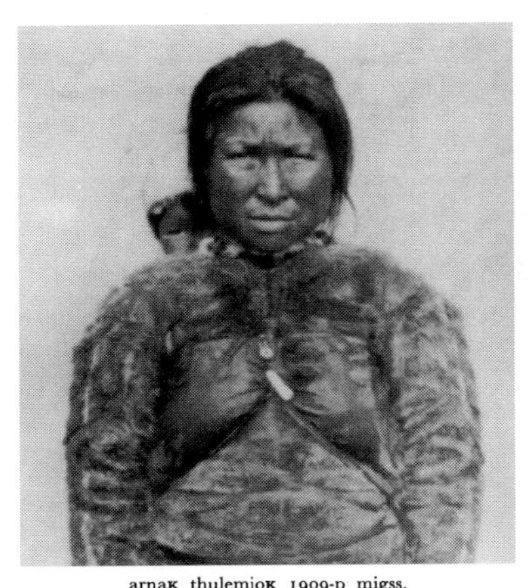

arnaĸ thulemioĸ 1909-p migss.
Kvinde fra Thule omkring 1909

avanerssuarmioĸ inûsugtoĸ
Ung polareskimo i pels

1. eskimût thulemiut

Europame sorssungnerit sivisoĸissut ĸângiungmata nunanut takornartanut angalassoĸartarĸilerpoĸ. Kalâtdlit-nunãnítaoĸ inuit nutât nunalo nutâĸ navssârineĸarput.
tuluit Amerika avangnarĸutdlugo avĸutânik navssârniarput. taimailivdlune imarsiortut nâlagârât, John Ross 1818-ime Thulemut ángúpoĸ, sikup sinâvanut pivoĸ avanerssuarmiutdlo takorĸârtûvdlugit. tikisait ersioĸaut agdlât tikerdlât patdligkumángitdluínardlugit. Rossip kalâleĸ Kujatânit ilaussorâ, ateĸartoĸ Zakæus, táunalo nunaliartitauvoĸ. avanerssuarmiut oĸaloĸatigisínauvai. avanerssuarmiut ersiorungnaeramik ĸimugsimik umiarssualiãput tuluitdlo niuverfigalugit.
ĸangarssuarujugssuaĸ avanerssuarmiut eskimûnik avdlanik nâpitsissáinarsimáput. eskimût ingerdlaortut Canadamêrsut tikerartuagãne nunaĸarput. eskimût Thulemit Kalâtdlit-nunât kaujatdlagdlugo ingerdlaorsimáput. siláinardle puerĸornerulermat K'imugseriarssûp migssâne sermeĸ savssarsimavoĸ angatdlavêrúsimavdlune. tamatuma kingorna thulemiut kujatâmiunik nâpitsísaersimáput.
1818-ip kingornagut ukiut 30 ĸângiútut avanerssuarmiut aitsât umiarssuaĸarĸigput. tuluit amêríkamiutdlo ilisimassagssarsiortut kalâleĸ piniartoĸ, Hans Hendrik Suersaĸmik taissagât ikiortitut ilagât. ilisimassagssarsiornerssuarne amerdlasûne peĸataussarame ilisimaneĸardlualerpoĸ. Thulimiumik nuliarpoĸ Kitâmiunitdlo sujugdlersauvdlune ukiune ardlalingne Thulime eskimût akornáne inûvdlune.

aperĸutit:

1. sôruna tuluit Avangnânut angalasimassut?
2. ĸanoĸ iliordlune John Rossip avanerssuarmiut umiarssuarminukâtípai?
3. sôruna avanerssuarmiut kujatâmiunik nâpitsísaersimassut?

34

5. Sample pages of a bilingual history of Greenland for the fifth, sixth, and seventh grades, 1968.

Fangstdyr og brugsgenstande tegnet af Thuleeskimoer ved kolonisationens start 1909
ûmassut piniagkat atortutdlo avanerssuarmiumit titartagkat nunasinerup nalâne 1909-me

1. Thule-eskimoerne

Efter de lange krige i Europa drog mennesker igen på opdagelse til ukendte egne, og også i Grønland blev der fundet nye mennesker og nyt land.

Englænderne ville finde vejen nord om Amerika, og en søofficer, John Ross, kom på den måde i 1818 helt op til Thule. Han sejlede ind til iskanten og mødte Thule-eskimoerne, som var så bange for de fremmede, at de ikke ville komme hen til dem. Ross havde en grønlænder sydfra, Zakæus, med ombord, og han blev sendt ind til de nye eskimoer. Det gik bedre. Han kunne snart tale med dem. Da de nu ikke mere var bange, kørte de i slæde ud til skibet og handlede med englænderne.

I meget gamle dage mødte Thule-eskimoerne tit andre eskimoer. De boede jo på det sted, hvortil nye eskimoer hele tiden kom fra Canada. Fra Thule gik de så videre rundt om Grønland. Men da der blev koldere i landet, bredte indlandsisen sig helt ud til havet i Melville-bugten og gjorde det næsten umuligt at rejse over den./Derefter mødtes Thule-boerne ikke længere med de andre grønlændere.\

Efter Ross' besøg i 1818 varede det mere end 30 år, før der igen kom skib sydfra op til de nordligste grønlændere. Det var engelske og amerikanske opdagere, som havde en grønlandsk fanger, Hans Henrik fra Fiskenæsset, med som hjælper. Han deltog i mange store ekspeditioner og blev meget kendt. Han giftede sig med en pige fra Thule og boede som den første vestgrønlænder flere år blandt Thuleeskimoerne.

Spørgsmål:

1. Hvorfor sejlede englænderne helt til Nordgrønland?
2. Hvordan fik John Ross Thule-eskimoerne til at komme ud til skibet?
3. Hvorfor mødte Thule-boerne ikke mere de andre grønlændere?

Professional development of teachers

> Teachers say that culture cannot be taught in schools, that it should be taught in the home. But they teach culture in the schools, in fact that is all they teach.[71]

This statement, by members of an Alaska Native association, suggests a long-standing difference in perspectives between the school and community. Because much of the success or failure of a school depends on the purposes and beliefs teachers hold to be important, the statement also draws attention to the type of outcome in the school that can be attributed to the extent and nature of a teacher's knowledge and values. These, we believe, transcend the significance of all other variables in a school's programs and policies. When the classroom door is shut, as pointed out by Arthur Combs, "there is no one but the pupils and the teachers to decide what is done. Under these conditions, unless the teacher has made ... society's purpose his or her own, it is almost certain it will not be carried out."[72]

This notion broaches two of the most provocative aspects of the professional development of teachers: the need for teachers to be thoroughly aware of and educated in the ways of the society in which they work and an awareness of their ultimate responsibility to that society.

Incidentally, but not unimportantly, we note that although teachers are by far the greatest in number and most important members of any school's staff, we include school administrators and professional support personnel in the generic category of teacher as well. Partly we do this for convenience, but mostly because all members of the professional staff should consider themselves teachers first and foremost.

It has become popular in recent years to find fault with teachers who were the first to go North in previous periods of history principally because of stern teacher attitudes and practices that were derived from their close alliance with conservative religious

71. Bristol Bay Native Association 1973, p. 1.
72. Combs 1965.

groups. However, by keeping our view of this criticism in the context of those times rather than our own, criticism becomes less creditable. During the 19th century and well into the mid-20th century, most teachers did not fail at what was expected of them; they were competent and they fulfilled the objectives of their school systems while enduring hardships unknown or seldom appreciated today.

Their shortcomings by contemporary standards were due in part to the goals of education that were set forth by society at large. Accordingly, the reputation of teachers from that time in history should not be disparaged simply because of the mistaken notions of society and the policies of those then in authority. Such policies, usually derived from the tenets of a strict fundamentalist Christian sense of right and wrong, were set forth with what were thought to be good intentions. Simply put, they were products of the ethnocentric ignorance of the time, especially ignorance of the validity and worth of other cultural and spiritual values. The tragedy of their extreme views is that they seldom had respect for the culture they set out to destroy. However, their actual behavior and practices in that time can never be completely known; all we have to go on are the written reports and plans in their chronicles. The only thing we can say for sure is that they were humans with both the good and the bad that that implies. Furthermore, while the motivation and educational practice of missionaries in the schools and other early teachers have often been criticized, it is only fair to point our that they were the first to venture into an extremely harsh, unknown environment and took responsibility for initiating education by default.

If we can overlook prior shortcomings of teachers because of what we know about the past, there should be no excuse for inadequate teacher training today. At issue, then, is the problem of how to be sure that teachers have all of the skills, attitudes, personal background, and motivation required to fulfill contemporary society's purposes, *and* the cultural needs of individuals trying to cope with a rapidly changing world. Examples of professional development programs from each of the countries we cover demonstrate what is now being done to resolve the need this problem suggests.

Scandinavia

Under this topic we look at Scandinavia first because it is there that the concept of training programs for the indigenous population was first put into practice, although the training of Saami, or Saami-speaking teachers, has waxed and waned over the years and never has kept up with demand.

As early as 1717, the Seminarium Scholasticum in Trondheim was founded for the purpose of training Saami to be teachers of their fellow Saami. The driving force behind this philosophy was the missionary Thomas von Westen. He was the first to institute the policy that the Seminarium undertake the responsibility to train missionaries to be fluent in the Saami language. As progressive as this concept appears, the Seminarium lasted only until 1727. It reopened in 1752 under the name Seminarium Lapponicum and actively prepared teachers until 1774 at which time it finally closed. Although it could not sustain itself beyond then, partly because the concept upon which it was founded was intrinsically controversial, during its life it was a stronghold for Saami culture and language in education and missionary work.

By the first half of the 19th century, there was renewed interest in a need for a Saami presence in the schools. In 1821 the Norwegian Parliament authorized a teacher training college dedicated to the training of Saami as teachers and to preparing Norwegian teachers to work in the Saami districts. The school opened in 1826 in Northern Norway at Trondenes. Remarkably, it was the first government teacher training college for any group of teachers anywhere in Norway. As had been the case with the earlier teacher training college, the value of appointing Saami to teaching positions was emphasized as well as the worth of the Saami language in the schools. By 1853, eight Saami students annually had all of their expenses for participating in the program covered by the state. And as a means to demonstrate a high level of professional standing of Saami teachers and Norwegian teachers working in the North, a special salary incentive was paid teachers in Saami districts as well as provision of extra money for school facilities.

It is important to be aware that for over 150 years the main body of teachers working among the Saami were Saami. At first they received their teacher training from priests and missionaries. This group of teachers drew their strength from their innate knowledge of the Native culture and communities and personal connections to their own people and students. Their weakness was due to their lack of a broad, formal education. The need to overcome this weakness was the justification for opening the first government teacher training college with a more inclusive and liberal curriculum in 1826, at Trondenes. (In a much altered form and now located at Tromsø, this college continues to train teachers.) Unfortunately, few Saami attended the college, with the result that there was little long-sustained benefit due to the effort. Poor planning and financial considerations account in part for the lack of success. The college was situated outside the main Saami districts, which created social and personal problems, and it was too expensive, especially for people who came from a subsistence economy. But possibly the most likely reason for its failure was that the college was constituted on Norwegian culture structural lines, not on those of the Saami.

In addition to the college at Trondenes, other colleges constituted along similar lines were established at Tana in the eastern Saami district of Norway and at Alta on the north coast. Their numbers of graduates were small and they ceased operation after a brief time. Thus, Saami-specific teacher training efforts that had begun in 1717 were discontinued in the 1870s. For the next 100 years teacher training programs that provided for the distinctiveness of Saami people and language were abolished. During the period from 1870 to 1970 the official policy, and what was perceived to be the most "realistic" policy, convinced the government to insist that Saami learn the Norwegian language. It was intended that this policy was to be carried out at the expense of the Saami language. As a result Saami students at teacher training colleges were given neither special training nor special financial incentives for their service.

Many of the problems of the previous era were addressed in 1973 with a reversal of the policy of the previous 100 years. The opening of a new teacher training college in Alta in the county of

Finnmark, the most populous Saami county in Norway, meant the issue of Saami-specific teacher qualifications had come full circle. In addition to teacher training the college was given the responsibility for the development of Saami curricula, instructional materials, and multilingual instructional methodology for Saami primary schools. Despite the growing awareness of the inadequacy of the Norwegian primary school serving Saami districts, the Alta College did not fully live up to expectations. It was therefore decided to start over by moving the college to a location more closely in touch with traditional Saami ways of thinking.

The new Saami Cultural College, located at Guovdageaidnu in the heart of Norwegian Saamiland, grew out of this need. It opened in 1989 under the leadership of Jan Henry Keskitalo as rector. In addition to the responsibilities inherited from the Alta Teacher College, the new college also became the teacher training school for the Saami in Finland. The college is now uniquely Saami in character, with Saami the main language of both instruction and administration. The core of the teacher training program reflects Saami culture in structure and values. Field-based training, with teachers situated throughout the district, has become routine. Student teachers practice teaching in both small and large schools in Finnmark, some of which have an almost exclusively Saami student population. The teacher-training and instructional-materials development programs at the Saami Cultural College have become a stimulating blend of Saami traditional values and modern communications technology; they serve as models for exploiting the indigenous capacity to adapt to change with confidence.

The development of formal education for Saami teacher training in Sweden started as early as 1596. With a general history not unlike that of Norway during the early years of schooling, it is natural that there are similarities in the way they were constituted. The priests used Saami assistants as much as possible to enable the Saami language to be used in their work. By so doing the priests selected promising Saami to be teachers and instructed them accordingly. By 1632 a special school, Skytteanska skolan (Skytteanian), at Lycksele was established to facilitate recruitment of Saami for service in the Church. This set the pattern for Saami education and teacher training until the end of the 18th century. Theology and the function of priests were the primary thrusts of the training program and there were numerous efforts to improve the performance of catechists. Furthermore, the state made special efforts to recruit Saami as priests and catechists since the daily work of teaching was carried out mainly by the Saami. Those who were not Saami were urged to develop a functional level of the Saami language since the methodology for teaching in Saami communities was Saami-pupil oriented. These policies were practiced as early as 1735.[73]

In addition to the general teaching of children, candidates for confirmation were the main focus of the Church, both in permanent schools and of itinerant teachers who moved with the migratory population. This ambulatory system of teaching, or nomad school, which was introduced in the School Reform Act of 1846, was unique to Sweden and lasted far into the 20th century. However, permanent schools were judged to be more effective since their programs were more extensive and their teachers better educated and established. But because of the migratory life style of the population they had fewer students. Conversely, the ambulatory system was extremely primitive with few adequate programs, due in part to insufficient education of the teachers. However, significantly more students were reached in these schools than in the permanently established schools, thereby justifying their continued use.

The course of study for both the nomad and permanent schools consisted of a two-year program and only a few pupils were selected for each class. The main purpose of the schools was to function as a rudimentary form of teacher training; those who finished were then expected to teach others to read and promote the fundamentals of Christianity. As crude as the system was, its effectiveness lay in the fact that those being trained were Saami.[74]

73. Henrysson 1993, pp. 16–17.

74. Ruong, I., "Lapp Schools, Teacher Education and Trans-Cultural Studies." In Darnell (ed.) 1972, p. 326.

This process had the positive effect of strengthening Saami as the language of instruction and eventually led to establishment of more formal teacher training programs. A teacher training college with special responsibility to Saami teachers was established at Mattisudden, close to Jokkmokk, in the Saami district of Lappmark. By the end of the 19th century, formal teacher training had replaced theology as the main subject of instruction and was continued until the end of World War II.

At this time, despite a number of attempts to prepare Saami to be teachers, the policy was reversed. Since then there has been no teacher training program in Sweden specifically designed for Saami teachers. Swedish Saami who want a Saami-specific program of teacher training attend the Saami Cultural College. Others take standard teacher training courses given for those who are preparing to teach in the regular Swedish state school system for non-Saami students. This situation has increased the influence of the Saami Cultural College, which now has the potential to become the center of teacher training for all Saami throughout Norway, Sweden, and Finland.

Greenland

The early years of schooling in Greenland have much in common with the first attempts to establish schools among the Saami. Since the missionaries came from the same places in Scandinavia and were of the same school of thought, this is as expected. As pointed out in Chapter 4, the motive of Lutheran missionaries in Greenland, as had been the case in Scandinavia, was the conversion of the population to Christianity. In both places the value of having local residents assist as teachers or catechists was recognized soon after their efforts to Christianize the population were initiated. Because the first priests and catechists were Danes who lacked a knowledge of the Greenlandic customs and language, their early attempts met with little success. Realizing that it was necessary to have Greenlanders who knew local customs and the language work as teachers, just three years after Hans Egede arrived in Greenland he sent two Greenlanders to Denmark to become educated in the ways of Denmark and to become catechists, initiating a trend that endured for years.

Even though this effort was started during the early history of formal schooling, its effect was minimal. There were just too few Greenlanders being trained and the geography of Greenland too vast to make much of a difference. Accordingly, in 1737, a teacher training college for Danes intended for Greenland, Seminarium Groenlandicum, was established in Copenhagen. Headed by Hans Egede, the college prepared both catechists and missionaries. The catechists were boys recruited from an orphanage, and the missionaries from secondary schools in Copenhagen.[75] Students in the college were given classes in Greenlandic culture and language. Later, the program was expanded to include Greenlanders who were sent to Denmark, some of whom attended regular Danish teacher training programs.

To avoid the necessity of sending Greenlanders to Denmark, plans for a full-scale teacher training college in Greenland were first made at the beginning of the 19th century. The school was to be comprehensive in character and courses were to be given in reading, writing, arithmetic, traditional craftsmanship, hunting skills, and health care. Because of external logistical and political factors, the plan was never put into effect.

However, by royal decree in 1844, two formal teacher training colleges had their beginning. Colleges at Nuuk and Illulissat adopted similar curricula that included writing, reading, arithmetic, Danish, religion, geography, natural history, choral music, organ, and kayaking. Probably among the courses offered, those given the most attention dealt with pedagogical subjects. The college at Illulissat lacked sufficient support; it closed in 1875, reopened in 1901, and permanently closed in 1905. However, the college at Nuuk, Ilinniarfissuaq, was successful and continues to function today. The first programs of the Nuuk college, although successful among individual students, trained an insufficient number of graduates and the scope of their education was inadequate, a situation that lasted until recent times.

75. Larsen 1976, pp. 14–15.

The Education Reform Act set out by the Danish Parliament in 1905 totally changed the emphasis on education and the training of teachers. Where there had been an idyllic and romantic appreciation of Greenlandic culture and language in the 19th century, the new emphasis was to be on the Danish language and modernization of the curriculum to reflect Danish culture. The same basic subjects were retained in the college, but given a Danish slant. And pedagogical studies in the theory and practice of psychology were added. Furthermore, priests were no longer given the responsibility for training catechists who were expected thereafter to get all of their training at the college.[76]

By 1925 the law had been modified to encourage Greenlandic students who did especially well at Nuuk to go to Denmark for supplementary education after their graduation from a college preparatory class at Ilinniarfissuaq. Since that time Ilinniarfissuaq has slowly evolved into a comprehensive teacher's college. During the 1940s the emphasis on religion in the curriculum was reduced, as were the number of classes given in Danish, although Danish remained the first language of instruction.

While the teachers trained at Nuuk were the titular mainstay of the schools of Greenland up until the early 1950s, their education remained inadequate in content and quantity.[77]

All through the years following World War II up until the present period under home rule, two-thirds to four-fifths of the teachers in Greenland came from Denmark. They, and most Greenlandic teachers who had been educated according to Western European pedagogical ideals, supported aspects of the Danish way of life which many Greenlanders considered anathema to Greenlandic culture.

Changes in the Danish constitution in 1953 ended Greenland's colonial status and made Greenland a county in Denmark. As reported by Greenlander Karl Kristian Olsen,

> the end of the colonial period and the transition to a free democratic society brought about the need for substantial changes in the institutions of

---

76. Berliner 1987, pp. 186–204.
77. Gunther, Bent, "The Pedagogical Situation in Greenland." In Darnell (ed.) 1972.

> the society. The content of schools and education were gradually brought in line with Danish standards. In order to implement the changes teachers and administrators from Denmark were hired. As far as the public schools were concerned, the Greenlandic School Act of 1967 was almost identical to the Danish public school law, and the Danish law concerning teacher education was applied to Ilinniarfissuaq in 1964, though with a few adjustments to the needs of Greenlandic society.[78]

Since the Home Rule Act of 1979, teacher training has, as has the whole of the Greenland education system, been directed toward the development of a modern Greenlandic education complex. Greenlandic culture and language have been focused with a two-fold aim: To establish a truly Greenlandic teacher training program in content, and one sufficient in size to meet the need for an increased number of Greenlandic teachers. This effort is now being developed as a three-year campus-based program or, alternatively, as a four-year field-based program.[79] In addition to this effort, the home rule government has also prepared the way for students to go to North American colleges and universities. And, most recently, Ilisimatusarfik, Greenland's new university, begun as the Inuit Institute in 1983, has entered into cooperative programs with universities in Scandinavia and North America.

During the 1992 school year, 835 persons were engaged in classroom teaching in Greenland, of whom 219 were part-time, hourly teaching assistants (the equivalent of 139 full time teachers). Of the full-time teachers, 498 were Greenlanders and 270 were Danish. Greenlanders accounted for 193 of the part-time teachers and 26 were Danish. Among the administrative staff, 28 were Greenlanders and 39 were Danish. The number of Greenlandic teachers is expected to increase within the next few years, due in large measure to the larger number of graduates expected in the improved secondary schools who will be eligible to attend Ilinniarfissuaq.[80]

---

78. Olsen 1993, p. 2.
79. Ibid., p. 5.
80. Ibid., p. 4.

Alaska and Canada

Professional development of teachers in North America has a shorter history than in Scandinavia and Greenland. As meager as the early efforts in Scandinavia and Greenland were, the first Church authorities recognized an advantage in utilizing teachers drawn from the Native populations as early as the 18th century. In North America, the value of innate Native knowledge and the need for teachers to understand local customs and needs was not broadly accepted until recent times.

Because the professional development of teachers in Alaska and Canada evolved along similar lines we have combined our discussion of this topic for these two locations under one heading. It was not until the 1960s that a serious effort was made to prepare teachers with special qualifications for village or settlement teaching in both Alaska and Canada. Prior to that time, most teachers assigned to village and settlement schools were recruited from those who underwent their professional preparation at standard teacher training colleges and universities in the South. Typically these teachers were given only brief orientation courses before they left for their assignments. Such courses usually lasted only a matter of days and consisted of no more than a review of the standard curriculum then in use throughout the country, logistical problems of living in isolated places, and the administrative regulations with which they were to comply. Except for the rare visit of an inspector, after that they were on their own.

In both Alaska and Canada awareness of the need to look for better ways to prepare teachers for schools serving the Native population came about in the early 1960s. All teachers being assigned to village and settlement schools were well qualified according to the standards for teachers required in the states and provinces from which they came. But certificates specifying certain qualifications to teach in a standard, urban or rural school did not attest to an ability to teach "across cultures." Recognition of this shortcoming at the University of Alaska Fairbanks and the University of Saskatchewan at Saskatoon gave rise to the first cross-cultural teacher education programs in North America.

The Alaska Rural School Project, developed by Professors Charles Ray and Frank Darnell in 1966, with financial assistance from the Ford Foundation, offered courses in anthropology of Alaska Natives, teaching English as a second language, and pedagogical aspects of cross-cultural classrooms, in a program focused on Native village life styles. Each teacher selected for the program was new to village teaching in Alaska and had recently been assigned to either a federal Bureau of Indian Affairs or state of Alaska school. Teachers who completed the program over the next several years became the vanguard of proponents for culturally sensitive, innovative programs throughout the state. Their influence persists today. Since then there have been several versions of the concept typified by the Alaska Rural School Project on the campuses of the University of Alaska at both Fairbanks and Anchorage and at Alaska Pacific University in Anchorage. However, it should be noted that these programs were designed primarily as orientation programs for non-Natives. Nevertheless, the need for such efforts continues today; a majority of non-Native teachers taking positions in village schools still exceeds the number of Natives who make up the professional staffs.

In Canada, it was a program developed at the University of Saskatchewan at Saskatoon that first set the precedent for a strong Canadian presence in teacher training programs that addressed Native needs. Professor Andre Renaud, first director of the program, designed the curriculum to reflect the cross-cultural nature of village teaching and the emerging needs of Canadian Native cultures in transition. In Saskatchewan, as in Alaska, the program was designed with the goal of familiarizing new teachers with the cultural nuances and values of Native societies while providing practical knowledge about how to cope with life and teach in small, isolated school sites. Unlike the first effort in this field in Alaska, the Saskatoon program had a mixture of Native and non-Native students. The tradition started in Saskatoon in the 1960s continues today in the programs of the Saskatchewan Indian Federated College.

The need for Native teachers for Northern schools was not recognized in North America until 1968, at which time the Northwest Territories Teacher Education Program at Fort Smith, especially developed for Native teachers, was initiated. This development was due primarily to an outgrowth of the civil rights movement of the previous decade, efforts of enlightened academics, and the emergence of the Native population as a political force. Since then, in both Alaska and Canada, there have been substantial efforts to design and implement teacher training programs that enable members of the Native population to become full-fledged professional teachers.

The school at Fort Smith was open to all Natives of the Northwest Territories; its graduates were trained in accordance with the standards of teacher training schools found in the South. The use of Native languages in schools had not yet become an issue, and much emphasis was placed on methods of teaching English as a second language. Because of its location most of its students were Athapaskan Dene; only a few Inuit were willing to attend. This situation and political pressure obligated authorities in the territorial government to establish a second teacher training program in the Eastern Arctic in 1979.[81]

Located at Iqaluit (at the time still called Frobisher Bay), the Eastern Arctic Teacher Education Program (EATEP) had a modest beginning as a two-year course of study developed in conjunction with a classroom aid training project already established there. Where the program at Fort Smith had put an emphasis on teaching English, EATEP quickly developed its own format and put an emphasis on teaching in Inuktitut. Furthermore, in 1981 EATEP introduced the concept of field-based teacher training which soon became a major focus of the college's delivery system. Moreover, the college had expanded its scope by incorporating the classroom teacher assistant training program into its structure, thereby making it a more comprehensive college.

Although the Eastern Arctic Teacher Education Project had become an institutional reality with both campus- and field-based students, there still was no way for its graduates to receive credits from a recognized university. To remedy this shortcoming, the

81. Ibid., p. 118.

field-based teacher education program at McGill University, already successfully under way in Arctic Quebec, was incorporated into EATEP. This created the means for the project to acquire higher academic standing and broaden its scope and field-based operations. This was made possible by a grant of almost half a million dollars made in 1981 by the Canadian Donner Foundation. Many students at that time did the equivalent of one year's study in the field over a period of two or three years coupled with one year on the campus at Iqaluit to complete a two-year program. In 1984 the program had added a third year, the entire program being recognized as part of McGill University's cooperative expansion into the Northwest Territories. In June 1985, the first Inuk graduated with the Bachelor of Education degree. By 1987 a total of seven graduates had earned this degree and two had been accepted at McGill University for graduate study. At the end of same year, EATEP had graduated 55 teachers in its two-year training program and more than 140 classroom assistants had registered for the McGill–EATEP Certificate in Native and Northern Education.[82]

Quebec is also recognized as being among the first governmental units in Canada to initiate a teacher training program in the Far North specifically for the Native population. The first provincial schools established in Arctic Quebec, the Kativik School District, drew their teachers from the South. But because these schools had assumed the responsibility for offering instruction in Inuktitut, it was apparent that only the resident Native population, with but few exceptions, had language skills sufficient to carry out this responsibility.

At the beginning of the 1970s there were several trained Inuit classroom assistants in Quebec, many of them highly competent, but none held teaching credentials. To meet the need created by the government's policy to offer classroom instruction in the Native language, 35 classroom assistants were given "tolerance" certificates by the Minister of Education to work as full-time teach-

82. Wilman, David, "Teacher Training in the Canadian Eastern Arctic." In Farrow and Wilman (eds.) 1989, pp. 88, 89, 93.

ers on the condition that they enroll in an authorized in-service teacher training program. Dr. Jack Cram, director of the Center for Native Studies at McGill University, was appointed coordinator of the program in 1975, and a formal relationship between the school district and the university leading to the professional certification of Inuit as fully trained teachers was initiated. McGill courses were offered on a regular basis in the summer and winter on an in-service basis. In 1978, the first eight Inuit teachers received provincial certification. The program became formally recognized by the university "after some hesitation and a certain amount of internal 'politicking'" by the McGill Senate in 1981.[83] The entry of McGill University in the work of teacher training in the Canadian Far North was not only among the first, but it established precedents in methods and standards that persist today.

Recent achievements notwithstanding, teacher training institutions have not produced near the number of Native teachers required for the growing number of classrooms. In 1992, Native teachers made up 14 percent of the qualified teachers in the Northwest Territories, while Native students made up 70 percent of the population. It is estimated that approximately 1,300 teachers will be required in the schools of the Northwest Territories by the next century. At present the goal is to have half of this number, 650 teachers, drawn from the Native population. Accordingly, new teacher training programs are being developed, especially programs carried out at the community level. In the Eastern Arctic, where the need may be the greatest, this work is being done on campuses of the Arctic College, especially at the Nunatta Campus of Nunavut Arctic College in Iqaluit[84] and, since 1991, in 11 of the 27 Nunavut settlement areas in newly developed community-based teacher education programs. These programs have proved to be even more popular than EATEP's earlier field-based programs. In 1993, 34 Inuit teachers were graduated, and in 1995, 47. Since its inception in 1979, EATEP/NTEP, in association with McGill University, has graduated more than 160 teach-

83. Cram 1985, p. 121.
84. Wilman 1993, and personal correspondence, 1993.

ers with the basic two-year certificate in Native and Northern Education. Of these, 40 have gone on to the McGill Bachelor of Education degree. There are similar successful developments in the western Northwest Territories. The goal of 80 percent of an aboriginal teaching force for the Northwest Territories is now realistic.[85]

In Alaska, as well as Canada, it has been found that field-based courses have become an essential way to attract and adequately prepare members of the Native community to become village teachers. It is more than coincidental that the first program in Canada based on this concept in 1968 was started about the same time in Alaska, in 1970. The nativistic movement for influence in formulation of school policies gained momentum in the two countries at the same time. Augmenting this development, the civil rights movement in the United States had given rise to the federal government's Teacher Corps Program, a program designed to bring members of minority groups throughout the United States into classroom teaching through innovative teacher training. Alaska became one of the first Teacher Corps sites in the United States. Started initially at Alaska Methodist University in Anchorage in 1970, the program moved that same year to the Fairbanks campus of the University of Alaska under the academic direction of Professor Raymond Barnhardt.

The program, originally called the Alaska Rural Teacher Training Corps (ARTTC), was established as a four-year experimental course of study to train Native elementary school teachers. Upon completion of the course work it was expected that students would have met the university's requirements for the Bachelor of Education degree. Since the program was field-based and experimental there was the expected objection to the program by traditionalists in the Education Department of the university and the academic council that policed the integrity of the university's degrees. By 1974, many of the objections to the program had been overcome and 42 of the original 60 students had graduated. The curriculum was expanded to include the prepara-

85. Wilman, personal correspondence, 1995.

tion of bilingual teachers and teachers for small rural high schools. Furthermore, the program by that time offered a non-teaching degree in rural human resource development for students interested in state-wide Native affairs and a Master of Education degree was approved. With the thrust of the program broadened, its name was changed to the Cross-cultural Education Development Program (or popularly called X-CED) to be more descriptive of its various functions.

X-CED today is looked upon as a well-established field delivery program that has grown beyond its experimental stages and has acquired a level of permanence that could not have been predicted during its early years. Barnhardt, writing about the program a few years after it had become institutionalized, opined as follows:

> We have learned that the training of educators, native or non-native, requires more than the inclusion of a few anthropology courses in the teacher training curriculum. Such a limited focus runs the risk of putting just enough information in teachers' hands to make them dangerous, even when well-intentioned. The development of a cross-cultural perspective in education requires that the persons being trained have extensive guided field experience in which the methods and concepts provided in the training are blended with actual working experience. Only after having coped with the uncertainty and confusion engendered in a cross-cultural experience, can a person fully internalize a perspective which transcends cultural boundaries, and only when such a perspective is fully internalized can the person use it productively.[86]

Experience from throughout the North supports Barnhardt's observations and gives credence to the notion that if pupils are to learn, teachers must have participated in culture-based and, where appropriate, linguistically relevant education programs. However, this does not necessarily mean that all teachers need to be recruited from the Native population. Although much effort is currently being expended on programs that rely on teachers who are a part of the Native population, ethnic minority status alone does not ensure that an individual will succeed. Conversely, non-

---

86. Barnhardt, Ray, "Field-Based Education for Alaskan Native Teachers." In Barnhardt (ed.) 1977, p. 96.

minority status does not invalidate the potential of teachers to succeed. In either case, it is the quality and appropriateness of the education and training that teachers acquire that is essential if one is to become an effective teacher.

Throughout this section we asserted that there is a clear need for teachers to have a thorough knowledge of the ways of the society in which they will work. At issue, therefore, is the problem of how best this requirement can be met. In all probability, if prospective teachers are indigenous members of the society this need is apt to be more easily met than otherwise. And of equal weight, it has been well demonstrated that Native teachers act as effective role models among their peers. Most importantly, they demonstrate that teachers of Native ethnicity can be expected to succeed as a Native in a school that is an institutional component of Western society. Therefore, when all other factors are equal, selection of a Native teacher over a non-Native teacher is not an unfair choice. But this choice should only be made, as the ordinance of the Northwest Territories provides, "to the extent that qualified personnel are available."[87] It is implied in this proviso that an *ability* to teach, rather than *entitlement* to teach, comes first.

There are many types of teacher certificates that attest to the suitability of their holders to assume responsibility to be teachers. These certificates, therefore, are credentials as well as licenses or authorizations to teach. They do not, unfortunately, certify ability. But it is this quality in teachers, Native and non-Native alike, that is the most important; it is the one that teacher training programs find the most difficult to engender. To do so requires that teacher training programs inculcate their trainees in the unique characteristics, needs, and values of the populations they serve as well as pedagogical techniques appropriate for a distinctive, multicultural population. This means there is a need to be aware of the traditional values and characteristics of both Native and contemporary urban society. For these needs to be met successfully it is necessary to disregard the highly structured model of teacher training institutions to the South in favor of an informal structure

87. Northwest Territories Legislative Assembly 1983, Section 58.

more akin to Native societies. Without the constraints imposed by traditional models of teacher training, the cultural nuances and predilection of the Native society can be better accommodated in teacher education programs.

As suggested in the opening paragraphs of this section, much of the success or failure of a school depends on the purposes and beliefs teachers hold to be important. What these are derive from the level and breadth of the education they have received. Without meaning to demean teachers as individuals or as a class, it can be said that few village teachers are educated to the extent that they could be considering the complexity of the relationships that exist between the school and community. In too few instances are any teachers, Native or non-Native, prepared to weigh the values of the society in which they work and use effectively the multicultural knowledge available to them.

Ultimately, implied in all aspects of teacher training and classroom teaching is the need to be aware of the responsibility that society places on teachers. It is, therefore, incumbent on both trainers of teachers and teachers themselves to constantly look for ways to improve both their academic and professional background. Failing this, it becomes the responsibility of community leaders and those at higher levels of government, especially those who certify individuals to teach, to insist on this in principle if not actually in law.

Pupil performance

Because of recent progress in Native control of policy making, improved curricula, and better and more accessible teacher training, it might be assumed that these developments have resulted in improved pupil performance. For some it has, but not nearly as many as might be expected. It is disturbing to note that many pupils continue to underachieve and are severely impaired both academically and socially. Compared with their innate ability and potential to attain a level of education required to succeed in a multicultural society, the results of schooling often are dismal. In all sectors of the Far North, many pupils continue to find schools frustrating and unfulfilling. Why this is so, and why the level of Native children's academic performance is recorded at the bottom of charts reporting school performance are questions that define the issue of inadequate school performance.

Throughout the history of education for Native indigenous pupils in the Far North the level of school performance has been much lower than comparable age groups in the majority population. For up to two hundred and fifty years, schools have been unable to raise the relative level of performance among pupils of the indigenous population compared with the level of the majority population. The gap in student performance between the two populations has always been great, although, for example, in Scandinavia during the 18th and 19th centuries it was less when Saami culture was a more pronounced element of the school than the century between 1870 to 1970 when Saami culture was neglected.

There have been but few attempts to measure school performance, and there is little agreement as to the best way to do it and even less about how to explain the poor showing in the findings. Assessment of student performance in Norway, Finland, and Alaska are examples of the studies that have been done in this field.

The most comprehensive effort to understand school performance among the Saami in Norway was made by Hoëm in the 1970s.[88] The purpose of the study was to clarify how the schools operating under a 1936 act of Parliament attempted to reach the goals specified in the law. His sample was taken from four municipalities of Finnmark where the majority of the population was Saami. Included in the sample was the whole school population in grades five and seven. Among those tested in the seventh grade, 78.7 percent were Saami and 21.3 percent were Norwegians and in the fifth grade 74.4 percent were Saami and 25.6 percent were Norwegian. It was found that the Saami pupils were far behind the schedule set for achieving the goals. It was also found that there were great differences between levels of achievement between schools, between classrooms in the same school, and

88. Hoëm 1976a, 1976b.

between subjects. Generally, pupils living in the most isolated places or who were children of nomads had the lowest level of performance. Saami children with a strong Norwegian cultural background performed better than those without. In subject matter, the more alien the subjects were from the point of view of the Saami culture, the poorer the outcome of the test, although there were exceptions to this generalization. The highest scores were in the study of Christianity, a traditional subject of Saami education; many pupils reached the goals set by the parliament for this subject. Not unexpectedly, it was found that pupils of Norwegian extraction, living in districts with a high concentration of Saami pupils, had a weak mastery of the Saami language.

From his analysis of the findings, Hoëm concluded that low pupil achievement was due to the inappropriateness of the Norwegian cultural system of education set in a different cultural milieu. The school system was well funded, the quality of facilities and equipment were adequate and were of a high quality. Teachers were well trained by high Norwegian standards. All that was needed for a good education had been provided by the government, but to little avail. Since the time of this study, inadequate pupil performance compared with the achievements of the majority population has remained the norm. Moreover, education officials, arguing that the best school system possible is in place, continue to ponder the question of why performance is so low. In terms of what they accept is the best, their argument is correct. It is not only the best system known to them, it is the only one. The question, What would the system look like if the present one was changed to reflect the environment and culture of the people where it is located? goes unasked.

Findings from a study in Finland, reported by L. Seitamo in 1988, resemble findings in Norway. In this study psychological aspects of trends in school achievement were investigated in Skolt Saami and Finnish children. The study focused on the effects of cognitive factors, self-concept, and child-rearing practices on school performance among Skolt Saami children from Sevettijarvi and a comparable sample of Finnish children from Northern Finland. The schools in which the data were collected all adhered to the standard Finnish curriculum and the Saami and Finnish children were all taught in Finnish. Pressure from an accumulation of difficulties, especially on boys, was great. Poor readiness for school and neglect of Saami culture and language in the curriculum contributed to reduced motivation, dislike of school, and lack of persistence in school work.[89] Seitamo concluded from the study that

> a question arises whether such [problems] would have emerged at all in a school system based on their own [Saami] culture and language. The results show very clearly the serious consequences resulting from any school policy not taking into account a group's own culture and language.[90]

Although their research was ten years apart, Seitamo's and Hoëm's findings are similar, as are findings from student performance assessments in other Circumpolar countries.

Findings from recent standardized testing programs in Alaska, for example, report the same kinds of results from which the same conclusions can be reached: student performance among Alaska Native pupils is woefully inadequate. In 1990, 9,010 fourth graders, 8,143 sixth graders, and 7,572 eighth graders in Alaska were tested with the standardized Iowa Test of Basic Skills, a test used throughout the United States. Results of the program revealed a marked disparity between Alaska Natives and the rest of the school population. Overall, Alaska students, Native and non-Native combined, scored just above the national average at the 50th to 56th percentile level. But when the population was broken down between Native and non-Native the gap between the two was extremely wide. The school district with the highest average rank scored at the 70.5 percentile level. The lowest ranked district scored at the 4.5 percentile level. This district had a student body comprised of 100 percent Natives, while the highest ranked district was made up of 100 percent non-Natives.[91] It is important to note that these districts are at the extreme ends of

89. Seitamo 1988, p. 97.
90. Ibid.
91. Alaska 1990.

the continuum. Nevertheless, the proportion of Native to non-Native students correlates positively with the lowest to the highest test scores among all districts throughout the state. This is to say, the higher percentage of Native students in the district the lower the aggregate test score and, vice versa, the higher percentage of non-Natives in the population, the higher the score.

With these findings in mind, it must be emphasized that achievement testing among minority populations has been persistently unreliable, not just in the Far North, but wherever there are multicultural minority populations. Several distinctly different minority cultures in the North, varying degrees of acculturation by members of the Native population, different levels of English-language competency, lower economic status, and extensive geographic isolation all skew the potential validity of the tests. Regardless of reasons given for the disparity in test results between Native and non-Native students, hasty conclusions can lead to groundless opinions, attitudes unfavorable to minority students, and stereotyping. Reliance on test data as indicators of academic achievement as shown on standardized test scores by Native pupils as individuals, in groups, or school systems as a whole, is tenuous at best. At its worst, misinterpretation can prejudicially demean a whole Native population. Unquestionably, scores on achievement tests should not be used to infer that the level of innate ability of any segment of the population, be it by gender, geographic region, or ethnicity, is superior to another. Reliable data from achievement tests that can be used to declare or predict ability among the indigenous population as defined, simply do not exist.

Low grade level attainment as a measure of student performance is equally disturbing. Current data show that in some school districts up to 30 percent of Native children are below grade level in the primary grades, and in excess of 40 percent are below grade level in grades 7 through 12.

Likewise, scores from the American College Test (ACT) are troublesome. In this test non-Native college students had an a average composite score of 20.7 on the ACT, while Alaska Natives at college had an average score of 12.2, or on average, 40 percent lower than non-Native students.[92] As reported, the reliability of the data can be brought into question because of the way it was collected. At the time the data were made known, the University of Alaska, the only source for such information, relied on self-reporting by students and the multiple and very ambiguous categories provided to students on university forms often result in students not responding at all.[93] Nevertheless, although completely reliable data on the ACT simply are not available, the results that are available indicate that student performance among Alaska Natives at the university level needs attention as well as a better system of evaluation.

The results of nationally standardized tests used in Alaska can be explained along lines similar to the reasons for low student performance given in the Saami studies: the inappropriateness of the majority culture's systems of education set among a different cultural milieu. Furthermore, Alaska districts with a high percentage of Native students are characterized by extreme poverty, low levels of education among adults, and traditions and values vastly different from the American population on which the tests were standardized.

These reasons, while they attempt to explain the causes for poor showing in standardized tests, are not sufficient to account for the extremes of the low scores. The poor showing may also be due, in part, to the dysfunctional nature of many Native communities. As pointed out in a recent report by the Joint State–Federal Commission on Policies and Programs Affecting Alaska Natives, stable Native community life has largely broken down in many locations. The commission, whose members, among others, came from a broad cross-section of the Native population, reported that

> exacerbating the complexities of transferring information and ideas from one culture to another are the social and economic conditions of the families and villages themselves. Many children come from homes where there is chronic abuse of alcohol and a frightening prevalence of domestic

---

92. O'Rourke 1989.
93. Barnhardt, Carol, School of Education, University of Alaska Fairbanks, personal communication, 1995.

> violence. They come from homes that have near total dependence on government for their economic survival, homes steeped in spiritual and economic poverty where the parents and other family members are too preoccupied with their own problems to pay adequate attention to the child and how he or she is doing in school.
>
> All too often the school is a place of rest for a child who does not sleep well and does not get the nurturing she needs at home. The school, then, is a place not for learning but instead a place to temporarily escape the less than fortunate realities of home.[94]

These realities are dramatically illustrated with the depressing statistics that reveal the consequences of the dysfunctional nature of many Native communities. In each of the Circumpolar countries, an extremely high incidence of alcoholism and suicide among the Native population attest to the problem. Both are among the highest in world; the most recent figures from Alaska are tragic, but typical throughout the Far North. During the 1980s, the mortality rate from alcoholism was three and one half times the rate for non-Natives. And loss of life due to alcohol related accidents was five times as great as deaths from the same cause among the non-Native population.

Suicide rates are equally or even more revealing of the devastating consequences of dysfunctional populations in the Far North, especially among young male Natives. The rate continues to rise; by 1990 it was 30 percent higher among this group than the national average for the same age group. It is now the fourth leading cause of death among all Natives. The Alaska Federation of Natives in their study of this phenomenon found that suicide mortality rates for Alaska Natives increased from 42 per 100,000 population in 1980 to 58 per 100,000 population in 1986.[95] Since then the rate has continued to escalate, especially among the young. Approximately half of all suicides by Alaska Natives are carried out by 15–24-year-olds, compared with one in four among non-Natives in this age group. In the Northwest Territories in Canada and in Greenland, statistics are very similar. The situation in those places parallels that in Alaska.

94. Irwin 1994, pp. 66–67.
95. Alaska Federation of Natives 1989, pp. 7–8.

Standardized achievement tests, levels of schooling attained compared with years in attendance, and dropout rates are the most common ways of assessing student performance. More recently, performance tests based on student competence have been developed, some at the local level. But these too have met with mixed results, for some essentially are based on goals of education typical of the non-Native society. For example, some measure competence in life skills, but, of course, in Native communities some of these differ markedly from urban locales and deciding on what are or are not appropriate life skills to measure becomes an issue in itself. Others measure such things as opinions of employers regarding performance of graduates or the number of graduates in specialized job training programs or higher education. Each of these types of measurement may determine the extent to which the school's goals have or have not been met, but the fact remains that such goals are not always consistent with the needs or values in the Native society. In such cases it is unlikely that measures of competency will be a fair indicator of innate pupil ability. However, in defense of competence-based testing it should be pointed out that this category of pupil assessment did not come into its own until the past few years and as such the very meaning of competency itself has become an issue.

In the Canadian Far North, there is little to go on to judge the extent of adequate student performance other than broad statements from government agencies attesting to the fact that performance is deficient. Dropout rates, one telling but indirect measure of performance, are kept in the Yukon Territory, Northwest Territories, and Arctic Quebec. In all three places they are unacceptably high, but their use is usually confined to administrative considerations rather than pedagogical.

The most urgent issue in student performance stems from the question how best to determine if the school is meeting its obligation to its students and the community in which it is situated, rather than testing to see if it is meeting the goals of an unrelated population from elsewhere. In the light of the failure of quantitative measures of testing, qualitative assessment may hold more promise. Even considering the subjective nature of such evaluations, they may say much about the appropriateness of the school's program. For example, the intuitive assessment made by the Yup'ik elder in Tununuk, cited at the beginning of Chapter 1, is an indicator, albeit obviously subjective, of one aspect of the school's program. Although his question was derived from an assumption and was based on a value judgment, he had concluded that children of his village had not learned things that he, and probably many of his peers, consider important.

Others have described what it is to be successful in the Native community and society at large in non-quantifiable terms. One such description was expressed by Janie Leask, at the time President of the Alaska Federation of Natives, when she asserted that "the real measure of success is not generated by the statistics of the people who run the institution. It is the quality of life lived by the people who emerge from it."[96] In elegant simplicity, she has defined the purpose of education as well as the ultimate measure of success of anyone, regardless of where or how it is acquired.

---

96. Leask 1985.

Part Three
Conclusions

Chapter 6

A Comparative Review and Lessons Learned

Historical development of schooling summarized

There is little need to dwell on the differences and similarities in the physiographic and climatic characteristics of the various political divisions of the Far North. In which country the most severe or strikingly beautiful physical environment can be found may be argued, but all countries share rugged terrain, long, dark, severe winters, compensated for only in part by brief, but bright, warm summers in some areas. Population numbers of each ethnic group are small and settlements are spaced far apart, a significant aspect of the population being its very low density, the number of people per square kilometer being among the lowest in the world in all cases. All of these extremes have shaped Native cultures and societies and exacerbate the problems of implementing and maintaining schools as much, or more, than any place in the world.

A review of historical developments in each country draws attention to the most prominent similarities and differences between the countries we cover. It is apparent that, fundamentally, the expansion of each school system has followed a pattern similar to the others, although circumstances and the chronology of each differed. Regardless of the age of the various systems, and they vary considerably, as recently as 25 years ago all school policies were made and administered from central capital cities, usually far distant from the schools themselves in each country we cover.

In Alaska, for example, in 1975, there were 175 village schools controlled and administered by centrally based agencies. The schools of the United States Bureau of Indian Affairs, administered from Washington, D.C., and Juneau, were found at 75 village locations. The Alaska State Operated School System administered schools at 100 remote sites from one central office in Anchorage. By 1976 there were no longer any centrally administered state schools and in 1985, after a presence of 100 years in Alaska, the last federal school was transferred to local, predominantly Native school districts. Now, there are 24 rural REAA and municipal school districts that have responsibility for all former federal and state operated schools. School board members by and large come from the local Native population. This vivid change came about because of a number of factors, but the most pervasive of them was the Alaska nativistic movement for self-determination at the political level.

In Canada, where all Northern schools were initially administered from Ottawa, the political dimension of schooling has undergone several changes during the past 25 to 30 years. It was in 1962 that these changes began with the creation of the Northwest Territories constituency (election district). This development enabled the entire population of the Northwest Territories to be represented in the federal government along with the southern half of Canada. As important as this step was, it was during the period 1965–74 that significant political changes in the government of the Northwest Territories came about. An increased number of representatives in the Territorial Assembly, more equitable distribution of constituency district membership, and elected rather than appointed assembly members all contributed to a stronger voice of Native peoples in government affairs. Some government functions were retained by the federal government, including education, but by 1970, education, always one of the most controversial of government services, was put under the jurisdiction of the new territorial government located in Yellowknife. As potentially promising as this development seemed at the time, little in the way of substantial education change took place at first. The system that emerged was a copy of the typical school system that was found elsewhere in Canada thereby reducing the likelihood that the school could truly serve the needs of Native communities.[1]

Although there was increased Inuit and Indian participation in political activities during this period, and "it was during the 1970s that the organizational capacity of the Inuit assumed national dimensions,"[2] it was not until 1979 that there was a shift from Euro-Canadians acting as mediators between the Inuit and the larger society in favor of the Inuit acting as their own mediators.[3]

While not all of these political developments were specifically related to education, it was during this period that education issues came to the forefront of territorial debate. And it was during this period that effective and respected Native organizations, such as Inuit Tapirisat of Canada (ITC), the Inuit Broadcasting Corporation (IBC), and the Inuit Cultural Institute (ICI) came into existence. It was at the close of this decade that ITC set forth its Nunavut proposal. This concept, calling for a separate territorial government in the Eastern Arctic, has many implications for Native involvement in the local control of education. Improvements in education now taking place had their beginning because of the devolution of central government that started 25 years earlier. Of special note, and somewhat as the culmination of this movement, the Nunavut Land Claims was finalized and passed into law in 1994. Nunavut, as a new political entity, will have an 85 percent Inuit population and thus, essentially, Inuit self-governance will come into being on April 1, 1999.

Elsewhere in the Canadian North, Native involvement in education in Arctic Quebec has made significant progress in the past 20 years. The Kativik School District has shown how well local groups can take on the responsibility for education. Among several innovative programs, the district has established a constructive relationship with McGill University and the Ministry of Educa-

---

1. Northwest Territories Legislative Assembly 1982.
2. Vallee, F.G., D.G. Smith, and J.D. Cooper, "Contemporary Canadian Inuit." In Damas (vol. ed.) 1984.
3. Vallee 1981, cited in Damas (vol. ed.) 1984.

tion in Montreal where Native curricula and language programs designed at the local level are supported.

Likewise, recent developments in the Yukon Territory are promising. In the late 1980s territorial officials, for the first time, took steps to provide an opportunity for Natives to participate in the development of the government's education programs. In a region where the Native population is small and the dominant Euro-Canadian majority for years was indifferent to Native needs, this development is in itself significant in Native–non-Native relationships. Even in Labrador, where Native interests were a long-neglected priority, consideration is now being given to Native needs.

Scandinavia

When missionaries introduced formal education in the 16th century in the North of Scandinavia, there was a twofold reason for the Crown to be engaged in missionary affairs. One was to use the missions to enforce the king's right to govern over ethnic minorities; the other was to Christianize and enlighten the heathens, in both cases the Saami. During the early years of the mission age income derived from the Saami, as tribute to the Crown, was levied through trade and direct taxation. At first, therefore, the Crown had an economic interest in allowing the indigenous people to utilize their land in traditional ways, primarily by producing trade goods. Later it was the land itself that was a source of income, not in traditional land use as it had been at first, but through the introduction of technology as a means to transform minerals, agricultural products, and marine resources into cash and political power.

This change, and its deleterious consequences, led to a different perception by the Crown of the role of the Saami population. Where indigenous knowledge, the culture of the people, had been the source of revenue at first, it became an obstacle to the king's accumulation of wealth. As the North became more developed the choice for the king, therefore, became one of deciding between a policy of cultural replacement, that is, transformation of the

Saami to the culture of the Crown, or of callously disregarding and overlooking the Saami's traditional rights to land and water. At times each of these alternatives was favored simultaneously. As elsewhere in the North, with cultural replacement the goal, formal schooling was seen as the way to achieve it.

Moreover, officials of the Church had their own reasons for establishing schools among the Saami other than those in the interest of the king. For Christians it was an imperative of their religious tenets to convert the heathen. For Protestants this first meant teaching them to read. Moreover, mission teachers had a strong belief in promoting the value of Western enlightenment and knowledge. This meant that the king and his fellow countrymen placed their culture in the dominant position by characterizing the indigenous people and their culture as inferior. Holding such a belief ostensibly gave the king a moral obligation to search for ways to promote cultural replacement.

The Saami perceived the situation in quite the opposite way. They were, after all, the majority population in their communities even though they were a small minority in the nation-wide society. In essence, they did not see themselves as inferior in any way. This difference in perspective combined with their deep-rooted, traditional interests explain why attempts to establish formal education systems among the Saami were often frustrating. For both the Saami and the state alike there were, at the macrolevel, conflicts in both short- and long-term planning. The state simply established a school among the Saami as it did any other school in the national system. Its organization and curriculum content were the same; everything about the school reflected the national society and its traditions. In some cases the minority population did not even want an education system at all.

At the microlevel, where the role of the school was unclear, there were other complicating factors. The interests and needs of individuals seldom overlapped or coincided with the needs of the community. Where parents saw the school as a threat to their community as a whole on the one hand, it could provide opportunities to some individuals on the other. For example, during times of food shortage or material scarcity, the boarding-school system meant both food and clothing for the children. But the most perplexing factor at the microlevel was the way the ultimate purpose of the school was perceived. Both the parents and the state believed that the only responsibility of the school and its teachers was to interact with individual pupils. This was largely due to the fact that the indigenous culture had no part to play in defining the role of the school, just as the state did not see itself as an agent in the management or development of the indigenous society. The state simply did not recognize the people as a distinct and unique body. Consequently, little thought was given to what the school was doing other than replacing the Saami society and culture as a whole. There is striking similarity between these perceptions and circumstances in Scandinavia and rest of the Far North.

This dilemma is now abating in Scandinavia, as elsewhere in the Far North. Over the past 20 years enabling laws favoring the Saami population have been enacted, primarily through the efforts of the Nordic-Saami Council, the Saami Education Council and the Saami Cultural College. The conceptualization of equality in terms of rights and in terms of humanitarian values is accepted by governments of all the Nordic countries. Today, it is, in principle, possible to allow the local society to be more and more the basis and the field of learning. But because Saamiland extends across three international boundaries the task of advancing Saami interests is more complex politically than elsewhere in the Far North; the process of achieving the present level of authority has been arduous. Two goals have been drawn up by the Saami Education Council as guides to further carry out this task: 1) the school must give the new generation of Saami possibilities to take an active part in societal interaction; and 2) at the same time and as part of societal interaction, the school must give the Saami the possibility both to conserve and further create their ethnic and cultural identity. These sweeping objectives apply equally to the rest of the Far North, just as they do to any society with ethnic minorities.

Greenland

While there are many similarities between Greenland and other Northern regions, school programs in Greenland at first developed along lines dissimilar from other Northern countries. Instead of the exclusive use of Danish teachers, most teachers were Greenlanders. Inuttitut, the first language of Greenlanders, was the language of instruction; in North America it was English, while in Scandinavia, the majority Scandinavian languages were alternated over the years with Saami. These early characteristics of schooling have made Greenland's history of education less similar to the other Circumpolar countries, but not so much so that problems there are different from elsewhere.

As early as the 1930s, prominent Greenlanders were working for the termination of the colonial status of Greenland. But it was not until the end of World War II and the new international order brought about by the creation of the United Nations that Greenland was recognized, in 1953, as an integral political unit of Denmark. Three years earlier a new school law had been passed that compelled a separation between the Church and the school system in an attempt to equalize educational opportunity between Denmark and Greenland. Consequently, many Danish teachers were introduced from abroad and Danish culture and language were reinforced through the Danification of the curriculum as never before.

Today in Greenland, issues in education go beyond schooling in the ordinary sense. Because Greenland has had home rule status and a significant amount of independence from Denmark since 1979, education is at the forefront of a new national purpose and character. At issue is nothing less than the means to develop a modern system of education that meets the needs of an emerging state. In this sense, Greenlanders are caught between their wish to be anchored to the traditional culture and value system and their desire to qualify the younger generation for a modern, internationally oriented society. The main dilemma in this regard, then, is to determine how to connect the past and the future in contemporary school programs while finding a balance in the content of each. A related problem, and one that sets Greenland apart from the other Circumpolar countries, is the debate that attempts to settle the argument whether Greenland should be more strongly connected to the culture and economy of North America or continue to be aligned with Denmark and Europe.

Four historical periods of educational development[4]

As we have seen, even though great distances and political boundaries separate inhabited places in the Far North there are more similarities in the historical development of education than differences. Likewise, problems associated with issues currently in contention are more alike than not from one country to the next. As Western society moved northward throughout the Circumpolar world, education programs were invariably implemented on the premise that members of that society knew what was best for the indigenous minority people found there. The need for "cultural replacement" and religious conversion were the prevailing reasons given for initiating most "civilizing" programs. Alternative programs that nourished cultural reinforcement were seldom tried. As a consequence, schools eventually became a source of discontent among the Native population resulting in the movement for Native self-determination the second half of the 20th century. Four historical periods common to all Circumpolar countries distinguish this movement.

The first period covers those years soon after Western contact with the indigenous population. It is characterized by missionary and government teachers who held conformist views of Western culture. These teachers were dedicated to strict adherence to inflexible rules of behavior, rules that were at great variance from traditional Native conventions. School policies decreed replacement of Native culture with Western practices and fundamental-

4. Adapted from Darnell, Frank, "Education and the Circumpolar Nativistic Movement: Twenty Years of Change for the Better." In Farrow and Wilman (eds.) 1989.

ist Christianity. Although this conflict of values resulted in confusion on the part of Native peoples, they accepted the coming of schools, in large part out of natural curiosity. This is not to say that schools were embraced, but they were not challenged. During this period the Native population did not know how to act collectively nor would they have necessarily wanted to. They were too widely dispersed and too worldly innocent to recognize the consequences schools of that period were eventually to have for their societies. Although attending school, which required sedentary, repetitious, and compulsory behavior, was unfamiliar to Native life style it was tolerated. Nevertheless, traditional Native customs continued to guide society; hunting and traditional subsistence life style were still the prevailing means to sustain life and were the focus of village activities.

In each country, missionary teachers were followed by government teachers who were strongly influenced by the type of school programs that had been implemented up to that time. Furthermore, in all cases, they had been selected and assigned to their positions by bureaucratic agencies located far from the scene of operation. Most importantly, however, teachers emulated the widespread conservative values of the majority society of that day; schools were expected to reflect, indeed, to promote them. It is important to keep the context of the times in mind when trying to assess the motives, means, and methods of school officials of those times in order to avoid unjust criticism of their practices.

In addition to the conservative nature of education institutions of that day, the Native population was far from prepared to suggest alternatives to school programs then being offered. Although complex Native cultures were to be found throughout the North, they were largely limited to uncompromising ancient life styles, life styles that were dictated by the extreme harshness of subsistence economics and constant battles with nature to overcome shortages of the basics necessary to sustain life. Little time was left for what could be called the necessities of Western life style such as a written language, let alone the amenities of the late 20th century. Depending on the particular historical growth of schooling in each country (or regions within countries), this period varied considerably in length; in parts of Greenland and Scandinavia it exceeded 200 years while in parts of Canada and Alaska, it lasted no longer than 20. Regardless of its length, this period started to come to a close *simultaneously* throughout the entire Far North during the 1950s.

Occasional statements of discontent with the content and methodology of education, especially during the latter part of the 1950s, marked the beginning of the second period and signaled a break with the Native passivity of the past. Dissatisfaction with the education system was first made known by a few scattered Native groups, but little heed was given to them by non-Native school authorities. In particular, this period, which was to last no more than ten years, was characterized by a heightened awareness of a need for change and increasingly the content and methodology of formal education were disputed. Such a level of discontent is an interesting paradox. Acquisition of the skills necessary to make an effective protest, literacy, and a sophisticated knowledge of the rest of the world, were learned through the schools that were being challenged. Nevertheless, central governmental authorities were able to deflect criticism and successfully defend their policies and programs or, alternatively, simply ignore them. With but few exceptions, non-Natives continued to make all of the major decisions affecting the educational policies in all of the countries of the Far North.

The third period, which commenced during the mid- to late 1960s, also lasted about ten years. This period saw the beginning of sustained assertiveness by Native groups and their rejection of what they perceived to be an inappropriate and inadequate school system. In each of the Circumpolar countries newly established Native political organizations sought to acquire political influence in the making of education policy or to have a say in the development of Native-specific programs. In some instances, efforts by Native groups were joined by academicians whose studies of schooling in Northern societies documented what Natives were learning through experience. In particular, findings of scholarly work at the Institute for Educational Research at the University of Oslo, the Institute of Eskimology at the University of Copenhagen,

McGill University in Montreal, the University of Saskatchewan at Saskatoon, and the University of Alaska Fairbanks confirmed the assertions of Native groups. This development, coming at about the same time all across the Far North illustrates the extent to which Northern Natives had become part of the movement for human rights and self-determination then taking place among ethnic minorities worldwide.

Government agencies charged with the responsibility of education were no longer able to defend their programs and practices or to ignore the growing discontent. Some agencies began looking for positive ways to respond to declared Native needs, others for ways to postpone implementation of the demands of Native groups, even as it became increasingly clear that change was inevitable. It was at the close of the third period, then, that two conflicting points of view emerged as the most vexing problem of the day. One side argued that the goal of formal education should be to straighten cultural continuity while the other advocated cultural replacement as the goal. Protagonists on both sides of the debate grew increasingly polarized. Cultural replacement was generally favored by those who were inclined toward Westernized exploitation of natural resources or were central government officials. They saw programs, in content and method similar to broad national programs, as the key to incorporate hitherto isolated peoples into Western society. The goal of cultural continuity was supported by those concerned with community improvement along local, traditional lines in which Native languages and culture in the classroom were favored and respected, especially as a means to strengthen individual self-respect and reliance.

The fourth and present period emerged in the mid-1970s. Although the issues discussed in the previous chapters remain unresolved, the current period is characterized by the attainment of a variety of political provisions that accommodate Native self-determination in all of the Western Circumpolar world. This period also is characterized by governmental awareness of Native needs and, in many cases, by cooperative programs in the development of Native-specific education. Moreover, it now appears that policies and programs that lead to attainment of a balanced combination of programs that support both cultural replacement and cultural continuity are the most promising. Ideally, it is argued, the two schools of thought taken in combination, aptly named "cultural synthesis," may provide the means for individuals to grow intellectually and succeed economically in the Western world while taking pride as members of a Native society. Furthermore, the other purpose of education – maintenance and improvement of society – will be advanced as well. However, even though gains made during the current period are substantial, they have yet to produce results to the extent predicted or sought.

Given that most political developments are now looked upon in a positive light in both Native and non-Native circles, it is perplexing that Native social conditions are so destabilized and that individual pupil achievements remain so far below the educational norms of the countries of which they are a part. This may be attributed in part to the fact that, historically, all Native groups have, to a greater or lesser degree, experienced some loss of their traditional way of life without acquiring a satisfactory replacement and have witnessed exploitation of their natural resources. But given the positive political developments of the past 10 to 20 years, these reasons do not sufficiently explain the dilemma. Thus, the two most vexing question of all remain:

1. Why is Native student performance still not on par with the national society at large?
2. Why does low self-image among so many pupils, often leading to destructive behavior, remain so prevalent?

Definitive answers to these question await the results of future developments and research, but the lessons we have learned from our personal observations over the years may contribute some background to the debate.

Lessons learned

Much of what we have learned has been woven into the preceding text so it is not necessary to labor the points made in the topics covered there. Rather, in this section we pick up on points that may fill out those topics in a more philosophical way as a means to conclude them.

Under the topics of organizational structure and locus of control we have little to add to what has already been covered except to introduce the subject of accountability. Schools now established for minority indigenous populations often are anomalies among the states' school systems of which they are a part. Nevertheless, they owe their existence to the national governments that give them credibility in law and support them financially; the reality is that they are creatures of the state and have certain obligations to that state as well as to the community they serve. Accordingly, the state has a vested interest in their performance, regardless of the degree to which districts may be locally controlled.

Although conflict resolution between local and state factions in recent years has preferred devolution of authority in favor of Native groups, as we believe it quite appropriately should, this does not abrogate the state's responsibility to oversee the results of this development. The interest of the state remains fundamental. This situation requires that the state employ a system of evaluation that is acceptable at both the local and central levels. Such a system is not necessarily easy to devise. As pointed out by Hans W. Weiler, "Modern, pluralist societies face increasingly a lack of consensus on the objectives of education, and hence on the criteria for evaluating the performance of educational systems."[5] This view is consistent with what we have learned in the Far North and suggests a problem that has the potential to interfere with the desires of the emerging Native-controlled boards of education.

Because the state has the ultimate responsibility for the education of its citizen, regardless of how much authority it has decentralized in favor of local communities, its oversight function remains essential to the well-being of the population at large. While devolution of authority is likely to improve decision-making opportunities at the local level, it creates the potential for school programs that fail to accommodate national interests. Moreover, as contended by Weiler, "redistribution of power seems largely

5. Weiler 1990, p. 7.

incompatible with the manifest interests of the modern state in maintaining effective control and in discharging some of its key functions."[6] Ultimately, decentralization without sufficient oversight raises the risk of the state's loss of its own legitimacy. Thus, with local and state interests often at odds, the perennial problem of how best to achieve balance between them will continue to confront opposing forces in multicultural national societies. Realistic expectations of schools by both Native groups and the state may be one means to eventually resolve this problem.

Of all the lessons learned over the years, we believe that teachers still are the most important link in the processes of formal schooling. As an extension to this belief we need also to stress that the right to this distinction carries with it a prodigious responsibility. By accepting the role of teacher, one becomes the surrogate for an entire community. This can best be illustrated with a statement from the Alaska Eskimo educational and cultural corporation, Yupiktak Bista:

> Before the erection of school houses and the introduction of professional teachers to whom Western civilization entrusts the minds of their children, education was growing up in a village. Education was done in the home with the father, mother, grandmother, grandfather, brother, sister, uncles, aunts, cousins, and friends. Education was also given by the weather, the sea, the fish, the animals and the land. Children at a very early age came to terms with the elements. We did not worry about relating education to life, because learning came naturally as part of living. Education was the process of living from the land, of subsisting, of surviving.
>
> The coming of Western civilization broke this unity and living. Suddenly survival depended upon knowing a new language, new skills and new ways of relating to people and the world. Today we have entrusted the minds of our young to professional teachers who seemingly know all there is to know. They are teaching a child how to read, write, repair a car, weld two pipes together. But they are not teaching the child the most important thing. Who he is: an Eskimo or Indian with a history full of folklore, music, great men, medicine, a philosophy, complete with poets; in short, there was a civilization, a culture which survived the harshest of environments for thousands of years. Now this culture and subsistence

6. Ibid., p. 10.

> way of life are being swept away by books, patents, money and corporations.[7]

Teachers, either experienced or newly trained, Native or non-Native, when accepting a place in the education of Native children, need to ponder this statement and assure themselves that they are both intellectually and psychologically prepared to assume the responsibility it implies. Good teachers, either Native or non-Native, come from many backgrounds. And, we should add, we believe that being Native, while that status may enhance a teacher's position in the classroom, is neither a sufficient nor a necessary condition for success as a teacher in a Native community. Nevertheless, it is an important characteristic that can provide the motivation for students to relate more positively to school and demonstrates that their patrimony is important. But given no more than the problem of supply and demand, recruiting a cadre of teachers that is 100 percent Native in any of the Circumpolar countries is unrealistic, although 85 percent is proving to be realistic in Nunavut. But that should not be an issue; all teachers, if their comprehension of what multicultural teaching entails is commensurate with the needs of their students, are likely to be successful.

As well as having responsibility for perpetuating the culture of a society, the intellectual and social development of individual students has always been a fundamental purpose of schools. On a daily basis, school personnel are compelled by the routine of the day to think in terms of individual pupils far more often than they think of society as a whole. Typically, this has always been a reasonable expectation of teachers everywhere. However, attention to individual needs too often is apt to be limited to mundane classroom exercises instead of dealing with ways to cope intellectually with individual learning problems. And taking responsibility for affecting long-term personality characteristics and the development of pupils' self-identity is usually beyond the training of most teachers. In schools for indigenous minorities this reality is a

7. Bista, Yupiktak, "Education and the Subsistence Way of Life." In Barnhardt (ed.) 1977, p. 71.

problem with greater personal consequences than it would be in a typical urban, Western school. Moreover, as Spindler has pointed out,

> the search for identity is a constant process in all human beings as members of cultural systems and ... this process becomes acute when divergent cultural systems come into contact. Education in such circumstances can foster identity conflict by forcing people to choose between two contrasting sets of values, role expectations, and models for identification, or it can promote cultural synthesis.[8]

This observation is analogous to our own perceptions; it is a blending of cultural synthesis with respect for other cultures in school programs that is among the most promising of all approaches to improved student performance in the Far North. Such an approach avoids the need for students to choose between two conflicting value systems. Schools constituted in this way take on the characteristics of the best of contemporary, restructured schools anywhere and thereby have the potential to resolve past problems as well as prepare students for the future.

In all of the domains of education in the Far North, problems associated with providing education that fits both the traditional and contemporary needs of the indigenous peoples grow increasingly complex each year. The role educational research can play in resolving these problems should be among the most important. And although much of this book, as explained in the first chapter, is derived from our personal observations and, as such, is a narrative about what we have learned, we have also been dependent on the work of many others. What we have learned about the processes of research among indigenous minorities may bear on future work of the research community.

Although the research community has become increasingly active in the development of educational systems and programs in the Far North during the past decade, research findings have not been without their limitations. When the influence of researchers has been most effective, it has been when they have refrained from playing the role of advocate for a particular position. Ideally, when

8. Spindler 1968, cited in Darnell (ed.) 1970, p. 49.

they have taken an objective and neutral position, and have described the pros and cons of a topic of contention, they have acquired influence in both the ethnic minority communities and the political and administrative systems of the nation-wide society. But gaining this influence has been limited to only a few researchers and their work has not been without its problems. To reach a position of influence, successful researchers have had to acquire the confidence of members of Native communities, officials in the education and social agencies of the nation-wide society, and colleagues in the research community, an undertaking that requires considerable sincerity of purpose and objectivity. Essentially, social scientists have had to demonstrate an ability to truly understand the Native society, to communicate within it in the context of Native cognitive style, and demonstrate that their findings are valid and relevant. This demands that researchers acquire a respect for the community in which they work and a perspective from both inside and outside their projects. This means that they must be able to demonstrate an ability to combine the role of scientist on the one hand with the role of participant in the local community on the other.

Furthermore, preconditions necessary to gain an effective position among these groups are tied to an ability to demonstrate close adherence to the rules of scientific ethics, competence in research methodology, and skill in solving practical problems in investigations in the fields. Of course, these are requirements of researchers everywhere, but in the Far North they are compounded because of their relationship to the ethnic dimension of Native communities and the ability of social scientists to deal with them. In short, this means there is a compelling need to have the ability to be both an insider and an outsider whenever possible. As pointed out by Spindler and Spindler,

> education is a cultural process ... [and] in every cultural setting, is an instrument for survival. It is also an instrument for adaptation and change. To understand education we must study it as it is – embedded in the culture of which it is an integral part and which it serves.[9]

9. Spindler, G., and L. Spindler, foreword to King 1967, p. v.

Over the years this is what successful researchers in the Far North have attempted to do.

> When education is studied this way, the generalizations about the relationship between schools and communities, educational and social systems, education and cultural setting that are current in modern educational discussions, become meaningful.[10]

Even when these aspects of research in ethnic communities are understood, research efforts still sometimes fail. When this happens, the obstacle to success is usually due to a focus that is limited to purely theoretical matters and lack of experience or understanding in ways theories can be implemented in practical situations. Typically, therefore, some researchers often have been portrayed as unduly idealistic, impractical, and out of touch with the reality of the situations they study.

Singularity of thought is another problem attributed to the research community. As a rule, social scientists confine their work to the tradition of a particular discipline; there is inadequate communication among scholars in the various fields and even less with practitioners. An equally troublesome shortcoming is how few researchers take into consideration the circumstances of educational systems as integral components of the society. As a means to develop a comprehensive body of knowledge concerned with education in Native communities, this is an essential.

The consequences of this situation are manifold. First, practitioners have to combine findings from various disciplines in order to use them to improve the educational system. Secondly, when social scientists from outside education fail to understand the practical side of education, the uniqueness of education as an object of study is inaccessible to them. Finally, as long as the field of education does not have a body of knowledge or theories of its own that are drawn from the field of education itself, the possibilities to improve school systems through research will remain few in number.

10. Ibid.

Having pointed out these shortcomings of research it is necessary to emphasize that there have, nevertheless, been several notable efforts that have contributed to our understanding of education. Research, especially research that was carried out during the third historical period of school development described above, has been especially important to an understanding of the evolution of the schools.

Conclusion

Probably the most profound characteristics of the indigenous peoples of the Far North has been their ability to adjust to change. This characteristic stands out as one of the most enduring qualities of Native culture, a quality derived from centuries of adjustments to the harsh vicissitudes of nature. Where the ability to accept change is resolute, flexibility comes naturally. It is this quality, when applied to the school, that reinforces the view of contemporary school-reform advocates that the need to be flexible in the development of the curriculum, professional development of the teaching staff, the language of instruction, and organizational structure of the school is essential.

Before turning to the last chapter and our notions about emerging theories of education in multicultural societies we return to the query of the Tununuk village elder on the first page of Chapter 1: "Why is it that the kids who finish school do not know any more than I do?" To decide whether we have answered this question requires that we first examine the premise upon which the question was based. That is, do graduates of the Tununuk school indeed know no more than he? The answer depends on what he meant by "know." If it is what he knows about Yup'ik culture, the intricacies of Tununuk society, and the ways of survival in a subsistence economy then it is certain that those now finishing school know less than he. Likewise, if by inference the elder's question is, Why do the kids who finish this school not know any more than I do *about how to be a contributing member of this community?* his premise is valid. In these instances, the answer to his question of why, then, simply put, is because the school, with its uniform Western philosophy, goals of education, and value system, was not designed with his traditional purposes of education, the perpetuation of his culture, an objective.

We have seen that when formal education was first introduced in Tununuk, as well as the rest of the North, school policies, programs, and the means for their implementation were decided without the involvement or consent of the people they were intended to affect. Western assimilationist education was seen as the means to Christianize and civilize a population in need of redemption. As recently as 25 years ago, educational policies were designed solely to accommodate the language, cultural values, economic systems, and general interests of the dominant Western society. Although this is no longer so and opportunities for promising improvements are now at hand, it remains a disturbing fact that student performance is still far from adequate.

Historically, education has been viewed as the primary arena through which states advance social agendas and establish terms of intergroup relations. Accordingly, goals of education define the philosophy by which these characteristics of society are shaped. As noted in Part One, when the culture of the society is the same as the culture of those that define the processes and programs of education, the two groups will be in accord. However, in communities with minority–majority relationships this accord may be lacking. Findings from research done in Scandinavia in the 1960s illustrate this phenomenon. Hoëm concluded from his investigation of the effects of state-defined and -provided schooling among the Saami population that

> investments in special training for teachers, printing of text-books and literature in Lappish, introduction of Lappish language and culture as subjects are efforts to raise the efficiency of teaching within the established system [that is, the Western model of school organization, curriculum and practices]. They are not efforts to adapt the school to the particular needs and values of the Lappish society. Therefore one will find different norms and values in the school and the home, and different behavioral standards. In fact, the more efficient is the teaching, the greater is the discrepancy between goals of education at home and in the school. This makes formal education an unnecessarily difficult process. The result is a

> cultural and social gap between the most successful pupils and the local Lapp society.[11]

This finding remains an accurate description of the situation in many locations today. It is a problem common in all countries we have studied and can be observed universally across the Far North, albeit not in like manner in all schools. Now, however, in each country, governments recognize that there is a need for the norms and values of the school and society to be brought more closely together. Unfortunately, recognition of this principle does not always guarantee that it will be put into practice. But where it has been possible for programs to be developed on this premise, invariably it will be found that there was some form of formal cooperation between the school and the society.

Perhaps the best way to summarize this concept is to turn to a statement made at the time of the first International Seminar on Cross-cultural Education in the Circumpolar North held in Fairbanks in 1976. Martha Teeluk, a Yup'ik Eskimo who was raised in a traditional Eskimo society but who was also a pioneer in the development of an orthography for the Yup'ik language while working as a linguist at the Alaska Native Language Center at the University of Alaska Fairbanks, captured the essence of traditional knowledge as it applies to schooling. In response to a discussion during the seminar in which the pros and cons of including detailed aspects of traditional material culture, life style, and Native languages in Native schools had been debated, Teeluk wrote the following to the seminar organizers:

> In my opinion, Natives as a whole are searching for something a little bit more abstract but in a sense have not found a means to express this. I have thought about this many times. What Native people are asking for is to introduce the *philosophy* of the Native cultures. It is that thing that made a Native a good useful Native. Learning about our traditional lifestyles is good for the sake of history, but may I dare say that most of the traditional life styles do not apply to the present day Native.

---

11. Hoëm, Anton, "Samer, Skole og Samfunn," as translated and cited by Ulsby, I.B., "Norwegian Cross-Cultural Programs for Lapp Societies." In Darnell (ed.) 1970, p. 272.

> I travel quite extensively to different areas all over Alaska. I come in contact with Native people in their own settings. True, some people still hunt and fish for subsistence, but let us look at the methods of hunting. At one of the villages, where I had the good fortune of being weathered in, I was taken on a moose hunt with my hosts. We went in a big tractor on a road that was built by miners in the early 1900s. We brought lunches of fruit juice, crackers, soda pop and candy. This was so different from former methods where the family left early in the morning and spent the day calling for moose and waiting for them to show up.
>
> The village had no electricity nor running water, but it does not stop the women from using gas-powered washing machines. There are radios almost in every house and out-board motors traverse the Yukon river. Children are in school from nine to four. When the weather permits there are planes coming in and out of the village. The people want electricity and running water and I am sure they will get them in the near future. What I am saying is that Native people are making progress every day whether they realize it or not....
>
> The Native's interpretation of a good Native was one who was responsible, one who took his responsibility (raising and supporting a family) seriously. He had respect for other people. Family problems were taken care of at that level.... Why can't we continue in the good philosophy of our ancestors. Isn't that what we are searching for? I do not see how romanticizing the study of our heritage and language can help us run the [business of our Native settlement] corporations. I think the Native people need to stop and take a good, hard, serious look at where to go from here. Let's stop living in the past, but let us look at the present situation and plan for the future.[12]

It is the depth of feeling for values and self-worth that Teeluk alludes to that holds hope for the future of Native societies. These features of a culture's basic nature may be intangible, unlike physical trappings that can be held or seen, but they are the essence of qualities that have the potential to eventually lead to better schools, and improved pupil performance and self-image.

With this understanding we conclude our narrative. However, by looking back over what we have covered, it affords us the opportunity to depart from the format we have used throughout the text and move into a more hypothetical world that may apply

---

12. Teeluk, Martha, personal communication, 1976, on file in the Archives of the University of Alaska Fairbanks.

to multicultural societies anywhere. In a way the next chapter stands on its own as an abstraction of what we perceive is the essence of our subject. At least, that is the way we hope our final chapter will be seen.

Chapter 7

Emerging Theories of Education in Multicultural Societies

From what has been said in the preceding chapters, education is seen as an ongoing process that imbeds or includes almost every aspect of the society and every dimension of man. The outcome of the process has a paradoxical character: it anticipates both continuity and change, conformity and originality, and submission and freedom.

Ideally, the processes of education affect the society and individual intentionally in a fundamental and permanent way. In the immediate, daily life of a community this result is hardly discernible. The community's cultural processes go on seemingly without any connection to the educational system. At the same time life in the schools goes on. In the school's relationship to students an immediate effect can be seen, while its influence on the culture can only be recorded over a much longer span of time. Some students are successful and they can not imagine a more relevant life than that of studying. They have chosen the school as their world. Others, as underachievers, become dropouts and much is forgotten the moment they have completed their final examinations. The most lasting outcome of their education is a determination to never again attend school. Through all this the school itself remains little changed as it meets new generations of students.

In daily life the school has the potential to provide all students, as well as society, with the opportunity for intellectual and personal experiences, but at the likely expense of what the student brings with him to the school if the background of the students differs culturally from that of the school. It is axiomatic that it is only to the degree that the school is able to release the potential intellectual growth of it students (or the community), that it is able to reach its goals. On the other hand, it is only to the degree that the student is able to trust his personal and cultural abilities that he is able to be successful. A comprehensive theory of the school, therefore, should at least include these fundamental notions.

The school as a social system

Rhetorically, it can be said that the school has to be a part of the world to function in the world. Theoretically, the meaning of this can be formulated as follows: On the macrolevel the school can be understood as a social system which constitutes a subsystem of the total society. When so composed, it is the degree of integration between the sub- and the total system that determines the way and extent to which the subsystem will function.[1]

The subsystem can be seen as the educational system and the total system as the society at large. Or the subsystem can be determined as a single school and the total system can be seen as the educational system of, for example, a municipality. Likewise, the subsystem can be seen as the school's relationship to an ethnic minority and the total system as the national system. The important part of this interpretation is that the school always has to be seen as a part of a larger system and that the total system can be made as small or large as is necessary, depending on the actual problem being dealt with. Accordingly, the basic principle for a school or an educational system is the same, independent of where the education process is taking place. Manifestation of this basic principle will, of course, be different depending on the circumstances, for example, in a multiethnic enclave, in a culturally homogeneous suburb, or in the most remote or isolated places of the nation. Thus, when dealing with educational problems where there is the greatest amount of difference between subsystems

1. Hoëm 1990b.

and the total system, the challenge will be how best to relate the different parts of the process to the basic principle of which they are a manifestation.

Relative size and power

The relative size of the parts, for instance the school and surrounding society, will have an influence on their function and capacity to be effective. And, of course, the influence of size works both ways, that is, the school will influence the society and the society will influence the school. But as a general rule the surrounding society will have a greater impact on the school than the school will have on the society. However, there is one impressive exception to this; it is the relationship between school and society in small villages of indigenous peoples. In these cases the very fact that the school is a local agency within a nation-wide system has an important bearing on the outcome of schooling; it is indifferent to the culture of the people it is intended to serve. As a consequence of this relationship, the school will be constituted and operated on its own, without community involvement. Since the school is unaffected by the indigenous society, it therefore lacks the ability to influence the local society in a meaningful and profound way. This is the case when the school is not a part of the world of which it should be, that is, when it is not integrated in the community.[2]

A standard school program in a rural, isolated ethnic community is an example of such a non-integrated system. The school and community do not have the same relationship found in a normal, functioning educational system. Rather they become a disintegrated system, although the school and the local community still have the capacity to maintain themselves and to affect each other. However, because situations vary so much from place to place, forecasting that effect is problematic at best. Furthermore, the sources of power on each side are of a different kind than is the case where there are typical urban schools in typical urban sur-

2. Hoëm 1976a.

roundings. However, the relative power of an integrated system is always strongest in the larger unit. In a disintegrated system, however, it is of no consequence to compare the relative parts as if they were a component of an integrated system. In such cases it is necessary first to identify the parts of the former system that are constituted in the new one. It then becomes possible to identify the relative power of the parts and the function of the new system.

Four vital dimensions of integration

The potential for integration between the parts in question, for example between a local school and the surrounding community, can be examined from several perspectives. In this case we have defined degrees of integration according to four categories or dimensions of the school and community: technology, economic systems, social order, and aestheticism (including spirituality). These dimensions are among the most important components of culture. They also cover or embody levels of insight and wisdom in the culture as well as levels of ability to perform any given task; accordingly each can be differentiated. These levels include all variations of technology from the simple to the complex, economic systems that range from subsistence to market, social orders from structure and values in an isolated rural community to a modern megalopolis, and the aesthetic from artistic sensitivity to the metaphysical. In short, the levels range from uniplex to multiplex components of society.

Communities, schools, and cultures vary in unique and primary potentialities. Therefore, the level of precision with which these dimensions are defined should be determined in accordance with the actual level of activity or programs being dealt with. For example, in a vocational school in an industrial region, technology and economics matters will have a high standing, just as myths, and supernatural and metaphysical beliefs will be almost non-existent. In a sectarian congregation and its associated schools the opposite may be the case.

Phenomena at the community level

At the microlevel of traditional societies the elders represent living history, thereby reminding the population of its obligations to maintain its cultural heritage. Members of the working age group, then, are caught between what seem to them to be the reality of today's employment and social opportunities on the one hand, and obligations to maintain traditions as defined by the elders on the other. Due to the nature of their indigenous culture, every conflicting situation has to be seen from a holistic perspective while simultaneously being judged in accordance with the mono-functional standards of the Western world.

Children and youth experience this conflict as cultural dissonance, similar to adults, but often with more long-lasting, unexpected, and even damaging consequences. The result of this conflicting perspective is that children find themselves in a world of their own, a world which is neither that of their parents nor the outside world.[3]

Differences in gender also are affected by this conflict. Boys and men have tended to be more traditional than girls and women. Boys have dropped out of school more often than girls and make their living in traditional subsistence pursuits rather than "white collar" occupations, although, paradoxically, boys and men are more apt to use technical equipment than women (except, in some cases, computers).

In dealing with everyday life, in all types of situations, people are constantly contrasting new and old ways. Community influences that argue for the preservation of ethnic traditions are set against the urge to adopt new and tempting alternatives. Moreover, discrimination from conservative elements within the community exerts pressure on village residents to retain traditional life styles. This is in contrast to pressure in the schools where pupils are provided with many alternative opportunities from Western society, if they are willing to forgo their heritage, a most unfair trade. Thus, we find that in Native villages there are two

3. Høgmo 1986, pp. 395–417.

primary contrasting or competing forces: patrimonial ethnicity which gives rise to local discrimination which in turn ties people to their past, and the forces of schooling and urbanization that draw people away from their origins and place them in a new and uncertain cultural context.

Throughout this book we have maintained that the optimal learning situation is when the integration levels between the school and society are equal, that is where they are culturally homogeneous. However, it will only be in rare situations when the school and society are found in such balance. The degree of integration and singularity of purpose in any given situation will usually differ among the four dimensions. Thus, it could be that a profile of the levels of integration among the four dimensions can be the best predictors of how well and to what degree a school will function adequately or be capable of achieving its goals. An example of an inadequately integrated system can be found where a community is still dependent on a subsistence economy, but where the school has a curriculum based on contemporary urban society, some instruction is given in the mother tongue of the indigenous society, teachers are recruited from outside the community, and the school building is of the most modern design. It can be predicted that in such cases the school will be functioning at inadequate levels of instruction and pupil achievement.

Conversely, if the general degree of integration between the system and the subsystem is above a certain or critical level, the culture of the units involved will reinforce each other and will have cultural vitality and ongoing, planned development will be possible.

If an adequate degree of integration between the units in the system is lacking, the units may impair or extinguish each other. In such cases the weakest unit of a system may decline in its cultural attributes accompanied by the strengthening of the culture of the other units. Which of the cultures will be weakened and which will be strengthened depends on the relative power or influence of the parts involved. For instance, where a community has modernized in relation to the outside world and the school is oriented in a substantial way toward the traditional ethnic society one will have to give way to the other to achieve equilibrium.

Balance within and between systems

Where the line between that point that causes systems to shift from cultural reinforcement to cultural extinction is located, for example from a predictable and highly effective school to an unpredictable and inadequately functioning school, is an empirical question. Nevertheless, it can be said that there has to be a balance between the interacting units that comprise the system. There also has to be a balance or equal proportion of the relative power of the interacting parts within a system or between systems to achieve equilibrium. This suggests, for instance, that there has to be at least a minimum of conformity between the development of society and the school. Furthermore it implies that a school has to maintain a balanced sense of importance for each subject taught. By this is meant that, although they may be given a different rank order of importance in the curriculum, all subjects must be accorded the status of a valid subject. Differences in quality of facilities and levels of subject importance notwithstanding, peripheral subjects should not be considered or made to appear inferior.

Change

Tension between units or components in a social system create incentives for change. Likewise, tensions between social systems in their entirety will result in change. Such tensions can be measured by the degree of congruence between the four dimensions that characterize all social systems, referred to above. Traditionally oriented culture and modern expressions of art can initiate change in the cultural orientation of the school, just as can modern technology and traditional norms and values. If there is a certain degree of congruence between the four dimensions there will be a movement for change that can lead in a planned direction. If the divergences between the four dimensions are out of proportion, change will not be manageable and the processes will get out of control.

For example, in a school where different subjects are recognized as basic but, nevertheless, are perceived as being of unequal importance by each interacting group, unplanned, and most likely, undesirable change is likely to occur. Furthermore, in a school where there is complete disagreement concerning the importance of different subjects by the interacting groups, the function of the school will be weakened and unpredictable. This will also be the case if the teachers give formal education high value while the parents strongly favor traditional Native knowledge. Thus, it can be seen that the outcome of interaction between the school and the local community, just as it will be between the educational system and the nation-wide society, will also depend on the profile of the four dimensions that characterize them. In short, and in either case, if there is a certain degree of continuity, each will reinforce the other in an intended and positive way.

Schooling as a socialization process

On the macrolevel it is said that the degree of integration between an entire system and its subsystems will determine how and to what degree the system will function. That is, different processes and levels of socialization will develop as a result of the levels of integration between its component parts. Where there is cultural homogeneity or a complementary relationship between the home and the school, each will reinforce the other. Furthermore, formal schooling will reinforce normal processes of socialization that typically take place in any societies.

Conversely, if the cultural background of the students and the culture of the school lack symmetry there will be conflict. The cultural influence of the school will tend to weaken the self-concept and identity of the students, render their patrimonial background irrelevant and desocialization and resocialization will occur. The socialization process taking place in a well-balanced school will connect the students to essential elements and sectors of the society in which the school is found. However, in a school where groups of teachers differ as to the purpose of the school, the resultant conflict will most likely make the outcome of formal socialization aimless, unintended, and unpredictable. This will especially be the case in minority situations if the culture of the school differs significantly from influential and/or powerful institutions such as mass media, the pop culture, and the credit card economy. In short, as the preceding chapters make clear, it can be stated that there must be a considerable degree of congruence between the values espoused by the school and the significant institutions of the society before the school can achieve its goals.

The macrophenomena of the school

Throughout the Western world the school is a specialized institution with one primary function: to educate children – regardless of how the purposes of education have been perceived, or the methods used to achieve those purposes. Historically those purposes have been to socialize students so that they adhere to the standards and customs of the majority society.

In the typical indigenous community in the Far North the upbringing of children is interwoven into most of the various kinds of activities that go to make up village life. These activities have at least two educational functions: one is to prepare children to qualify as members of their society, the other is to contribute to the requirements of daily living. As a consequence, village schools organized on the Western model face the dilemma of how best to achieve credibility among members of the society they serve; they need approval from the local community, on the one hand, while clinging to the idea that education is a specialized, Westernized function, different from traditional indigenous ways and purposes of bringing up children, on the other.

Furthermore, the school as an alien institution is organized principally as a reflection of schools in an urban society. This assumes that its clientele come from a dense, specialized, vocationally differentiated population devoid of child labor. Because these features of society are not found in indigenous societies in the Far North, there are attempts to compensate for them with provisions such as boarding schools, bussing to central locations, or schools too small to be organized on an urban model, but nevertheless are.[4] Such efforts simply have failed to fit the community. By making the terrain fit the map rather than the map fit the terrain, they invariably create new problems. This may best be demonstrated by examining how the aims or goals of the school are formulated. If the school is to contribute to the development and maintenance of the indigenous culture it means that the school must take on the many different functions imbedded in the traditional rearing of children while simultaneously functioning as a modern, specialized educational institution. Consequently, to be able to deal with education in a contemporary indigenous society, planners have to be aware of the main characteristics of traditional child-rearing customs and combine them with the functions of a modern school. To do this requires a basic understanding of the social meaning of education in both the traditional Native and Western senses.

One strategy school officials have used to cope with the complexities of this situation has simply been to ignore them. A less frequent but more constructive way has been to introduce Native languages in the curriculum, in part as a means to improve communication between teachers and students, but also to utilize the Native language as the mode of instruction where the language is still viable. Where the language is no longer in daily use, it has been introduced as a subject for study. Still another solution has been to add subject matter related to Native culture, such as Native arts, crafts, and lore, and the use and fabrication of the material culture, in the curriculum. Because this approach has its focus on the individual person, but the problem has it roots at the macrolevel, namely, the disparity between the school and surrounding society, it tends more to deprive the school of solutions to their problems than to remedy them.

Differences between school-year calendars and the seasonally determined working year illustrate this difference, as do differences between the social structure of the society and structure of the school. Likewise, differences between the community's conception of what constitutes adequate knowledge and some of the

4. Hoëm 1976a, 1976b, 1990b.

subjects offered at school, as well as the practical, tangible goals and aspersions of parents for their children compared with abstract qualifications offered by the school, are other examples of discrepancies between the community and the school.

The microphenomena of the school

As can be seen in the preceding chapters, the framework of the school in the Far North has been much the same as in the majority society from which it derived. In short, a school is a school. However, in Native villages the school is something else as well, for it is the place where the culture of the outside world and the culture of the indigenous society meet. It, therefore, is where conflicts between cultures are the most persistent. It is also where the most significant trials have been made between what some consider the most idealistic pedagogical approach to learning, the use of the Native first language, and what others consider the most realistic and practical, the official language of the nation-wide society. And in recent years much attention has been given to implementation of more structured classrooms and numerous contemporary pedagogical innovations have been tried. What is striking about these attempts to improve education, as well-meaning as they are, is that every one has been an effort to improve on the Western model of the school without concern for the consequences which that model leads to. Unfortunately, the more numerous and varied these attempts are, the greater the trouble in which the schools finds themselves.

This dilemma can be attributed to two conditions: lack of understanding or respect for the culture of the ethnic group as the foundation for an education system, and lack of confidence in the ability of parents to function as equal partners in the education process. This has led to what we believe we now find in many locations in the Far North: education systems that often are inappropriate or inadequate and inferior to what they could be.

Results and consequences

On the macrolevel it is generally the function of an educational system to maintain and refine the culture of the society. Therefore the curriculum has to reflect the comprehensive cultural heritage. By 'comprehensive' is meant that elements of the curriculum reflect both international and national fields of interest. Of even greater importance, however, from the perspective of the indigenous minority peoples of the Far North, the cultural heritage of the people needs to be included in the curriculum. This principal, as pointed out earlier, when used excessively, is apt to result in an overloaded school program and a curriculum in disarray. Nevertheless, to ignore it may result in an equally deleterious effect.

The outcomes of this dilemma usually are both planned and unplanned. Since, in general, the school is dealing with culture, that is, the range of knowledge that makes up the various societies of which it is a part, which of the outcomes prevails over the other is often determined by random circumstances. Planned results will be the fulfillment of the school's goals; unintended results will be due to lack of coordination and integration of the various units of the school. The consequences of planned results are mastery of formal knowledge. Unplanned results often are expressed as discontent with society and self in general.

A school or educational system that fulfills the requirements presented so far will manifest a system that maintains, vitalizes, and increases the store of knowledge of the society; that is, it will enhance its culture. If it does not, and depending on the extent to which there are unplanned results, the system will be out of control to varying degrees. Figure 1 illustrates this point graphically. The entire system, which is dynamic and complex, is represented by the figure as a whole. Subsystems, such as political and administrative components, are shown by the different units in the circle. The arrows indicate the four dimensions (technological, economical, social, and the arts). Likewise, cultural processes are shown by the same arrows, indicating that they have the same relationship to the whole as the four dimensions. Within each item many subparts may be found. For example the family and local social network are components of local, ethnic processes.

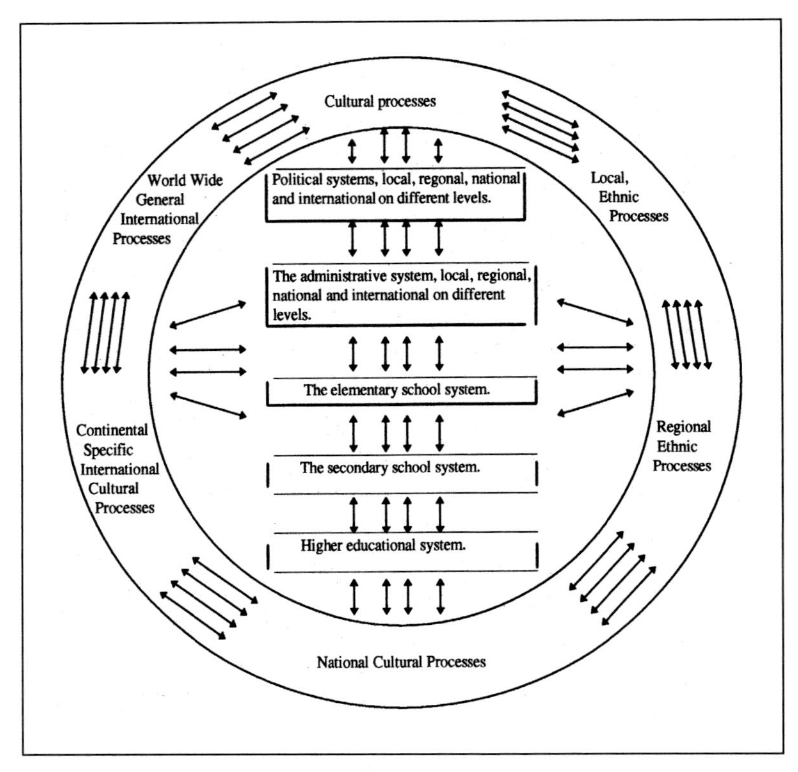

Figure1. School and society. A theoretical model.

Schooling as interaction

In schools there will always be interaction between individuals and between groups. These forms of interaction can be planned, or take place at random, and will interfere with or complement the individuals or groups involved. Factors that determine the outcome of these ongoing contacts such as prestige, authority, and ability are expressed in different forms of behavior. During such interaction, the actors behave in accordance with their perception of the situation. In this sense they are autonomous, self-determining units. Students, for instance, are active or not in any given situation in accordance with their immediate or more distant values, goals, and sense of ability.

Another important consideration in attempting to understand the activities of everyday life in the school is to recognize the fact that members of the school community have little influence over what happens on the macrolevel. Examples of this can be seen in the way the school has been organized, the curriculum developed, the recruitment of teachers undertaken, and the locus of control exercised with, or without, the involvement of the entire school community.

Values

Social values are among the most basic of human forces controlling the interaction of people. Shared values make cooperation possible, just as a lack of them makes it difficult for people to work together. However, when common values are lacking, common interests, which are precursors of values, may substitute for them, and in daily life often are a significant driving force. Both social values and interests in this sense are seen as something that are personally accepted as good. A social phenomenon which has this quality creates an incentive to reinforce itself; thus values and interests have the potential to free pent-up action.

Furthermore, social values connect people to what is commonly felt as good or worthwhile. When a place or situation has a shared quality of goodness or togetherness, people want to stay there or to continue a relationship with friends. In short, you are connected to a place and to people. But people living together or working together do not always share values or interests. In fact, not infrequently, there will be a divergence of interests from situation to situation, especially in schools in multicultural societies, making the effort for cooperative working arrangements unlikely. Teachers differ in values toward the purpose of schooling and single subjects, as do the students and their parents.

Diagrammatically, values and interest, according to this notion can be shown as in Figure 2. In ideal situations there will be complete correlation between values and interest. In such cases everyone is working for the same reason. External pressures or controls to get the work done are unnecessary. The box to the upper left represents this situation. The opposite situation, in which there are neither common or shared interests nor values, is seen in the lower right-hand box. In this case none of the interacting parties believe in what they do and resist cooperation. This situation is not unusual in a nationally or centrally planned school situated in a remote Native village. Without a means to accommodate local values and interests, the work of the school will conflict with the needs or wishes of the community. In this type of situation the school must assert strong pressure and discipline if its position is to prevail.

VALUES / INTERESTS	Shared	Conflicting
Shared	+ +	− +
Conflicting	+ −	− −

Figure 2. Positive and negative working conditions in schools as determined by relationship of values to interests.

The most common situations found throughout the North, however, are those where interests and values are both common and conflicting, as shown in the upper right and lower left boxes. At first notice, it may seem that the two boxes indicate equal educational situations and opportunities. However, the school situation will differ in each case. Where there are common values and conflicting interests, an education program will be relatively difficult to initiate. Although values are more difficult to develop or to activate in the school, once programs based on values are started they stabilize and are able to sustain themselves over time. Conversely, where there are common interests and conflicting values, the education program will be relatively easy to initiate, but there will be a constant need to stimulate the interest for the subject being taught. In this case, programs of education are less stable and not as long lasting as those where values are in common but interests are not. In either case, relevance of the program to the local situation or individual student is essential. It is this requirement that bears most heavily on student motivation.

Motivation

One of the most often-noted shortcomings of formal education, especially among indigenous and immigrant minority peoples, is the dearth of learning programs appropriate to local interests and needs. Often the local community is of the opinion that students should be engaged in more meaningful activities than schooling, or at least that there are some subjects that are just a waste of time. There are a number of ways to respond to this argument and these attitudes. One of the most frequently used is when the school attempts to motivate its students and their parents at the same time. Motivation in this sense requires that subjects in the school are shown to be relevant to the value system of the parents. An often-used strategy in this context is to relate the subject to something well known in the students' environment, thereby attracting the students' interest in a topic about which their parents are likely to have either understanding or expertise.

When this approach has been successful, the subject can then be turned to the primary subject. By so doing the students' culture has been used as a pedagogical tool to make the lesson more attractive and relevant. This has become an accepted and often-used strategy. However, this method is just a tool; it is less acceptable where the school does not actually accept the culture and background of the students and the main goal of the school is to replace the local, or Native, culture with an urban, nation-wide culture. When used in this way, the strategy is superficial and indicates only quasi-acceptance of the culture of the people since it is used as a means to extinguish it. Unfortunately, schools often function in this way. The sure way to deprive this approach of credibility is to accept the indigenous culture on equal terms with others. In this way, school programs will integrate elements of the local culture with national and international cultures, the strategy used most often in functional and successful school systems.

Identity

Just as there can be social dissonance as a result of the introduction of cultural items from the outside world, so too can this phenomenon negatively affect the self-identity of individual members of the society, especially children and youth. Mass media, the market economy, the educational system – all of the agents of change – affect the identity of single individuals as well as society in general. When new innovations infringe on relatively stable societies at a rapid rate, people's values are apt to become confused. In such cases self-identity formation is affected by a number of factors, persons, and events of the most diverse kind.

The degree of changes in individuals varies, of course, but as a rule the process of change itself reinforces specific change. Thus changes, once under way, are hard to cancel. Accordingly, processes of change that are taking place constitute preconditions for socialization in general and sub-processes accordingly. When the culture and the social climate are of traditional character, they will reinforce each other and the formation of identity will be more stable and traditional. The person will identify himself in much the same way as his forefathers. If the different elements and forces are radical, heterogeneous, and fundamentally different from the traditional culture and society, the effect can be both desocializing and resocializing. This means that both children and adults will develop identities quite different from what has been traditional ethnic identity. Or, they will simply protect themselves and develop other identities accordingly. In these cases, an individual may have a personality system consisting of several identities as a means of coping with adversity. Which of these becomes an individual's frame of reference at any given time depends on the actual situation at hand.

In societies undergoing rapid and radical change such as is now apparent, the culture, as well as individual identities, will also change. What the character of the culture and individual identities will be at any particular time remains an empirical question.[5]

Therefore, one of the most permanent, but unpredictable, effects of schooling may be its personal impact on individual students as human beings. When the school is successful it provides the person with a way of understanding and internalizing subject matter. More importantly, however, it serves as a means to enable mastery of life. Thus, the ultimate effect of schooling, for better or worse, is an important factor in the development of self-identity. Identity in this case is defined as the conscious self, that is, how a person is able to perceive or explain himself to himself and to others. The extent of insight or knowledge individuals have that enable themselves to understand who they are is largely achieved through the process of socialization. Thus, schooling when functioning as planned will be a significant part of this process. When education is perceived as a meaningful experience by students, teachers and parents, the outcome of the experience will be as intended and the students' positive self-identity will be reinforced. When not, self-identity will be confused and depressed.

As part of this process, every subject that the school offers has the potential to be transformed into a social value. When this happens students will work on their own, compelled by the forces of their own interests and the intrinsic value of the subject.

Every subject in the school should have the potential to become of value, and thus of interest to someone. If the teacher is dedicated to a subject and competent in it, it is likely that his or her interest and enthusiasm will be transferred to the students. Moreover, if a group of students likes a subject, there is a fair chance that each individual student will also. The opposite will be the case if the teacher lacks interest – so too will the students. If the class as a group lacks interest it will, through peer pressure, discourage the interest of students who might otherwise have found the subject of importance. Both teachers and classmates, therefore, play an important role in deciding the value and functions each will have on the other. It is in this aspect of the school-

---

5. Hoëm 1972, pp. 245–63; Hoëm 1979.

ing process that the cultural distance between the students' background and culture of the school is of importance.

If the contrast of cultures is too sharp and the gap too wide, the students are faced with educational challenges with which they are unable to cope. In such cases neither the school, the teacher, nor the subject will be of interest. The result of this is that students acquire a negative attitude toward themselves, believing that they are losers and eventually most become dropouts and social dissidents. This may partly explain the phenomenon of inadequate school performance typically found among students as discussed in Chapter 5.

If cultural contrasts are reasonable and the cultural gap manageable, the school situation will be manageable. Students will experience success and their self-image will be that of students who are comfortable with the school and themselves. In situations where the cultural gap between the school and local community are manageable for the students and the school, but not the parents, the students will experience schooling as a constant choice between their traditional life style and the outside world. In this case education will weaken the pupils sense of belonging to their home environment, thereby necessitating a new frame of reference existentially. What this will be like is hard to predict, but it will not be the traditional one of the local community. The students will no longer be able to see themselves as ordinary members of their traditional society, but, nevertheless, as persons with values, interests, and life styles that more than likely will link them to a different world, a world which they do not really know.

The effect of this ostensibly successful school in a community with indigenous culture will create existential tensions between the identities of the younger and the elder generations. This situation can be attributed to both ordinary tensions caused by the generation gap, but more importantly to tension caused by an existential orientation that includes their patrimonial values.

Education as cultural process and identity formation

The final point that we need to make in this chapter concerns a universal principle: the school in a multicultural society has to be part of the world at large if it is to fulfill its intended goals. This implies as well that the school must acquire the qualities of a well-functioning society. A basic premise that must be accepted along with this concept is that every unit and every culture in the society should be recognized as having equal importance to the people with whom they are connected. It is only then that members of each group will have the wisdom to know what is best for themselves in their local communities.

Each of the principles described in this chapter should bear on the planning that goes into the development of goals of a statewide or local system of education, especially when plans for the educational system include schools for indigenous or immigrant minorities. In the single school, as well as in each classroom, preparatory work and daily planning should be carried out with the same principles in mind. By so doing, every individual will have the opportunity to make determinations as free and responsible members of a society operating under the fundamental law that all human beings, within their capacity to do so, are the ones best prepared to determine their own fate.

Bibliography

Aikio, Marjut. 1991. *Language Conditions and Role of Language among the Indigenous Sami Population.* Unpublished paper, University of Lapland, Rovaniemi, Finland.

Alaska. *Constitution* – Article VII, Section 1.

———. 1920. *Report of the Alaska Commissioner of Education.* Juneau, Alas.: Territorial Department of Education.

———. 1943. Office of the Attorney General. *Opinion No. 38271-1943-803.* Juneau, Alas.

———. 1954. *Report of the Alaska Commissioner of Education.* Juneau, Alas.

———. 1968. Files of the office of the Commissioner, Alaska Department of Education. Juneau, Alas.

———. 1969. *Report of the Commissioner of Education, Department of Education.* Juneau, Alas.

———. 1972. Seventh Legislature, Second Session. Codified as AS 14.30.400. Juneau, Alas.

———. 1990. Alaska State Department of Education. *Report of the State Student Testing Program.* Juneau, Alas.

———. 1991. *New Directives in School Performance: The Legislature as Advocate and Guarantor.* Juneau, Alas.: Seventeenth Alaska State Legislature.

Alaska Federation of Natives. 1989. *The AFN Report on the Status of Alaska Natives: A Call for Action.* Anchorage, Alas.

Anderson, H. Dewey, and Walter C. Eells. 1935. *Alaska Natives, A Survey of Their Sociological and Educational Status.* Stanford, Calif.: Stanford University Press.

Armstrong, Terence, George Rogers, and Graham Rowley. 1978. *The Circumpolar North.* London: Methuen and Co.

Balto, Asta. 1990. *The Sami Language in School, Its Teaching and Its Status.* Paper presented at the meeting of the Northern Nations Ministers of Education, Umeå.

Banks, James A., and Cherry A. Banks (eds.). 1989. *Multicultural Education: Issues and Perspectives.* Boston: Allyn and Bacon.

Barnhardt, Ray (ed.). 1977. *Cross-Cultural Issues in Alaskan Education.* Fairbanks, Alas.: University of Alaska, Center for Northern Educational Research.

Battiste, Marie, and Jean Barman (eds.). 1995. *First Nations Education in Canada: The Circle Unfolds.* Vancouver: UBC Press.

Berliner, Peter. 1987. *Afhængighed og udfordring. Skolen i Grønland og i den tredje verden.* Copenhagen: Danmarks Lærerhøyskole, Institut for dansk skolehistorie.

Birket-Smith, Kaj. 1971. *The Eskimos.* New York: Crown Publishers, Inc.

Borg, Edward (ed.). 1981. *Readings in Education 1979/80.* Guilford, Conn.: Duskin Publishing Group.

Bristol Bay Native Association. 1973. *A Modest Proposal: An Expression of Children's Needs by People in Rural Alaska.* Anchorage, Alas.: Alaska State Operated School System.

Broadbent, Noel D. (ed.). 1992. *Nordic Perspectives on Arctic Cultural and Political Ecology.* Umeå: Umeå University, Center for Arctic Cultural Research.

Carney, Robert. 1970. *Relations in Education Between the Federal and Territorial Governments and the Roman Catholic Church in the Northwest Territories.* Unpublished doctoral dissertation, University of Alberta.

Cashmore, Ellis, and Barry Troyna. 1990. *Introduction to Race Relations.* London and New York: The Falmer Press.

Chubb, John E. 1988. "Why the Current Wave of School Reform Will Fail." *The Public Interest,* No. 90, Winter.

Combs, Arthur W. 1965. *The Professional Education of Teachers.* Boston: Allyn and Bacon, Inc.

Cooke, Alan, and Clive Holland. 1978. *The Exploration of Northern Canada, 500 to 1920: A Chronology.* Toronto: The Arctic History Press.

Cram, Jack. 1985. "Northern Teachers for Northern Schools." *McGill Journal of Education,* Vol. 20, No. 2, Spring.

Cremin, Lawrence A. 1977. *Traditions of American Education.* New York: Basic Books.

Dahl, Helge. 1957. Språkpolitikk og skolestell i Finnmark. 1814–1905. Oslo: Universitetsforlaget.

Damas, David (vol. ed.). 1984. *Arctic.* Vol. 5 of *Handbook of North American Indians.* Washington, DC: Smithsonian Institution.

Darnell, Frank. 1970. *Alaska's Dual Federal–State School System: A History and Descriptive Analysis.* Unpublished doctoral dissertation, Wayne State University.

———. 1980. *Financing, Organization and Governance of Education for Special Populations.* Paris: Organization for Economic and Community Development, Centre for Educational Research and Innovation, CERI/SF 80.23.

——— (ed.). 1972. *Education in the North.* Fairbanks, Alas.: Arctic Institute

of North America and University of Alaska.
Darnell, Frank, Kathryn A. Hecht, and James M. Orvik. 1974. *Prehigher Education in the Unorganized Borough.* Fairbanks, Alas.: University of Alaska, Center for Northern Educational Research.
Demmert, William G. (ed.). 1986. *Indigenous Peoples and Education in the Circumpolar North.* Juneau, Alas.: University of Alaska; and Nuuk: Greenland Seminarian.
Education and Resources Group. 1994. *Newsletter*, Vol. 5, No. 1. Chelsea, Maine: The Roger Lang Clearinghouse for Circumpolar Education.
Egede, Ingmar. 1976. "Educational Problems in Greenland." *Pedagogik*, Vol. 6, No. 2. Copenhagen: Gjellerup.
Farrow, Malcom, and David Wilman (eds.). 1989. *Self-Determination in Native Education in the Circumpolar North.* Yellowknife: Government of the Northwest Territories, Department of Education.
Finnie, Richard. 1942. *Canada Moves North.* Toronto: Macmillan.
Fitzgerald, Joseph H. 1967. *Alaska and Its Land.* Unpublished speech delivered at the International Symposium on Circumpolar Health Related Programs, College, July. Fairbanks, Alas.: University of Alaska, Archives.
Fredrickson, George M. 1993. "No Foreigners Need Apply." *New York Times Book Review*, August 22.
Gibson, Margaret A., and John U. Ogbu (eds.). 1991. *Minority Status and Schooling.* New York: Garland Publishing Inc.
Harjunpää, Toivo. 1967. "Education and Schools in Russian Alaska." Offprint, *Historica II.* Jyväskylä.
Helm, June (vol. ed.). 1981. *Subarctic.* Vol. 6 of *Handbook of North American Indians.* Washington, DC: Smithsonian Institution.
Hendrick, Klimmis. 1968. "U.S. Indian Life Changes – Slowly." *Christian Science Monitor*, June 5, 1968, p. 1.
Henrysson, Sten, et al. 1993. *Samer, präster och skolmästare. Ett kulturellt perspektiv på samernas och Övre Norrlands historia.* Umeå, CUR nr 23.
Hetling, Knud, et al. (eds.). 1975. *Greenland Past and Present.* Copenhagen: Edvard Henriksen.
Hoëm, Anton. 1972. "Kunnskapsoverføring som sosialt fenomen." *Tidsskrift for samfunnsforskning*, Vol. 13, pp. 251–63.
———. 1976a. *Makt og kunnskap.* Oslo: Universitetsforlaget.
———. 1976b. *Yrkesfelle, sambygding, same eller norsk?* Oslo: Universitetsforlaget.
———. 1979. *Samfunnsrettet pedagogikk.* Oslo: Universitetsforlaget.
———. 1989a. "Intensjoner og realiteter. Samenes skolegang 1716–1988." *Nordisk pedagogik*, Vol. 1, pp. 9–16.
———. 1989b. "Skoleordning og skolegang blant samene." In *Skolen 1739–1989.* Oslo: NKS-Forlaget, pp. 159–66.
———. 1990a. "Ny giv for minoritetsgruppene." In *Med viten og vilje mot et lærerikt samfunn?* Oslo: Universitetsforlaget.

———. 1990b. *Sosialisering. En teoretisk og empirisk modellutvikling.* Oslo: Universitetsforlaget.

Høgmo, Asle. 1986. "Det tredje alternativ. Barns læring av identitetsforvaltning i Samisk – norske samfunn preget av identitetsskifte." *Tidsskrift for samfunnsforskning*, Vol. 27, pp. 395–416.

Irwin, Mike. 1994. *Alaska Natives Commission Final Report*, Vol. 1. Anchorage, Alas.: Joint State–Federal Commission on Policies and Programs Affecting Alaska Natives.

Jackson, Sheldon. 1880. *Alaska and Missions on the North Pacific Coast*. New York: Dodd Mead and Company.

Jenness, Diamond. 1962. *Eskimo Administration: I. Alaska*. Montreal: Arctic Institute of North America, Technical Paper No. 10.

———. 1964. *Eskimo Administration: II. Canada*. Montreal: Arctic Institute of North America, Technical Paper No. 14.

———. 1965. *Eskimo Administration: III. Labrador*. Montreal: Arctic Institute of North America, Technical Paper No. 16.

Jenness, Stuart E. (ed.) 1991. *Arctic Odyssey, the Diary of Diamond Jenness 1913–1916*. Hull: Canadian Museum of Civilization.

Johns, Robert E. 1976. "History of Administration of Schools, NWT." *The Musk-ox*. Saskatoon: Institute for Northern Studies, University of Saskatchewan.

Kawagley, Angayuqaq Oscar. 1993. *A Yupiaq World View: Implications for Cultural, Educational and Technological Adaptation in a Contemporary World.* Unpublished doctoral dissertation, University of British Columbia.

King, Richard A. 1967. *The School at Mopass*. New York: Holt, Rinehart and Winston.

Kleivan, Inge. 1992. "Monolingualism, Bilingualism, or Multiculturalism in the Arctic?" In Lise Lyck (ed.), *Nordic Arctic Research on Contemporary Arctic Problems.* Nordic Arctic Research Forum, Institute of Economics. Copenhagen: Aalborg University Press.

Kluckhohn, Clyde. 1966. *Culture and Behavior*. Toronto: The Free Press (The Macmillan Company).

Krauss, Michael. 1980. *Alaska Native Languages: Past, Present and Future.* Fairbanks, Alas.: University of Alaska, Alaska Native Language Center.

Larsen, M. S. 1976. *Skoleutvikling og lærerutdannelse i Grønland. En historisk oversikt 1721–1950*. Copenhagen: University of Copenhagen, Institute for Theoretical Pedagogy.

———. 1977. *Komparativ pædagogogisk undersøgelse af læreruddannelser etablered med henblik på sproglig-kulturelle minoriteter.* Copenhagen: University of Copenhagen, Institute for Theoretical Pedagogy.

Leask, Janie. 1985. "Defining the Meaning of Success in Native Education." *Anchorage Times*, November 3.

Lee, Sharon M. 1993. "Racial Classifications in the US Census." *Ethnic and Racial Studies*, Vol. 16, No. 1, January.

Linton, Ralph (ed.). 1980. *The Science of Man in the World Crisis.* New York: Columbia University Press.

Lyck, Lise (ed.). 1992. *Nordic Arctic Research on Contemporary Arctic Problems.* Nordic Arctic Research Forum, Institute of Economics. Copenhagen: Aalborg University Press.

McBeath, Gerald A., et al. 1984. *Patterns of Control in Rural Alaska Education.* Fairbanks, Alas.: University of Alaska, Center for Cross-Cultural Studies and Department of Political Science.

McCarthy, S. J., and P. L. Peterson. 1989. *Teacher Roles: Weaving New Patterns in Classroom Practice and School Organization.* Unpublished paper presented at the annual meeting of the American Educational Research Association, San Francisco.

MacLean, Edna Ahgeak. 1990. *Alaska Native Language Development, Identity and Success in Schooling: One Perspective.* Paper presented at the meeting of the Northern Nations Ministers of Education, Umeå.

Macpherson, Norman John. 1991. *Dreams and Visions: Education in the Northwest Territories from Early Days to 1984.* Yellowknife: Government of the Northwest Territories, Department of Education.

Meriam, Lewis. 1928. *The Problems of Indian Administration.* Baltimore: Johns Hopkins University Press.

Meriot, Christian. 1984. "The Saami Peoples from the Time of the Voyage of Ottar to Thomas von Westen." *Arctic,* Vol. 37, No. 4.

Murphy, Joseph. 1991. *Restructuring Schools: Capturing and Assessing the Phenomena.* New York: Teachers College Press, Columbia University.

Nieto, Sonia. 1992. *Affirming Diversity.* New York: Longman Publishing Group.

NORD 1990: 8. *Skola och skolförvaltning i Norden.* Copenhagen: Nordiska Ministerrådet.

Northwest Territories Legislative Assembly. 1982. *Learning Tradition and Change in the Northwest Territories.* Yellowknife.

———. 1983. *The Codified Education Act of the Northwest Territories.* Yellowknife.

Okun, S. B. 1951. *The Russian American Company.* Cambridge, Mass.: Harvard University Press.

Olsen, Karl Kristian. 1993. *Education in Greenland.* Unpublished essay. Nuuk.

O'Rourke, Patrick. 1989. Unpublished University of Alaska, Fairbanks chancellor's convocation address. Fairbanks, Alas.: University of Alaska, Archives.

Orvik, James M. 1977. "Definitions of Bilingual Education in Alaska." In Ray Barnhardt (ed.), *Cross-Cultural Issues in Alaskan Education.* Fairbanks, Alas.: Center for Northern Educational Research.

Oswalt, Wendell H. 1967. *Alaskan Eskimos.* San Francisco: Chandler Publishing Company.

Paine, Robert. 1994. *Herds of the Tundra: A Portrait of Saami Reindeer Pastoralism.* Washington, DC: Smithsonian Institution Press.

——— (ed). 1977. *The White Arctic*. Toronto: University of Toronto Press.

Pelly, David F. 1993. "Dawn of Nunavut." *Canadian Geographic*, March/April.

Perlman, Joel. 1988. *Ethnic Differences*. Cambridge: Cambridge University Press.

Quality Education for Minorities Project. 1990. *Education That Works: National Goals for the Education of Minorities and How to Achieve Them*. Cambridge, Mass.: Massachusetts Institute of Technology.

Rasmussen, Knud. 1927. *Across Arctic America*. New York and London: G. P. Putnam's Sons.

Ray, Charles K. 1959. *A Program of Education for Alaska Natives*. Fairbanks, Alas.: University of Alaska.

——— et al. 1971. *Time for Change in the Education of Alaska Natives*. Fairbanks, Alas.: Center For Northern Education, University of Alaska Fairbanks.

Rogers, George W. 1962. *The Future of Alaska*. Baltimore: Johns Hopkins Press.

Roland, Grete. 1993. "A University in the 'Fourth World': The Self-Determination of the Norwegian Saami." *Dialectical Anthropology*, Vol. 18.

Schlesinger, Arthur M., Jr. 1992. *The Disuniting of America*. New York: W. W. Norton and Company.

Seitamo, L. 1988. "Trends in School Achievement in Skolt Lappish and Northern Finnish Children as a Function of Cultural and Psychological Factors." *Arctic Medical Research*, Vol. 47: Suppl. 1.

Simon, Mary. 1989. "Inuit Control of Inuit Education." In Malcom Farrow and David Wilman (eds.), *Self-Determination in Native Education in the Circumpolar North*. Yellowknife: Government of the Northwest Territories.

Simpson, D. W., and D. K. F. Wattie. 1968. "The Role and Impact of the Educational Program in the Process of Change in Canadian Eskimo Communities." In *Educational Process and Social Change in a Specialized Environmental Milieu*. Occasional Publication No. 4. Edmonton: University of Alberta, Boreal Institute.

Sizer, Theodore R. 1985. *Horace's Compromise: The Dilemma of the American High School*. Boston: Houghton Mifflin Company.

Slobodin, Richard. 1966. *Metis of the Mackenzie District*. Ottawa: St. Paul University, Canadian Research Centre for Anthropology.

Spindler, George D. 1968. "Psychocultural Adaptation." In Edward Norbeck, Douglas Price Williams, and William M. McCord (eds.). *The Study of Personality. An Interdisciplinary Appraisal*. New York: Holt, Rinehart and Winston.

Stefansson, Vilhjalmur. 1921. *The Friendly Arctic*. New York: The Macmillan Company.

Tiffany, Warren I. 1966. *Education in Northwest Alaska*. Juneau, Alas.: Bureau of Indian Affairs.

Tikhmenev, P. A. 1978. *A History of the Russian–American Company.* (First published in 1861–63 in two volumes in Russian.) Translated and edited by Richard A. Pierce and Alton S. Donnely. Seattle: University of Washington Press.

Tschanz, L. 1980. *Native Languages and Government Policy: An Historical Examination.* Native Language Research Series No. 2, Center for Research and Teaching of Canadian Native Languages. London, Ont.: University of Western Ontario.

United States. 1884. 23 Stat. L., 24.

United States. 1905. 33 Stat. L., 277.

US Congress. 1886. *Report on Education in Alaska.* Washington, DC: US Government Printing Office.

———. 1968. House of Representatives, 90th Cong., 2nd sess. Dec. No. 272.

US Department of Commerce. 1992. *Statistical Abstracts of the United States, 1992.* Washington, DC: US Government Printing Office.

US Department of Interior. 1886. *Annual Report of the Commissioner of Indian Affairs.* Washington, DC: US Government Printing Office.

———. 1934. *Report of the Commissioner of Indian Affairs.* Washington, DC: US Government Printing Office.

———. 1962. *Report to the Secretary of the Interior by the Task Force on Alaska Native Affairs,* Washington, DC.

US Department of Interior, Bureau of Education. 1918. *Report of the Governor of Alaska.* Washington, DC: US Government Printing Office.

———. 1926. *Biennial Survey of Education, 1924–26.* Washington, DC: US Government Printing Office.

US Office of Education. 1967. *Draft Guidelines for Title VII, Elementary and Secondary Education Act.* Washington, DC: US Government Printing Office.

Vallee, F. G. 1981. *Inuit Participation in the Canadian Policy.* Unpublished manuscript in Social Science Data Archives, Carleton University, Ottawa.

Vallee, F. G., D. G. Smith, and J. D. Cooper. 1984. "Contemporary Canadian Inuit." In David Damas (vol. ed.), *Arctic Handbook of North American Indians,* Vol. 5. Washington, DC: Smithsonian Institution.

Vorren, Ørnulv, and Ernst Manker. 1962. *Lapp Life and Customs.* Oslo: Oslo University Press, pp. 165–66.

Walle-Hansen, W., and Anton Hoëm. 1992. "Glimt fra misjonen i Varanger." In *Varanger årbok.* Alta: Vadsø Historielag, pp. 94–107.

Walsh, John E. 1973. *Intercultural Education in the Community of Man.* Honolulu: East West Center, The University Press of Hawaii.

Washburn, Wilcome E. (vol. ed.). 1988. *History of Indian–White Relations.* Vol. 4 of *Handbook of North American Indians.* Washington, DC: Smithsonian Institution.

Weiler, Hans N. 1990. *An Exercise in Contradiction? Comparative Perspectives on Educational Decentralization.* Paper delivered at the Annual Meeting of the American Political Science Association, San Francisco.

Wilman, David. 1993. *Teacher Training in the Northwest Territories.* Yellowknife: Northwest Territories Department of Education, Culture and Employment.

Woollacatt, Martin. 1992. "Learning to Live Together in the World's Attic." *Guardian Weekly*, September 6.

Zaslow, Morris. 1971. *The Opening of the Canadian North, 1870–1940.* Toronto: McClelland & Stewart.

Index